SUCCESS!
THE TOTAL PACKAGE

RE-DEFINING THE TRUE MEANING OF SUCCESS

DR. CASSIUS V. STUART

COPYRIGHT © 2025. All rights reserved.
Dr. CASSIUS V. STUART
SUCCESS!
THE TOTAL PACKAGE
Re-Defining the True Meaning of Success

No part of this publication may be reproduced, distributed, or transmitted in any form or by any means, including photocopying, recording, or other electronic or mechanical methods, without the prior written permission of the publisher, except in the case of brief quotations embodied in critical reviews and certain other non-commercial uses permitted by copyright law.

Dr. CASSIUS V. STUART
Printed Worldwide
First Printing 2025
First Edition 2025
ISBN # 979-8-218-16590-1

Cover design © 2025 Cassius V. Stuart.

This publication contains the opinions and ideas of its author. It is intended to provide helpful and informative material on the subject matter covered.it is sold with the understanding that the author and publisher are not engaged in rendering professional service in the book. If the reader requires professional assistance or advice, a competent professional should be consulted.

The author and the publisher specifically disclaim any responsibility for any liability, loss, or risk, personal or otherwise, which is incurred as a consequence, directly or indirectly, of the use and application of any of the content of this book.

DEDICATION

TO MY GRAND-FATHER,

You may be gone, but your love and guidance will always remain with me. You taught me the importance of hard work, determination, and a never-give-up attitude. Your wisdom and unwavering support have inspired me to pursue my dreams and strive for excellence in everything I do. This book is dedicated to you, in loving memory of the impact you had on my life.

TO MY MOTHER, IDA STUART,

You are the rock of our family, always there to offer love and support no matter what. Your strength and resilience have been a constant source of inspiration, and I am grateful for all that you have done for me and my siblings. This book is dedicated to you, as a testament to the love and gratitude I have for you.

TO MY WIFE, SHARMAINE STUART,

You are my soulmate, my partner, and my best friend. Your unwavering love, support, and encouragement have been the driving force behind all my achievements. Thank you for always being there for me and for being a constant source of inspiration. This book is dedicated to you with love and gratitude for all that you bring into my life.

TO MY BEAUTIFUL GIRLS,

You are the light of my life and my greatest joy. Your laughter and love have brought immeasurable happiness into my life, and I am grateful for every moment I get to spend with you. This book is dedicated to you, my precious daughters, with the hope that it will inspire you to pursue your dreams and achieve greatness in all that you do.

With love and gratitude,
Cassius

ACKNOWLEDGMENTS

Dear Readers,

It is with great joy and gratitude that I present to you my book, "Success: The Total Package." This project has been a labor of love and a culmination of years of hard work and learning. I could not have made it to this point without the unwavering support and encouragement from the most important people in my life - my wife and kids. They have been my strength and my reason for pushing forward, even in the toughest of times.

I would also like to extend my heartfelt appreciation to the late Dr. Myles Munroe, who has laid a strong foundation in my life through his teachings and guidance. His wisdom and insights have been invaluable in shaping my understanding of success and the impact it can have on our lives.

Thank you to all who have supported and believed in me on this journey. I hope this book will inspire you to pursue your own path to success and help you achieve all that you desire in life.

With gratitude,
Cassius V Stuart

CONTENTS

Introduction *1*
Chapter One *6*
Understanding Success 6
   INTRODUCTION 7
   THE MAKE-UP OF MAN 8
   WHO IS MAN? 9
   THE SOUL OF MAN 11
   EMOTIONS OF MAN 14
   WHERE DO EMOTIONS COME FROM? 16

Chapter Two *20*
Developing Yourself Mentally *20*
   THE POWER OF EDUCATION 21
   BEN CARSON 24
   HOW READING SAVED ME 26
   DEVELOPING P.M.A 29
   THE SUBCONSCIOUS MIND 30
   THE SENSE OF SIGHT 34
   THE EGO 35
   THE IMPORTANCE OF SELF-LOVE 37
   UNDERSTANDING THE POWER OF THE SUBCONSCIOUS 39
   BEHAVIORAL PSYCHOLOGY TEACHES 42
   REFLECTIONS 44

Chapter Three *46*
Developing Yourself Emotionally *46*
   EMOTIONS - WHAT ARE THEY? 47
   CASSIUS'S THEORY OF EMOTION 51
   THE EVOLUTION OF MEN/WOMAN 53
   NEW YORK 55

UNDERSTANDING YOUR EMOTIONS 56
LOVE 57

Chapter Four 60
Developing Yourself Physically 60

THE GOOSE THAT LAID THE GOLDEN EGG..............................62
THE IMPORTANCE OF VITAMINS 63
VITAMIN A...65
VITAMIN B1 (THIAMINE) 67
VITAMIN B2 (RIBOFLAVIN)...69
VITAMIN B6 (PYRIDOXINE) 71
VITAMIN B12 (COBALAMIN)..73
BIOTIN (COENZYME R OR VITAMIN H) 75
VITAMIN C (ASCORBIC ACID, CEVITAMIN ACID) 77
CALCIUM PANTOTHENATE (PANTOTHENIC ACID, PANTHENOL, VITAMIN B5) 79
CHOLINE 81
VITAMIN D (SUNSHINE VITAMIN) 82
VITAMIN E 83
MINERAL TABLE 84
PROSTATE CANCER...87
PROSTATE CANCER IN AFRICAN AMERICAN MEN...................89
PROSTATE CANCER IN WHITE MEN 90
PROSTATE CANCER IN ASIAN MEN..91
PROSTATE CANCER IN LATINO MEN 92
BREAST CANCER 93
BREAST CANCER AMONG WHITE WOMEN 94
BREAST CANCER AMONG BLACK WOMEN................................95
BREAST CANCER AMONG ASIAN WOMEN.................................96
BREAST CANCER AMONG LATIN WOMEN 97
FACTS ABOUT BREAST CANCER..98
STROKE..99
SYMPTOMS OF STROKE 101
STROKE & RACE... 102
EXERCISE ROUTINE 103
RESTROUTINE 106
REST, FROM A RELIGIOUS PERSPECTIVE................................. 107

Chapter Five 110
Developing Yourself Socially 110
- INTRODUCTION 111
- WHAT ARE SOCIAL SKILLS? 114
- IMPORTANCE OF IMPROVING SOCIAL SKILLS 115
- ADVANTAGES OF SOCIAL CAPITAL IN THE SOCIAL MEDIA AGE 117
- DISADVANTAGES OF SOCIAL CAPITAL IN THE SOCIAL MEDIA AGE 118
- OVERCOMING FEAR AND SOCIAL ANXIETY 125
- TRUE FEAR VS. PHYSICAL FEAR 126
- SOCIAL ANXIETY 128
- PHYSICAL FEAR EQUALS SOCIAL ANXIETY 129
- SITUATIONS THAT TRIGGER ANXIETY 130
- SIGNS AND SYMPTOMS 131
- CAUSES 132
- TREATMENT 133
- FREEDOM FROM FEAR 135
- SOCIAL SKILL AND ITS ADVANTAGES TO YOUR CAREER 137
- SOCIAL SKILLS AND EFFECTIVE COMMUNICATION 138
- WHAT IS AN EFFECTIVE COMMUNICATOR? 139
- WHY IS EFFECTIVE COMMUNICATION IMPORTANT? 141
- HOW TO BE AN EFFECTIVE COMMUNICATOR 142
- LEE KUAN YEW 144
- CONFLICT RESOLUTION 146
- WHY IS CONFLICT RESOLUTION IMPORTANT? 147
- SOCIAL ISOLATION 148
- SIX NEGATIVE CONSEQUENCES OF SOCIAL ISOLATION 151
- SIX STRATEGIES FOR OVERCOMING SOCIAL ISOLATION ... 152
- CONCLUSION 153

Chapter Six 154
Developing Yourself Economically 154
- INTRODUCTION 155
- IMPORTANCE OF ECONOMIC DEVELOPMENT 156

- UNDERSTANDING YOUR FINANCIAL SITUATION 158
- ASSESSMENT OF CURRENT FINANCIAL STATUS 159
- SETTING FINANCIAL GOALS 163
- (SMART) GOALS 166
- BUDGETING AND SAVING 171
- THE STUART RULE 173
- 40/30/20/10 173
- BUILDING AN EMERGENCY FUND 175
- STRATEGIES FOR SAVING MONEY 177
- INVESTING 179
- UNDERSTANDING THE STOCK MARKET 181
- INVESTING INCRYPTOCURRENCY 186
- BITCOIN, IS IT A GOOD INVESTMENT? 187
- ETHEREUM, IS IT A GOOD INVESTMENT? 188
- WHAT IS BLOCKCHAIN? 189
- DIFFERENT TYPES OF INVESTMENTS 190
- REAL ESTATE & AIRBNB 192
- DIVERSIFYING YOUR INVESTMENT PORTFOLIO 194
- BUILDING WEALTH 195
- ENTREPRENEURSHIP AND SMALL BUSINESS OWNERSHIP 196
- BUILDING PASSIVE INCOME STREAMS 198
- MANAGING DEBT 199
- UNDERSTANDING DIFFERENT TYPES OF DEBT 201
- PAYING OFF DEBT EFFICIENTLY 202
- AVOIDING DEBT TRAPS 204
- CONCLUSION 205

Chapter Seven *208*

Developing Yourself Spiritually *208*

- INTRODUCTION 209
- DEFINITION OF SPIRITUAL DEVELOPMENT 210
- IMPORTANCE OF SPIRITUAL DEVELOPMENT 213
- UNDERSTANDING YOUR SPIRITUALITY 215
- WHAT IS SPIRITUALITY? 218
- SPIRITUALITY WITH A PURPOSE 232
- ENHANCING YOUR SPIRITUAL AWARENESS 233
- PRAYER AND FASTING 234
- NATURE AND SPIRITUAL DEVELOPMENT 238
- BIBLIOGRAPHY 244

PREFACE

"A person cannot do right in one department of life whilst attempting to do wrong in another department. Life is one indivisible whole."

PROLOGUE

"Take heed, and beware of greed: for a man's life consisteth not in the abundance of the things which he possesseth." - Luke 12:15

Throughout history, teachers, philosophers, and spiritual leaders have echoed a profound truth: true fulfillment comes not from material wealth but from balance, wisdom, and purpose. This principle is deeply rooted in religious and philosophical teachings, guiding countless individuals toward a more meaningful existence.

Luke 12:15 underscores this wisdom: "And he said to them, 'Take care, and be on your guard against all covetousness, for one's life does not consist in the abundance of his possessions.'" This biblical passage serves as a powerful reminder of the dangers of greed and the fleeting nature of material wealth. It challenges us to prioritize meaning over materialism, urging reflection on what truly constitutes a rich and fulfilling life.

Buddhism echoes this sentiment, teaching that attachment to material possessions leads to suffering. Buddha emphasized moderation and detachment, seeing them as essential steps toward enlightenment and inner peace. The Four Noble Truths and the Eightfold Path reinforce that by relinquishing material desires, one can achieve Nirvana—a state free from suffering and worldly attachments.

Similarly, Confucianism warns against the perils of greed, emphasizing the virtues of balance, righteousness, and moral integrity. Confucius believed true fulfillment comes not from wealth but from virtuous living—cultivating kindness, respect, and empathy. Despite their cultural differences, Buddhism and Confucianism converge on the idea that material wealth often leads away from true happiness, advocating instead for spiritual growth, ethical conduct, and inner virtue.

The teachings of Buddha, Confucius, Jesus, and Gandhi collectively caution against the illusion of fulfillment through material wealth. While their philosophies differ in expression, they share a common understanding: a meaningful life is not defined by possessions but by virtues such as compassion, integrity, and wisdom. Buddha teaches liberation from desire, Confucius promotes moral living, Jesus prioritizes spiritual wealth, and Gandhi exemplifies simple living and high thinking. Each perspective reinforces the notion that true success is measured not by what we accumulate but by how we live and what we contribute to the world.

The desire for success is universal. Those who have it strive for more, while those who lack it relentlessly pursue it. However, modern society often misconstrues success, equating it solely with wealth and status. Ancient Chinese philosophy offers a different perspective, asserting that success is not just about material gain but about living virtuously and harmoniously with oneself and others.

True success is built on sacrifice, discipline, and perseverance. Failure is not the opposite of success but an integral part of it—every setback serves as a steppingstone toward achievement. As the Chinese proverb states, "Failure is the mother of success." History has shown that even the most successful individuals have encountered numerous failures before reaching their goals.

Traditionally, success was measured by a blend of wealth, social status, family legacy, and physical strength. However, Gandhi's assertion that "Life is one indivisible whole" suggests a more holistic approach—one that values personal growth, relationships, and ethical living alongside material accomplishments. Wealth without morality, strength without wisdom, and success at the cost of well-being are incomplete victories.

A truly successful life is one of balance. If financial success comes at the expense of relationships or health, can it truly be called success? If a person possesses immense wealth yet lives in isolation or inner turmoil, is that fulfillment? Success should not be confined to economic prosperity but should encompass all aspects of life—mind, body, spirit, relationships, and purpose.

My journey through literature on achievement, prosperity, and personal growth has revealed a recurring omission: the absence of balance. Many texts emphasize material success while neglecting the broader picture of holistic fulfillment. This realization inspired me to explore success through a more comprehensive lens.

Deepak Chopra articulates this idea brilliantly, warning that material possessions are mere symbols, not the essence of success. He likens the pursuit of wealth without self-awareness to chasing a map instead of experiencing the actual destination. Many individuals, including high-profile figures such as Elvis Presley, Marilyn Monroe, and Michael Jackson, seemingly had everything yet struggled with profound emptiness. Their stories highlight the dangers of prioritizing external success over internal well-being.

This book seeks to uncover the root causes of discontent and debunk the notion that success is purely economic. True success is found in aligning with one's authentic self—nurturing mind, body, and spirit in harmony. By embracing a holistic approach to fulfillment, we can redefine success beyond material wealth, recognizing that true achievement lies in a life rich with purpose, integrity, and inner peace.

"Try not to become a person of success, but rather try to become a person of value."
– Albert Einstein

Chapter One
UNDERSTANDING SUCCESS

Success is not final; failure is not fatal: It is the courage to continue that counts."

Winston Churchill

INTRODUCTION

As we explore the concept of success—a widely discussed and often misunderstood idea—it is essential to first define what it truly means. According to traditional dictionary definitions, success is often described as the attainment of wealth, favor, or distinction, or as the achievement of a goal or purpose. While these definitions offer a general understanding, they fail to capture the full depth of what success truly entails.

Historically, success has been equated with financial prosperity and social status. However, this narrow perspective overlooks the deeper, more meaningful aspects of achievement. The world is filled with individuals who, despite their wealth and influence, struggle with failed marriages, declining health, or a profound sense of loneliness. These examples challenge the notion that success is merely about external accomplishments and highlight the need for a more holistic understanding.

True success extends beyond material wealth or recognition. It encompasses personal fulfillment, meaningful relationships, well-being, and the positive impact one has on others. A life centered solely on financial gain often leads to imbalance, where personal happiness and purpose are sacrificed for external validation. To truly grasp the essence of success, we must shift our perspective, recognizing that it is not solely about accumulation but about living with integrity, intention, and a deep sense of purpose.

This distinction between external success and true fulfillment is often overlooked, leading many to chase wealth at the expense of what truly matters. A compelling example of this is the story of a traveling salesperson who set a goal to earn one million dollars in a year.

This relentless entrepreneur was convinced that with the right idea, he could sell anything. Fueled by ambition, he poured his heart and soul into developing and patenting a cutting-edge recreational product, determined to turn his vision into reality. He spent countless hours on the road, traveling from city to city, chasing his dream with unwavering dedication.

Occasionally, he would bring one of his children along, eager to share the excitement of his journey. But his wife watched with growing concern. Each time they returned home, she noticed subtle yet unsettling changes. Their once-grounded children began to drift—neglecting their prayers, ignoring their schoolwork, and losing sight of the values they had been raised with. Her warnings went unheard as the man remained fixated on his goal.

At the end of the year, he triumphantly declared that he had achieved his dream— he had made his million dollars. But his victory was short-lived. The celebration was overshadowed by heartbreak as his world crumbled around him. His marriage collapsed, two of his children turned to drugs, and another spiraled into deep turmoil. His once-strong family was now in ruins.

He had won the financial battle but lost everything that truly mattered. The world saw him as a success, yet in the most profound sense, he had failed.

This individual failed to grasp the wisdom imparted by Gandhi, who stated, "A person cannot do right in one aspect of their life while simultaneously attempting to do wrong in another. Life is an indivisible whole." The man's relentless pursuit of financial success at the expense of his family and personal values ultimately led to his downfall, highlighting the necessity of balance and holistic growth to achieve true success.

As you read this book, it is crucial to understand that success cannot be measured solely by wealth and social status. The story of the traveling salesperson serves as a powerful reminder that neglecting one area of life while excelling in another leads to an incomplete and fragile foundation. Gandhi's insight reinforces the idea that "Life is an indivisible whole." To truly achieve success, one must strive for balance in all aspects of life, ensuring that professional aspirations do not come at the cost of personal fulfillment and well-being.

We often overlook the crucial role that physical health plays in our overall well-being. Neglecting proper nutrition, exercise, and rest can lead to significant consequences, affecting both our bodies and our mental clarity. Rest is essential for rejuvenation, and its absence can have detrimental effects on our health and overall quality of life. Likewise, relationships and emotional connections are often taken for granted until they are tested in difficult times. Mental health and self-care are equally important, yet they are frequently neglected, even though a healthy mind is vital for lasting success.

Perhaps the most essential yet frequently overlooked aspect of success is spiritual development. Our spiritual well-being is fundamental to holistic growth, influencing how we navigate challenges and find purpose in our lives. (This will be explored further in the book.) Success should be viewed as an interconnected lifestyle that acknowledges the total person, rather than a series of compartmentalized achievements. If we strive for success in our professional endeavors, we must also nurture our social relationships, emotional health, and personal development.

Economic success should not be pursued in isolation but as part of a broader, well-rounded approach to life. True success encompasses spiritual, mental, and emotional well-being in addition to financial stability. To attain meaningful and lasting success, every aspect of our being must be considered and cultivated. Seeking wealth without attending to mental, emotional, and spiritual growth leads to an unbalanced and ultimately unfulfilling life.

One of the greatest misconceptions about success is the belief that it is a destination to reach or an object to be grasped. In reality, success is not a tangible end goal—it is a way of life. By embracing success as a continuous journey, it becomes the driving force that motivates us to wake up each morning with purpose and intention. Without this perspective, we risk feeling perpetually unfulfilled, always searching for something more. True success is found in the journey itself, in the balance we cultivate, and in the life we build holistically.

THE MAKE-UP OF MAN

Every human being is made up of three distinct parts: the **spirit**, the **soul**, and the **body**. These components are not three separate lives fighting for space; they are inter locking pieces of a single design, each with a clear purpose that supports the others.

The **spirit** is the life giving core—the invisible spark that makes a person truly alive and aware. Our deepest convictions, our moral compass, and our capacity to reach for something beyond the visible world all flow from the spirit. When the spirit is healthy, a person feels anchored, purposeful, and hopeful—even in difficult circumstances.

The **soul** sits between spirit and body, acting as the interpreter. It includes the mind, emotions, and will. Through the soul we think, feel, choose, remember, dream, and imagine. A clear, well ordered soul takes the quiet insights of the spirit and translates them into balanced thoughts and steady decisions; a cluttered soul can distort those same insights and leave a person confused or anxious.

The **body** is the physical vessel that carries both spirit and soul through everyday life. It allows us to move, work, speak, and experience the world through our senses. Because the body is tangible, it often shows first when something inside is out of balance—fatigue, tension, or illness can signal deeper spiritual or emotional strain.

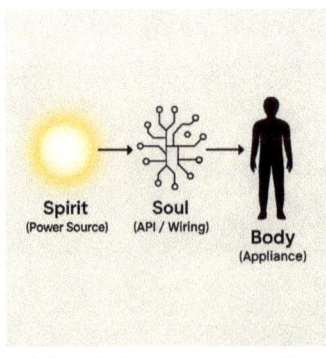

Each part has its own role, yet none can function at its best in isolation. The body cannot live without the spirit, and the spirit cannot fulfill its purpose on earth without the body. **The soul serves as the living interface—an inner "API"—that channels the wisdom of the spirit into thought, emotion, and choice, then translates those choices into physical action; likewise, you can picture it as the wiring in a house, with the spirit as the power source and the body as the appliance—when the wiring is intact, power flows and the appliance works as designed, but if the circuit breaks, even the strongest generator and the finest appliance sit idle.**

When spirit, soul, and body work together, a person experiences whole life wellness—clarity of thought, emotional stability, physical vitality, and a deep sense of meaning. When any link weakens, the entire system feels the strain, showing up as stress, restlessness, poor health, or lack of direction.

Synchronizing these three parts is essential to lasting success and an abundant life. Alignment does not happen by accident; it requires self examination, practical habits, and consistent care in all three areas. This book is designed to guide you through that process. By the end, you will understand how to nourish your spirit, steady your soul, and strengthen your body—so each can perform its unique task in harmony with the others.

WHO IS MAN?

First of all, we are going to look at the word "human," which is a grammatical construct that is derived from two words, "hu-man" or "humas-man," meaning "earth" or "ground" in Latin. This origin of the word gives us a clear understanding of the concept of a human being as a physical vessel, or "dirt suit," that houses the spirit. From this word, we can also derive related words such as "humus," "humanity," and "humility." The word "humility" comes from the Latin word "humilitas," which is related to the adjective "humilis," meaning "humble" or "grounded."

The origin of the word 'human' also suggests that the word has a connection to the idea of being grounded, connected to the earth, and humble. It emphasizes the idea that human beings are not separate or above nature but are a part of it. This understanding of the word "human" highlights the reality that we are all made of the same earth and will ultimately return to it.

In order to achieve success, it is important to understand that we are all connected, and that true success is not only about personal achievements, but also about contributing to the well-being of humanity.

Looking at the Humas of man or the biological body of man, we can see that it is made up of the same components as the earth.

The human body is composed of various chemical elements, with the most abundant being oxygen, carbon, hydrogen, and nitrogen. According to scientific data, oxygen makes up about 65% of the human body, while carbon makes up 18%, hydrogen makes up 10%, and nitrogen makes up 3%. The body also contains trace amounts of other elements such as calcium, phosphorus, potassium, sulfur, and chlorine. In total, the human body is composed of about 60 different chemical elements. It is important to note that the exact composition of the human body can vary depending on factors such as diet and overall health; for example, a person's weight can affect the body's composition.

This composition of the human body is based on the average percentages of elements, but the exact percentages may vary depending on the individual. For example, the levels of elements like sodium and chloride may vary depending on diet and hydration. Additionally, the body also contains trace amounts of elements like iron, zinc, copper, and iodine, which are essential for various bodily functions.

It is also important to mention that the body also contains water, which is composed of hydrogen and oxygen, making up to 60% of the body weight.

The human body is composed of various chemical elements, many of which can be found in the earth. This fact highlights the close connection between the human body and the earth and suggests that the body must be sustained by the earth in order to survive. This concept is reflected in the universal principle that all things are nurtured by their origin. As the human body is composed of elements from the earth, it needs to obtain vital nutrients from the earth to operate effectively.

The source of sustenance for the human body comes in the form of plants, animals, water, minerals, vitamins, and other elements. These essential nutrients are derived from the earth and are necessary for maintaining optimal health and well-being. The human body requires a balance of these different elements in order to function properly, and a lack of one element can lead to a wide range of health problems.

Therefore, it is important to understand that the human body is intimately connected to the earth and that in order to achieve optimal health and well-being, we must take care of the earth and consume the nutritious substances that it provides. This includes eating nutrient-rich foods, drinking clean water, getting enough exposure to sunlight, all of which are essential for maintaining optimal health and well-being.

THE SOUL OF MAN

... "and breathed into his nostrils the breath of life; and man became a living soul."

The soul is an essential aspect of human existence that connects the body and the spirit. It is the consciousness of a person, their ability to "know" and understand their existence. The famous philosopher René Descartes famously said, **"I think, therefore I am,"** emphasizing the connection between consciousness and being alive. The mind is the central processing unit of the soul; it is the driver of the will and emotions. (Descartes, 1641.)

The soul of a person is made up of three elements: the mind, the will, and the emotions. These elements, like the body, require constant development and maintenance to function properly. Many people do not understand that the issues or source of life come from the soul, which is why King Solomon advised to **"guard your heart with all diligence because out of it comes the issues of life."** This means that taking care of the soul is just as important as taking care of the body. If you were to substitute the word heart with the word mind, then the sentence would read like this "guard your **mind/soul** with all diligence because out of it comes the issues of life."

The soul, also referred to as the mind, is the link that connects the body and the spirit, and it is essential to maintain a balance between these three parts of the human being. This balance can be achieved by developing a healthy body, mind, and spirit, which can be obtained by following the right diet, exercise, meditation, and spiritual practices. King Solomon's advice to **"guard your heart with all diligence because out of it come the issues of life"** emphasizes the importance of being mindful of what we allow into our minds as the issues of life flow from the mind. He emphasizes the importance of guarding the mind with diligence, similar to how one would guard a prisoner.

Humans were created with a will, and it is one of the most powerful forces on the planet. Even God cannot violate the will of man. Once a decision is made, God cannot stop a person from carrying it out. It is important to keep in mind that every decision we make is not a final but rather a "seed" that will yield its consequences, whether positive or negative. Therefore, it is important to remember that the choices we make today will have an impact on our future, and it is essential to be mindful of the potential outcomes before making any decision. This emphasizes the importance of making conscious and well-informed decisions for our lives.

It is crucial to understand that the will of man is a powerful tool that can be used for good or for bad, and it is our responsibility to use it wisely.

The story of Eve in the Garden of Eden, as found in the Bible's book of Genesis, is a well-known story that explores the concept of free will. According to the story, God created Adam and Eve and placed them in a garden where they were free to eat from any tree except for the tree of knowledge of good and evil. However, Eve was tempted by a serpent to eat from the forbidden tree, and she chose to disobey God's command. This decision, made by Eve, ultimately led to the fall of mankind.

This story is often used as an illustration of the power of human will. Even though God is all-powerful, He could not interfere with Eve's decision to eat from the forbidden tree. He was bound by her free will to make her own choice. In this sense, the story highlights the importance of personal responsibility and the idea that everyone is responsible for their own actions.

We can see further elaborations and dialogue on this concept of free will, which is also discussed in various philosophical and religious texts, including the works of philosophers such as St. Augustine and St. Thomas Aquinas. They argue that free will is a fundamental aspect of human nature and that it allows individuals to make moral choices.

It is crucial to acknowledge that the story of Eve might be perceived differently across various cultures and individuals, leading to diverse interpretations of free will. Nonetheless, the narrative of Eve in the Garden of Eden unmistakably serves as a compelling example of the strength of human will and the significance of individual accountability.

In order to grasp a deeper and clear understanding of the will of man, I will seek to elaborate further on St. Augustine's writings with some context.

St. Augustine, also known as Augustine of Hippo, was a 4th-century Christian theologian and philosopher who wrote extensively on various topics, including the concept of free will. His most famous work on this topic is on Free Choice of the Will, which is considered one of the most important texts on the subject in Western philosophy. (Augustine, 397-400.)

In **On Free Choice of the Will,** Augustine argues that free will is a fundamental aspect of human nature and that it is necessary for moral responsibility. He maintains that without the ability to make choices, there can be no moral responsibility and that individuals are responsible for their own actions because they have the ability to make choices.

Augustine also addresses the problem of evil, which is the question of how to reconcile the existence of evil with the belief in a benevolent and all-powerful God. He argues that God created humans with free will, which allows them to choose between good and evil. However, because of the original sin of Adam and Eve, all humans are born with an inclination to sin, but they still can make choices and act differently.

Augustine also believes that God's grace is necessary for individuals to make good choices and that without it, individuals would be unable to overcome their inclination to sin. He argues that grace and free will are complementary and that God's grace does not take away an individual's freedom to make choices.

Augustine's ideas on free will have had a significant impact on Western philosophy and theology. Many later philosophers, including St. Thomas Aquinas, have been influenced by his ideas and have built on his arguments. His work on free will remains an important text for those interested in the philosophy of religion and moral responsibility.

Looking at a similar story of Cain and Abel, as found in the book of Genesis, is another example of the power of human will and the role of free will in relation to God. In this story, Cain, the firstborn son of Adam and Eve, becomes jealous of his brother Abel and ultimately kills him. When God asked Cain why he appeared downcast, God inquired, **"Why are you angry? Why is your face downcast? If you do what is right, won't you be accepted? But if you don't do what is right, sin is crouching at your door. It desires to have you, but you must rule over it."** In essence, you must "will" to do what is right.

This passage is often interpreted as God warning Cain about the power of sin and the importance of making the right choice. God is telling Cain that he has the power to control his actions and that he is responsible for his own decisions. God is not going to interfere with his will but rather advise him. This passage also illustrates the idea that sin is always present and that individuals must make the conscious decision to resist it. Out of the five questions God asked Cain, the most important one was, **"If you do what is right, will you not be accepted?** But if you do not do what is right, sin is crouching at your door; it desires to have you, but you must rule over it." (Genesis 4:7) Indication that it is possible to make the right choices.

Both stories have many parallels in that it highlights the power of human will and the importance of personal responsibility. It also illustrates the idea that God has given humans the ability to make choices, but it is ultimately up to them to make the right ones. Both stories also reinforce St. Augustine's idea that God's grace is necessary for individuals to make good choices and that without it, individuals would be unable to overcome their inclination to sin.

EMOTIONS OF MAN

The soul of man is a complex and multifaceted concept that encompasses many different aspects of the human experience. One key aspect of the soul is the emotions of man. The word "emotion" derives from the Latin "emotio," meaning "to move." It is through our emotions that we are moved to act and respond to the world around us.

As we examine the soul of man, we can see that there are three distinct parts that require development. The first is the mind, which needs to be cultivated through education. The mind is like a muscle that must be constantly exercised through reading and studying about the creator, life, and who we are. Developing the mind demands discipline and concentration, for it is by nurturing our mental faculties that we gain the ability to steer our own destiny.

The second aspect of the soul is the will, which we discussed earlier in this chapter, is the power to choose and act. We can see the power of the will in the stories of Eve in the Garden of Eden and Cain and Abel, as they were given the freedom to choose, but with that freedom came the responsibility to make the right choices.

The aspect of the soul which we are attempting to elaborate on is the emotions, which are the feelings and reactions that we have towards the world around us. Emotions are powerful and can move us to act, but they must be controlled and channeled in the right direction.

To develop the soul, it is necessary to work on all three aspects simultaneously, as they are interconnected and mutually influential.

The cultivation of the mind, the control of the will, and the regulation of emotions are all crucial elements for the overall development of the soul.

It is important to note that the development of the soul is a lifelong process and requires constant effort and self-reflection. By working on developing the mind, the will, and the emotions, we can gain a greater understanding of ourselves and the world around us and ultimately gain control over our destiny.

The brain is a complex and intricate organ that plays a crucial role in human behavior and emotions. One important aspect of the brain is the presence of two hemispheres, the left and the right. In early studies, it was believed that the left hemisphere was dominant for language and logical thinking, while the right hemisphere was responsible for emotional processing and creativity. However, recent research has shown that both hemispheres are involved in emotional processing and that the distinction between the two hemispheres is not as clear-cut as previously thought. (Brain., 2014.)

Current understanding reveals that the two brain hemispheres collaborate in managing emotions. The left hemisphere plays a role in analyzing emotional data, whereas the right hemisphere is tasked with creating emotional reactions. The two hemispheres communicate with each other through a bundle of nerve fibers called the corpus callosum, which allows for the integration of emotional information.

Emotional processing in the brain is a complex process that requires the participation of various brain regions, such as the amygdala, the hippocampus, and the prefrontal cortex. These regions work together to process different aspects of emotions, such as the recognition of emotional stimuli, the generation of emotional responses, and the regulation of emotional states.

Furthermore, it is understood that the decision-making process is closely linked to emotions, as emotions can influence the choices we make. The prefrontal cortex, a region located in the front of the brain, is an essential part of the decision-making process. It is responsible for evaluating the emotional significance of information and for making decisions based on that information.

In summary, recent studies suggest that both hemispheres of the brain are responsible for controlling emotions and that emotional processing in the brain is a complex process that requires the participation of various brain regions. (Brain., 2014.) Furthermore, the decision-making process is closely linked to emotions, and the prefrontal cortex plays an essential role in this process.

WHERE DO EMOTIONS COME FROM?

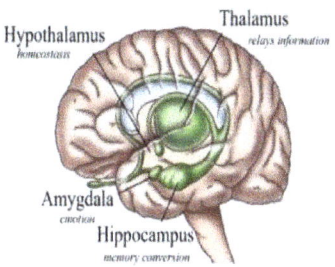

The part of the brain that is responsible for behavioral and emotional responses is the limbic system. This system is a group of interconnected structures located deep within the brain.

While most scientists have not reached an agreement about the full list of structures that make up the limbic system, the following structures are generally accepted as part of the group:

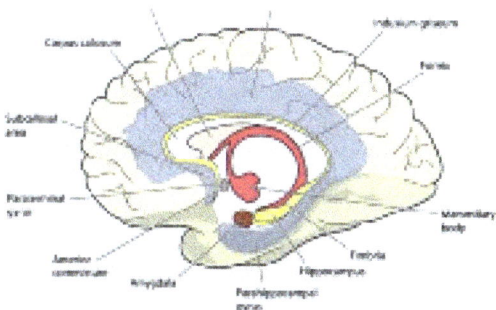

Hypothalamus. In addition to controlling emotional responses, the hypothalamus is also involved in sexual responses, hormone release, and regulating body temperature.

Hippocampus. The hippocampus helps preserve and retrieve memories. It also plays a role in how you understand the spatial dimensions of your environment.

Amygdala. The amygdala helps coordinate responses to things in your environment, especially those that trigger an emotional response. This structure plays an important role in fear and anger.

Limbic cortex. This part contains two structures, the cingulate gyrus and the parahippocampal gyrus. Together, they impact mood, motivation, and judgment. When you are unsettled or anxious, your cingulate gyrus is active. It helps you express your emotional state through gestures, posture, and movement.

As a result of indebt neurocognitive and cognitive studies of the brain, the cingulate gyrus has become a very important piece of the puzzle when understanding human emotions. Surprisingly, in their studies, scientists are discovering that this part of the human brain is involved in a variety of brain functions as well as in some disorders. A case in point for consideration, Alzheimer's disease and depression are two important disorders that have been identified with the cingulate gyrus. This, however, does not exclude disorders such as schizophrenia, bipolar disorder, some anxiety disorders, and addiction. (Smith, 2015.)

Attaining mastery over one's mind, will, and emotions is key to achieving true success in life. This type of success, often referred to as "soul-acle success," is particularly challenging to attain because the mind is a complex and largely unexplored territory. However, understanding the purpose and role of the soul is crucial for achieving success in this area.

One of the most important steps in achieving soul-acle success is to take control of what comes into and out of your mind. Your mind is the central point of all your decisions, and it is these decisions that will shape your future in either a positive or negative way. Therefore, it is essential to cultivate and condition your mind in order to make sound decisions.

This process of cultivation and conditioning starts with mastering the art of self-discipline and developing the ability to regulate one's emotions. The ability to control and discipline the mind, will, and emotions is the key to finding inner peace and fulfillment. It is also important to find a balance in your life, a place where you can be at peace and content.

In summary, true success in life is achieved by attaining mastery over one's mind, will, and emotions. This type of success, referred to as "soul-acle success," is challenging to achieve because the mind is a complex and largely unexplored territory. However, by understanding the purpose and role of the soul, taking control of what enters and exits the mind, and cultivating and conditioning the mind and emotions, one can attain inner peace and fulfillment and ultimately shape their future in a positive way.

The emotions aren't always immediately subject to reason, but they are always immediately subject to action." - William James.

"The mind is everything; what you think, you become." - Buddha (Buddha, 1993)

This quote by Buddha highlights the importance of the mind in shaping one's thoughts, emotions, and, ultimately, one's life. It emphasizes the idea that the mind is a powerful tool that can be used to shape one's reality and that one's thoughts have a direct impact on one's actions and, ultimately, their future. It aligns with the idea that the one who can master his mind and discipline his will and emotions is the one who will enter the realm of true success and inner peace, and fulfillment.

Chapter Two
DEVELOPING YOURSELF MENTALLY

"The man who acquires the ability to take full possession of his own mind may take possession of everything else to which he is justly entitled."

Andrew Carnegie

THE POWER OF EDUCATION

"Stone walls do not a prison make, nor iron bars a cage, mind innocence and quiet takes that for a hermitage; if I have freedom in my love, and in my soul I'm free, angels alone that stores above enjoys such liberty." (Lovelace).

The concept of true freedom is not limited to physical constraints but encompasses the freedom of the mind as well. In fact, true success in any aspect of life starts with a state of mind. The traditional understanding of mental development is often associated with formal education, but it is important to note that formal education is only one aspect of mental development. While education is essential in expanding one's knowledge and providing access to new information, it is not the sole determinant of mental development.

Education is a critical component of mental development as it provides individuals with access to knowledge and information, which serves as the foundation for a new mindset. The word "educate" comes from the Latin word "educo," meaning to draw out and develop from within. This understanding of the word emphasizes the idea that education is not just about acquiring knowledge but also about the ability to effectively utilize and communicate that knowledge to others.

An educated individual is not only one who has acquired knowledge but also possesses the ability to effectively communicate and apply that knowledge to benefit others. These transferable skills are crucial for success in any field, as they allow an individual to not only understand the information but also to use it in real-world situations.

Education is not only the key to acquiring knowledge but also to utilize it to make informed and successful decisions. Economists argue that having access to the right information is essential for making the right decisions, which in turn leads to financial success. However, it is also important to note that formal education is not the only path to success, as there are countless examples of individuals who have achieved financial success without a traditional education.

It is a common misconception that a university education is a requirement for success. In fact, there are numerous examples of successful individuals who did not graduate from university. Some of the most famous ones include Steve Jobs, co-founder and former CEO of Apple Inc; Mark Zuckerberg, founder and CEO of Facebook; Richard Branson, founder of Virgin Group; Bill Gates, founder of Microsoft; Oprah Winfrey, media executive, and television host; Michael Dell, founder, and CEO of Dell Technologies; Larry Ellison, founder of Oracle; Elon Musk, CEO of SpaceX and Tesla; Walt Disney, founder of The Walt Disney Company; Ralph Lauren, founder of Ralph Lauren Corporation; Steve Wozniak, co-founder of Apple Inc; Larry Page, co-founder of Google; Sergey Brin, co-founder of Google; David Geffen, co-founder of Dreamworks; Barbara Corcoran, founder of The Corcoran Group. These are only a few examples, but there are countless more successful individuals who have not graduated from university; these people may not have a formal education, but they took the time to develop their minds through other means such as private study, reading, and learning from others. Their graduation came from the **"University of Life,"** which provides lessons that cannot be taught in the classroom.

While education plays a crucial role in personal and mental development, it is important to recognize that it is not the be-all and end-all. There are many examples of highly educated individuals who have not achieved success. Education should be viewed as a means to an end rather than the end itself. It is important to remember that success is a journey, not a destination, and education is the same way. Education or knowledge should be the tool that guides you towards your desired outcome. Education alone does not guarantee personal freedom, but it does provide access to knowledge which is key in releasing oneself from the restrictions of ignorance. Plato once stated that **"the direction in which education starts a man will determine his future life."** Education serves as a compass for guiding our lives and charting our future. It is important to remember that one's education is never truly complete, and it is essential to incorporate a well-planned reading program as a daily habit. Reading is essential for mental growth as it nourishes the mind. As the saying goes, **"You are what you eat,"** it is important to be mindful of what we feed our minds just as we are with our bodies.

Being mindful of the information we consume is crucial, as our thoughts significantly influence our lives. The adage **"As a man thinks in his heart, so is he"** aptly captures this concept, emphasizing that our thoughts and beliefs profoundly shape who we are and the trajectory of our lives. Both positive and negative, the results we encounter are deeply connected to the strength and character of our thoughts.

Our thoughts are indeed one of life's most potent creative forces. They have the ability to shape our perceptions, influence our decisions, and ultimately determine the path we take. This is why the type of media we expose ourselves to – be it literature, music, or video – plays a significant role in shaping our mental landscape. Consistently engaging with negative or unproductive content can lead to its manifestation in our lives, affecting our attitudes, behaviors, and overall well-being.

The saying **"Just as a man thinks in his heart/mind, so is he,"** suggests that our inner world reflects in our outer reality. We become what we contemplate and internalize. Therefore, it is essential to guard our hearts and minds by being selective and intentional about the information we absorb. This does not only apply to media consumption but also to the ideas, conversations, and even the environments we choose to engage with.

To maintain a healthy and positive mindset, it is important to seek out information and experiences that uplift, inspire, and contribute positively to our growth. This approach not only helps in nurturing a positive outlook but also in fostering a life that is aligned with our values and aspirations. The content we consume should reinforce our goals, encourage constructive thinking, and contribute to a productive and fulfilling life. Remember, the mind is the gateway to the heart, and it is through this gateway that the issues of life flow.

Winston Churchill once famously stated that **"the empires of the future are the empires of the mind."** (Churchill, Speech, Unknown.) This highlights the immense power of the mind in shaping our reality. The world around us, both the one we desire and the one we do not, is a creation of our thoughts. The ancient emperor Marcus Aurelius also recognized this when he said, **"The soul becomes dyed with the color of its thoughts."** (Aurelius., 19XX.) Our thoughts shape us and shape the world we live in. The mind is the foundation of everything, and it is through our thoughts that we can manifest our reality. Your thoughts create you.

To cultivate a prosperous and fulfilling life, it is critically vital that we tend and constantly cultivate the garden of our minds with extreme care and plant only those thoughts that will bear positive fruit. Wisdom, the fruit of knowledge, is the ultimate outcome of this process. Knowledge is the tree that springs up as a result of the information we allow into our minds. We must actively work to cultivate our minds through reading and meditation in order to produce healthy and fruitful thoughts. The man that develops his mind by reading and meditating will be a man **"like a tree planted by streams of water, yielding its fruit in season, whose leaf does not wither, and who prospers in all he does."**

BEN CARSON

Ben Carson, a renowned neurosurgeon, author, and former presidential candidate, shares his story of personal transformation in his book "Think Big." He recounts how he used to be the dumbest kid in the fifth grade until his mother intervened. Fed up with her son's constant failure, she implemented a strict reading program for both him and his brother, requiring them to read two books a day and write a report on each one. This seemingly small change made all the difference in their lives. Ben Carson went from being the lowest performer in his class to graduating at the top of his class. This new voluntary reading program sparked his love for reading and gave him a competitive advantage over his peers as he was exposed to more information than they were. It served as a crucial step on the road to his success.

This newfound love for reading propelled Ben Carson to excel in a way that set him apart from his peers. As he grew older, he went on to become one of the top surgeons at John Hopkins Hospital. Ben Carson was instrumental in the development of the surgical technique for separating conjoined twins, particularly those joined at the head, a procedure known as craniopagus separation. He led several teams of surgeons in successfully separating multiple sets of conjoined twins, including the highly publicized separation of the Binder twins in 1987, which was considered one of the most difficult and complex craniopagus separations ever attempted at that time. His success rate for these surgeries was very high, and many of the separated twins went on to lead normal lives. Dr. Carson's work in this field has been widely recognized, and he is considered a pioneer in the field of neurosurgery; his surgical skills and knowledge helped to save many lives. (Carson, 1992)

Ben Carson's life is a prime example of the transformative power of mental conditioning. By cultivating his mind from a young age, he was able to make a significant impact on the lives of others as he grew older. Many sought out his wisdom in areas such as medical advice, special operations, and life in general. To achieve mental success, it is essential to continually condition the mind. As the saying goes, **"A book a day keeps ignorance away."** Parents, if you are reading this, it is crucial to encourage your children to start reading at an early age. Reading exercises the mind, and for young people, developing a daily reading ritual can lead to significant changes in their life. It is important to note that when I mention reading, I am referring to reading informative books or educational materials, not just light, entertaining reading material.

A well-crafted reading plan is just as important as a balanced diet when it comes to self-improvement. Education is the key that unlocks the door to knowledge and prosperity. Martin Luther King Jr. famously stated, **"Education is that particular something that will lift men from the dark depths of ignorance to the majestic heights of knowledge and prosperity."** (King Jr.) Similarly, another prominent civil rights leader, Malcolm X, believed that **"Education is the passport to the future."** (X., 1965) Education is our ticket to a better and brighter future. Unless you educate yourselves today, you will always be stopped in the future at the airport of life by the immigration of your ignorance. Without a commitment to ongoing education and self-improvement, individuals may find themselves held back in the future by their own lack of knowledge and understanding. Just as being halted at airport immigration for not having the right documents can impede your journey, insufficient education can similarly obstruct individuals from achieving their aspirations and realizing their fullest potential in life. It is like being held back at life's own airport.

It is important to actively seek out opportunities for learning and personal growth to overcome the "immigration of ignorance" and pave the way for a successful and fulfilling future. Education is the bridge between who we are today and who we will become tomorrow. It is essential that we take the time to carefully plan our reading and educational pursuits, much like we would a diet plan, to ensure that we are constantly growing and developing as individuals. (Carson, 1992)

HOW READING SAVED ME

The impact of reading on my personal life has been significant. As a child, growing up in a neighborhood plagued by drugs and crime, I had little inclination towards reading, despite my grandfather's constant encouragement to do my homework and read books. I failed to see the value of reading, and it was not until I entered college that my perspective shifted. My freshman year in college was challenging, particularly in subjects such as English. However, as I began to delve deeper into my coursework and engage with various texts, I began to understand the power of reading. It was through reading that I was able to gain a deeper understanding of the world and myself, and it was through reading that I was able to improve my writing and communication skills.

I came to realize that reading was a crucial tool for personal and intellectual growth.

I struggled with English in college, specifically with organizing my thoughts and expressing them in a structured manner on paper. This problem was rooted in the fact that I had not taken the time to develop my mental capabilities through reading. This deficiency manifested itself in my writing, which lacked coherence and had poorly structured sentences. I struggled with sentence structure, verb-subject agreement, and other language mechanics. My problems were so severe that I failed English 1100, a college-prep course, three times. I became discouraged, but my determination to pass the course kept me going. I knew that I could not move on to higher-level English classes until I passed this one. So, on my fourth attempt at taking English 1100, I decided to change teachers. My new teacher was Professor Raeya, a red-headed man with an unorthodox teaching style. On the first day of class, he announced that the class would be held outside by the lake.

The change of location to the lake situated in the middle of the campus significantly impacted the class dynamic. Professor Raeya introduced a new method called brainstorming, where he asked us to take a piece of paper and write whatever came to mind for 45 minutes. This technique proved to be highly effective as it allowed us to explore our thoughts freely without fear of judgment. The most striking aspect of this exercise was the ability to read our thoughts after the writing session was over. I strongly recommend trying this method for at least 20 minutes, as you may be surprised by the insights and ideas that surface. It was through this exercise that I was able to improve my writing skills and pass English 1100. This experience taught me the importance of being open to new methods and being willing to try new things in order to improve oneself.

Professor Raeya's unorthodox method of teaching English changed my perspective on the subject completely. It was through his class that I developed a newfound appreciation for the English language. One day, he said something that made me realize the key to becoming a good writer. He said, **"If you want to be a good writer, you must be a good reader."** In other words, a person's writing ability is directly linked to how much they read. If a person does not read, their writing will reflect their lack of reading. This statement had a profound impact on me, and as a result, my grades in English improved from a D to an A. I started reading books, newspapers, Time Magazine, Forbes Magazine, and other literature that I believed would benefit me personally.

My writing skills underwent a significant transformation as a result of Professor Raeya's class. I was now able to construct coherent sentences, organize my thoughts, and effectively compose essays. I went on to take English 1101 and 1102 and felt confident in my abilities, earning A's in both classes. I was proud of my accomplishments in English, as I had seen a clear improvement in my skills. The statement made by my professor, **"If you want to be a good writer, you must be a good reader,"** has stuck with me to this day, and as a result, I have implemented a regular reading program as a crucial aspect of my personal development and growth. Thanks to Professor Raeya's teaching methods and my newfound love for English and reading,

I am now the author of several books, which include "A New Start, New Business," "Dividing the Earth," and the book you are currently reading, "Success: The Total Package." This experience has taught me the value of education and the impact that a dedicated teacher can have on a student's life.

I am grateful for the role that Professor Raeya played in my personal and intellectual growth, and I will always carry the lessons he taught me with me.

As a student, I never fully appreciated the fact that I was paying university professors to teach me the importance of reading. However, once I came to understand the power of reading, I no longer needed to be told to read because I fully understood its significance. I have read hundreds of books throughout my life, all of which have enriched my life in countless of ways.

For me, reading has become more than just a hobby; it has become a method for conditioning my mind. Books are like dumbbells for the mind; if you continue to exercise your mind through reading, you will be amazed by the mental strength and capabilities you will possess. Reading has become an integral part of my self-improvement journey, and I encourage others to make it a regular part of their lives as well.

Let me stress that the importance of reading cannot be overstated. As W. Somerset Maugham so eloquently put it, **"To acquire the habit of reading is to construct for yourself a refuge from almost all the miseries of life."** Reading has the power to transport us to different worlds, introduce us to new ideas, and help us better understand ourselves and the world around us. It is a tool for personal and intellectual growth and a means of escape from the stresses and challenges of daily life. I encourage you to integrate reading into your daily routine, to immerse yourself in unfamiliar realms, and to acquire fresh viewpoints. The advantages of reading are boundless, and it could become the most enriching habit you ever develop.

DEVELOPING P.M.A. – POSITIVE MENTAL ATTITUDE

A well-trained mind is the driving force behind every lasting achievement, and one of its most powerful disciplines is **Positive Mental Attitude (PMA).** You will hear the term in business seminars, sports locker rooms, and pulpit messages alike, because experience keeps proving the same truth: **education plus PMA equals success.** Knowledge supplies the "horsepower"; PMA grabs the reins and steers that power toward constructive ends. Without education, energy lacks direction; without attitude, knowledge stalls. Together they move like a horse and carriage, each incomplete without the other.

What PMA Really Means

PMA is not wishful daydreaming or a thin coat of cheerfulness painted over real problems. It is a deliberate discipline that trains you to interpret events through a lens of possibility rather than limitation. Where pessimism asks, "Why even try?" PMA insists, "How can I turn this to my advantage?" It shifts your internal narrative from victim to problem-solver, from obstacle-focused to opportunity-focused. At its core, PMA declares that your thoughts are the architects of your reality—what you consistently dwell on shapes the emotions you feel, the decisions you make, and ultimately the results you experience.

The Mind Behind the Attitude

Psychologists describe the mind as two interlocking systems

Aspect	Share of Mind Power	Key Function
Conscious Mind	~20 %	Voluntary thought, reasoning, immediate choices
Subconscious Mind	~80 %	Habit formation, emotional memory, automatic beliefs

Your conscious mind is the front office, handling daily decisions and deliberate learning. Powerful as it seems, it controls only about one-fifth of your total mental capacity. The subconscious mind is the vast production floor humming out of view. It records every belief you accept—positive or negative—and quietly turns those beliefs into habits, reflexes, and expectations. PMA works because it feeds the subconscious with constructive instructions. Repeated optimistic thoughts become default settings, guiding you automatically when willpower is low.

Cultivating PMA in Daily Life

1. Guard the Gate – Treat every thought like a visitor to your home. If it does not uplift, instruct, or inspire, refuse it entry.
2. Affirm Intentionally – Speak life-giving statements aloud: "I am resourceful," "I adapt quickly," "Solutions come to me." Repetition imprints these truths on the subconscious.
3. Visualize the Outcome – Spend a few minutes each day vividly picturing your desired future—finishing the degree, launching the business, completing the marathon. The clearer the picture, the stronger the subconscious pull toward it.
4. Curate Your Circle – Surround yourself with people, books, and media that reinforce possibility. Attitudes are contagious; choose your company the way an athlete chooses fuel.
5. Convert Setbacks into Feedback – When obstacles arise, ask, "What is this teaching me?" and, "How can I leverage this lesson?" A PMA reframes failure as raw material for growth.

Why PMA Matters

A disciplined positive attitude does more than boost morale; it amplifies every other investment you make—time spent studying, hours logged at the gym, prayers whispered in the dark. It sustains momentum when motivation dips and opens creative channels the moment conventional answers fail. In relationships, PMA breeds empathy and solution-oriented dialogue; in business, it sparks innovation; in health, it accelerates recovery by reducing stress hormones and fortifying immune response.

Possessing a Positive Mental Attitude is therefore not optional for anyone seeking whole-life success. It is the operating system through which spirit, soul, and body upload their combined potential into daily action. Master PMA, and you master the art of turning inner possibility into outer reality.

THE SUBCONSCIOUS MIND

On the other hand, the subconscious mind is considered the true powerhouse of the mind and is responsible for shaping our beliefs, attitudes, and emotions. PMA is a practice that helps individuals to tap into the power of their subconscious mind, to overcome limiting beliefs and negative thoughts, and to develop a more optimistic outlook on life. It is a tool that helps to improve mental well-being and to achieve success in all aspects of life. In short, PMA is not just a concept, it is a discipline that can be trained and developed, and it is a key to unlocking the true potential of the human mind.

The subconscious mind operates similarly to an air traffic controller, effortlessly coordinating the intricate activities on the ground and in the air, much like handling the landings and departures of various airplanes. It functions independently, frequently outside our conscious perception or direct approval.

This behind-the-scenes role of the subconscious is crucial in various aspects of our physiology and psychology. For example, it plays a significant part in the body's natural rejuvenation processes, overseeing the replacement of worn-out cells with new ones and ensuring efficient distribution of nutrients and blood. It also meticulously manages the intricate workings of various body organs.

Beyond its physiological functions, the subconscious mind orchestrates a myriad of activities without requiring our conscious effort. It functions behind the scenes, significantly influencing our beliefs, attitudes, and emotions. While it might not be the primary agent in direct physical healing processes, such as cell regeneration and nutrient distribution, it nevertheless plays a supportive role in facilitating these vital operations.

Additionally, the subconscious is responsible for controlling automatic bodily functions, including breathing, heart rate, and digestion. It acts as a vast repository for memories, processes our emotions, and interprets sensory inputs, all of which are essential for our daily functioning.

Harnessing the power of the subconscious mind can have profound implications for our mental and emotional well-being. By cultivating a positive mental outlook, we can tap into this underutilized resource, leveraging its potential to enhance our overall health and quality of life.

The power of the subconscious mind is vast and multifaceted, acting as a recorder for all sensory input received through the five senses. Additionally, it plays a crucial role in maintaining the body's physical functions, such as the continuous beating of the heart, the filtration systems of the kidneys, and the proper functioning of the lungs and neurological balance in the brain.

Furthermore, the subconscious mind houses two other important functions:

1. It is the source of the ego or the sense of self, which guides a person's thoughts and actions.
2. Some spiritual or religious traditions suggest that the subconscious mind can access deeper levels of consciousness, such as the spiritual realm or the divine, and can be used as a tool for spiritual growth and understanding.

The ego, or sense of self, is shaped by the information that is absorbed through the five senses, with the senses of hearing and sight playing particularly important roles. The ears are the primary organs through which sounds are received, and these sounds are then processed and interpreted by the brain.

The brain then converts these sounds into symbols and images that are stored in the subconscious mind.

Research has shown that the sounds and language we are exposed to from a young age can significantly impact our beliefs and attitudes. For example, a study published in the Journal of Child Language in 2001 found that children exposed to more complex language in their environment had better language skills and cognitive development compared to those exposed to less complex language. (A., Journal of Child Language, (2001))

Additionally, according to a study published in the Journal of Experimental Psychology in 2010, our environment can shape our beliefs about the world, and it is likely that this happens through the sounds and language that we are exposed to.

Furthermore, the Bible says, **"Faith comes by hearing, and hearing by the word of God"** (Paul). This supports the idea that what we hear can play a significant role in shaping our beliefs and faith. Therefore, it is important to be mindful of the sounds and language we are exposing ourselves to, as they can have a powerful impact on our thoughts, beliefs, and actions.

The power of the subconscious mind to shape our thoughts, beliefs, and actions is significant, and the information we absorb through our senses plays a crucial role in shaping our ego. Negative inputs like self-doubt and pessimistic self-dialogue can adversely affect how we see ourselves and our capacity to attain success.

A well-known poem by Napoleon Hill, taken from his book,

"Think and Grow Rich" captures this concept perfectly. It states, **"If you think you're beaten, you are; if you think you dare not, you don't. If you like to** win, but you think you can't, it is almost certain you won't. If you think you'll lose, you're lost, for out in the word we find; Success begins with a fellow's will; it is all in the state of mind.

If you think you're outclassed, you are; you got to think high to rise, Got to be sure of yourself before you can ever win a prize.

Life's battles don't always go to the stronger or faster man,

But sooner or later, the man who wins is the man who THINKS HE CAN!"
(Hill, 2010)

The poem emphasizes that life's battles are not always won by the strongest or fastest person but by the person who believes they can win. This poem highlights the importance of the mind in shaping our thoughts, beliefs, and actions, and it is worth committing to memory as a reminder of the power of the mind.

The subconscious mind plays a crucial role in shaping our thoughts, beliefs, and actions, and the information we absorb through our senses can have a significant impact on our ego. It is important to be mindful of the sounds and language we expose ourselves to, as it can shape our faith and beliefs. Committing a poem like Napoleon Hill's to memory can be a powerful reminder of the power of the mind to shape our thoughts and beliefs. Also, it crystallizes the spirit of this chapter.

The subconscious mind plays a crucial role in shaping our thoughts, beliefs, and actions, and it is essential to guard it with diligence in order to maintain a positive and healthy mindset.

One way to do this is by avoiding toxic individuals, who can contaminate our minds with negative and unhealthy information.

Just like cancer, toxic people can start out small but eventually consume our entire being, affecting our mental and emotional well-being. They have the ability to 'suck our energy' out of us. It is essential to be mindful of who we allow in our circle of influence and to be selective in the individuals we choose to surround ourselves with. These individuals can have a significant impact on our thoughts, beliefs, and actions, and it is important to surround ourselves with individuals who will uplift and encourage us.

Proverbs 4:23 says, **"Above all else, guard your heart, for everything you do flows from it."** This is a reminder of the importance of protecting our subconscious mind from negative influences. By being mindful of the people we surround ourselves with, we can ensure that our thoughts, beliefs, and actions are guided by positivity and healthy information.

It is important to be mindful of the thoughts and beliefs that we allow to take root in our subconscious mind, as they can have a powerful impact on our actions and, ultimately, our success. Sometimes, bad experiences can lead us to become our own worst enemies, limiting our potential and self-sabotaging our efforts.

When we adopt negative self-talk such as "I cannot," "I will never be able to," and "I am a failure," we are setting ourselves up for failure. It is essential to remember that success and failure are both born in the mind. To achieve success, we must train our minds to focus on the positive aspects of our abilities and potential. We must tell ourselves, "I can," "I shall be," and "I am a winner."

By learning to lean more on the positive aspects of our minds and embracing a positive mental attitude, we can unlock the power that lies within us and reach our full potential. It is important to remember that positive thinking is not just a nice idea; it is a powerful tool that can help us achieve our goals and live a happier, more fulfilling life.

THE SENSE OF SIGHT

Our visual sense is the master validator of experience—shaping ego, confirming what our other senses report, and anchoring abstract ideas in concrete images. The eye functions like a high-resolution camera, but it is the brain that edits, labels, and stores the footage. In less than a tenth of a second, light reflected from an object reaches the retina, travels along the optic nerve, and forms an electric pattern the brain interprets as shape, color, depth, and motion. Within that instant, we decide whether to trust, fear, desire, or ignore what we see.

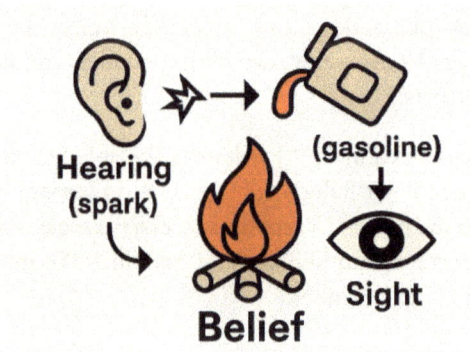

Just as hearing can kindle belief, sight can supercharge it. We often say, *"Seeing is believing,"* or, *"I won't believe it until I see it,"* because vision supplies the final proof that transforms data into conviction. Think of hearing and sight like a campfire: hearing strikes the spark of possibility, but sight pours gasoline on the flames, causing belief to leap higher and burn brighter.

Psychologists have shown that **visual cues powerfully influence judgment.** In one set of experiments, participants who merely glimpsed an image that aligned with an unfamiliar statement rated that statement as more credible than participants who heard the same words without a picture. Even simple graphs or photographs can bias us toward accepting information we would otherwise question—a phenomenon marketers and social-media influencers exploit daily. Vision, in short, is not a passive window; it is an active persuader.

Yet the sense of sight is also vulnerable to error. Optical illusions reveal that our brains sometimes "correct" raw data to match expectations, filling gaps or bending lines that are, in fact, straight. This built-in shortcut helps us navigate a fast-moving world, but it can also mislead. Witnesses to the same accident often deliver conflicting reports, each certain their eyes did not deceive them. Brains interpret; interpretations differ.

To harness sight rather than be manipulated by it, practice **mindful looking:**

1. **Slow Down** – Pause an extra second before deciding what a scene or headline means. That second recruits higher-order reasoning instead of reflex judgment.
2. **Cross-Check** – Verify what you think you saw with another sense: read aloud a chart you're viewing, or touch an object you believe is hot. Multisensory confirmation reduces error.
3. **Curate Inputs** – Surround yourself with images that elevate purpose—art, photography, environments—because what the eyes feast on, the mind eventually believes.
4. **Guard the Gate** – Limit sensational visual media designed to provoke fear or envy. A steady diet of such images distorts reality and dims gratitude.

When integrated with hearing, taste, smell, and touch, sight becomes the orchestra's lead violin—rich, expressive, but most powerful when tuned and playing in concert. By learning to see thoughtfully, we strengthen our ability to judge wisely, believe rightly, and act decisively.

THE EGO

A man's ego can be his greatest asset or his greatest liability, depending on the way he conditions it. The ego is comprised of all our thought and internal scripting by society and family. It comprises everything we have learned, our habits, and our beliefs about who we are. We develop our thoughts through the things we hear and see. This is why being on your guard about what you hear is important. It has been said that if you hear something more than three times, you will start to believe it. This highlights the importance of being selective about the information we expose ourselves to, as repeated exposure can lead to the internalization of false or harmful beliefs. It is important to be selective about the information we take in and to be mindful of the sources of this information, as it can shape our thoughts and attitudes. This is particularly important to avoid internalizing false or harmful beliefs.

Negative self-talk and societal biases can have detrimental effects on our self-esteem and beliefs about ourselves. For example, if parents consistently tell their children from a young age that they are "nothing" and "will never be anything," it is likely that those children will internalize those negative beliefs and grow up with low self-esteem. Similarly, suppose a certain race of people is consistently told through societal messages that they will never rise as a people. In that case, it can lead to the internalization of these negative beliefs and affect their self-esteem and motivation.

Would that not damage the ego of these people? Would they and their children and their children's children not believe this? This kind of negative internal scripting can lead to a lack of self-value and self-appreciation. It has been said, "Just as a man thinks, so is he," and "a man is a sum total of his thoughts." Can you imagine what these people would have to live with mentally? The thoughts we think about ourselves play a significant role in shaping our self-worth, self-esteem, and our perception of ourselves. The harmful effects of internal negative narratives are a major contributor to low self-esteem and diminished self-worth. It is essential to confront these pessimistic thoughts and beliefs, and to immerse ourselves in positive, uplifting messages that can elevate us and enable us to achieve our utmost potential.

The beauty of habits, whether good or bad, is that they can be unlearned, and negative internal scripting can be replaced with positive thoughts. Just as the mind can be programmed to think negative thoughts, it can also be programmed to think positive thoughts. A positive mental attitude is crucial in understanding and appreciating oneself as an individual. A person who displays a positive mental attitude is someone who has learned to love themselves. In line with this, Jesus said, **"Love your neighbor as you love yourself."**

It is important to recognize that changing negative habits and thoughts takes effort and time, but developing a positive mental attitude and loving oneself is worth it. Positive thinking and self-love are interconnected, and both play a crucial role in personal growth and well-being.

THE IMPORTANCE OF SELF-LOVE

Self-love is the foundation for developing a positive mental attitude and for being able to love others. Loving oneself means accepting and appreciating one's faults, flaws, strengths, weaknesses, and imperfections. Many people struggle with self-love due to insecurities about their physical appearance. Some people may dislike themselves because they are short, while others may develop depression due to weight issues. Others may feel uncomfortable with certain aspects of their physical appearance, such as their nose or eyes.

However, it is important to understand that these insecurities are often fueled by comparing ourselves to the unrealistic standards portrayed in the media, such as famous magazines (Perfect People). These standards are often unrealistic and unattainable, and when we feel that we do not measure up, it can lead to self-esteem issues, depression, and even suicide.

To develop a positive mental attitude and to love oneself, it is essential to appreciate and accept who we are rather than constantly comparing ourselves to others. We are all unique and special in our own ways, and it is important to focus on our strengths and work on improving our weaknesses. By loving ourselves, we can improve our self-esteem and our attitude towards ourselves and others. If my kids ever make jokes about my legs or nose, I always remind them that we only have one of each and that we should love and accept them. This has led them to adopt this mindset, and they now use it when their friends try to make fun of them.

In my opinion, to truly understand and appreciate ourselves, it is important to know what the creator thinks about his creation. According to Genesis 1, we were made in the image of God, vs.3 says, **"In the image of God he created him male and female he created them,"** and the book of Psalms states that we are **"fearfully and wonderfully made."**

Knowing this, the opinions of others should not hold as much weight. We are not evolved from lower life forms but were created by a higher one.

"All of creation, including fish, birds, plants, and angels, were all created by the word of God. However, man, me, and you were created with His hands."

All of creation was created by **the word of God,** including fish, birds, plants, angels, the planets, the solar systems, and the universe as a whole. At the beginning of the creation, the book of Genesis states that God spoke the world into existence with the phrase, **"Let there be light."**

The vastness and complexity of the universe are beyond human comprehension. The universe contains an estimated **2 trillion galaxies,** each with billions of stars and planets. The laws of physics and chemistry that govern the universe are incredibly intricate and precise, and scientists are still discovering new phenomena and understanding how everything works together. Overall, the universe is a vast and complex place, and it is impossible for the human mind to fully understand or comprehend its enormity and intricacies. It is a reminder of the limitations of human knowledge and understanding and the vastness of the creator's creation. All of this came into being through His spoken word.

When considering the vastness and magnificence of the universe, it is humbling to think about humanity's place within it. The universe is so immense and complex, yet despite its grandeur, humanity is still at the forefront of God's thoughts. This realization also serves as a reminder of the importance and uniqueness of mankind. It also shows the majesty of the creator, who created all this splendor and complexity, yet He is always thinking about His creation, **Mankind.**

It is uplifting to realize that, despite the vastness and complexity of the universe, humanity is still considered special and unique in the eyes of the creator. According to the book of Genesis, God formed man from the dust of the earth and breathed life into him, physically shaping and creating him with His own hands. This highlights the special and unique nature of humanity compared to the rest of creation and emphasizes the idea that man is a unique and special creation, created with a purpose and a special relationship with the creator. It is something to smile about, knowing that we are not just a small insignificant part of the universe, but we have a special place in it. (2:7.)

UNDERSTANDING THE POWER OF THE SUBCONSCIOUS

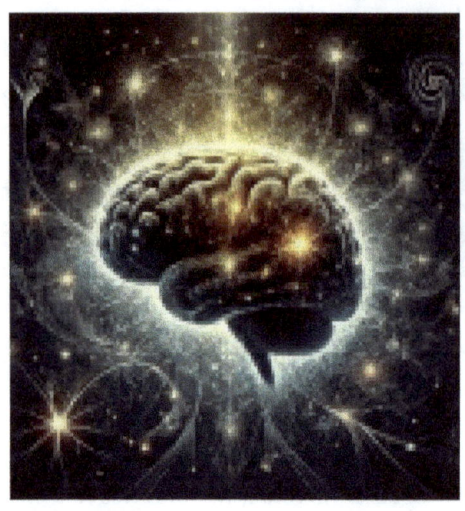

The human brain is an incredibly complex organ composed of an estimated 10 billion neurons. These neurons are interconnected through a network of electrical and chemical signals, allowing the brain to perform a wide range of functions. One of the least understood and explored aspects of the brain is the subconscious mind.

The subconscious mind is believed to be responsible for various automatic processes that occur within the body. For example, it is responsible for regulating vital functions such as heart rate and lung function, as well as the regeneration of cells throughout the body.

Despite its importance, the subconscious mind remains one of the least understood aspects of the human brain.

It is worth noting that scientists do not universally accept the concept of a "subconscious" mind, and it is still a subject of debate and research. Some scientists argue that the subconscious mind is not a distinct part of the brain but rather a concept used to describe the workings of the brain as a whole. Additionally, much research still needs to be done to fully understand the nature and function of the subconscious mind.

The subconscious mind plays a vital role in the healing process of the body, whether it occurs instantaneously or over time. This healing process is often referred to as a "miracle" when it happens quickly or "nature" when it takes place over a longer period. In reality, all healing is carried out by the subconscious mind. For example, when a person receives a wound on their hand, the body will naturally heal itself. However, the process by which this occurs is much more complex than it may appear. The subconscious mind takes action without the person's conscious awareness. It dispatches white blood cells to destroy foreign bacteria entering the body and initiates the healing process.

This process, often referred to as "nature," is actually a complex series of actions carried out by the subconscious mind. The body secretes a substance that forms a clot to stop bleeding and later forms a scab to protect the wound until it is fully healed. Many people do not pay attention to this process, but it is a true work of genius carried out by the subconscious mind.

As previously mentioned, the human mind is made up of two spheres: the conscious and subconscious mind.

The first sphere of the human mind is the conscious mind, which is often referred to as the seat of reason and the gatekeeper. This sphere is responsible for all conscious thoughts, beliefs, and decision-making. According to the book **"The Power of Your Subconscious Mind"** by Dr. Joseph Murphy, the conscious mind is where the action begins, and it is through the conscious mind that we can direct our thoughts and focus our attention. (Murphy, 1963)

The second sphere of the human mind is the subconscious mind, which is often referred to as a garden of fertile soil that is ready to incubate any thought that enters its domain. The subconscious mind is responsible for automatic processes such as breathing and digestion, as well as regulating emotions, memories, and habits. The subconscious mind can be thought of as a fertile soil that is always ready to nurture any thought that enters it. Whatever is planted in the subconscious mind, whether positive or negative, will take root and grow.

The subconscious mind requires constant monitoring as it is unable to distinguish between what is real and what is not. It accepts whatever thoughts and beliefs are fed into it, making them a reality. This is why it is crucial to be diligent in guarding the subconscious mind, as it is the source of all the issues in our lives. The relationship between the conscious and the subconscious mind is fascinating; it operates like a camera where the conscious mind acts as the body of the camera, and the subconscious mind acts as the film or negatives. Whatever images, concepts, or thoughts the conscious mind accepts, or the body captures, are then prominently placed in the subconscious mind, similar to an image on a film negative. After processing, the results can be seen in the form of our behavior, which is a reflection of our life.

The most interesting aspect of this process is that there is no discrimination in the outcome; whatever is captured in the negatives, whether good or bad, will be seen in the final picture. If an individual does not like the picture of their life, they can change the film by being mindful of the thoughts and beliefs that they allow to be ingrained in their subconscious mind. Our behavior and attitude are directly related to the images that have been embedded in our subconscious mind over time.

BEHAVIORAL PSYCHOLOGY TEACHES

Sensory-Subconscious Behavior

Sensory Input → Subconscious Mind → Behavioral Responds

In behavioral psychology, the process of behavior is represented by the flow of sensory input through a "black box" to produce a behavioral response. Sensory input encompasses not only external information from the environment but also internal information about the self, such as thoughts, emotions, and memories. The "black box" represents the subconscious mind, which is responsible for processing and interpreting this information. The subconscious mind stores and accumulates thoughts, ideas, and beliefs, and these shape our perception and interpretation of the world, as well as our behavior and response to the environment. The final step is the outcome, or manifestation, of this input as a behavioral response, and all behavior is believed to have a strong connection to the accumulation of thoughts and ideas in the subconscious mind.

The subconscious mind remains one of the great mysteries of the human experience. Despite its elusive nature, understanding the power of the subconscious is crucial for achieving success in life. When a person discovers the power that lies within the subconscious, they can begin to walk the path of success. This is because the subconscious is a direct reflection of a person, and as the saying goes, **"Just as a man thinks in his heart (subconscious), so is he."** In other words, if success is not present in one's mind, it will not manifest in their life. To begin the journey towards success, the first step is to adopt the right mental attitude.

A mind that embraces positive and uplifting values such as truth, honesty, justice, purity, and loveliness can lead to an abundant and fulfilling life. When these seeds are planted in the garden of our mind, our lives begin to reflect this abundance. This chapter is one of the most important in the book as it lays the foundation for all the other chapters. Before reading further, it is crucial to understand the significance of developing one's mental self, as the mind controls the entire body.

Thus, mental development is a key element in achieving overall success. The full understanding of the subconscious mind may take thousands of years to achieve, but the knowledge we have now can already make a significant impact on our lives. It is important not to waste the potential of the mind and to continue to develop it through reading and meditation. This can be achieved by reading literature that promotes personal growth and meditating on pure thoughts.

"The mind is everything; what you think you become." – Buddha.

REFLECTIONS

The power of the subconscious mind is an essential aspect of achieving success in life. Understanding the workings of the subconscious mind and developing a positive mental attitude through reading and meditation can lead to an abundant and fulfilling life. The quote above by Buddha emphasizes the idea that our thoughts shape our reality, and therefore it is important to be mindful of the thoughts we allow to take root in our minds. Remember that the mind is a powerful tool, and it is important to use it to our advantage by developing it and keeping it in a positive state.

Chapter Three
DEVELOPING YOURSELF EMOTIONALLY

"Emotional development is a lifelong process, requiring continuous self-reflection, learning, and growth. It is the key to cultivating healthier relationships and a more fulfilling life."

Unknown

EMOTIONS - WHAT ARE THEY?

Before delving into the topic of emotional development, it is important to first understand the nature of emotions. What are emotions? Where do they come from? And how can we control and channel them to lead us to greater success? These are important questions to address in order to fully understand the concept of emotional development.

Emotions are often considered abstract and elusive concepts, and writing about them can be challenging. Even scientists who dedicate their lives to studying emotions are still not entirely sure of what an emotion is, and there is much debate on the subject. However, one thing that is agreed upon is that emotions originate from the brain. They are a fundamental part of the human experience that adds depth and richness to our existence.

In this chapter, we will explore the nature of emotions and how they are generated in the brain. We will also discuss the importance of understanding and managing emotions as a key aspect of emotional development. We will examine how emotions can be controlled and channeled to lead us to greater success in life. Additionally, we will discuss how our emotions play a role in our overall well-being and how they can impact on our daily lives.

This chapter will be challenging to write, but it is essential to understanding emotional development and how we can improve our overall well-being and success.

A person without emotions is not truly alive; they are like a zombie, lacking vitality, ambition, and the capacity for love or fear. Unfortunately, our society has become one where many individuals have evolved into creatures without feeling. We rely heavily on the cognitive side of our brain but have severed the connection to the emotional aspect of our mind.

Emotions are a vital part of the human experience; they are what makes us human and what gives our lives meaning. Without emotions, we would be unable to connect to others, experience joy or sorrow, or have any sense of purpose. The detachment of our emotional aspect of the mind has led to a society of individuals that are emotionally disconnected, and this can have a negative impact on our overall well-being and relationships.

It is crucial to reconnect with our emotions and integrate them into our lives. We must strive to understand and manage our emotions, develop empathy and emotional intelligence, and build healthy relationships. This is the true path to living a fulfilling life and being truly human.

Cognitive thinking is solely focused on thinking, reasoning, and decision-making without considering emotions. It is the ability to analyze situations and make decisions based on logic and reason. This part of the brain functions like a computer, processing information and providing logical output. However, the problem arises when we rely solely on cognitive thinking and disregard our emotions. This is known as the Split-Brain theory, where individuals focus on either the cognitive or emotional side of the brain.

I believe that much of the crime and violence in our society is a result of this cognitive way of life. When we rely only on cognitive thinking, we tend to focus on the concept of "an eye for an eye" rather than considering the emotional and moral implications of our actions. Emotions and empathy play a crucial role in our decision-making and actions; without them, we become disconnected from our humanity. Therefore, it is essential to integrate both the cognitive and emotional aspects of our mind to make sound decisions and lead a fulfilling life.

Without compassion and forgiveness, which are emotions that do not stem from cognitive thinking, individuals may become cold-hearted and capable of causing harm or even taking a life. This is an indication that these individuals have severed the connection to their emotions and have evolved into creatures without feelings.

In our society today, we see examples of this behavior all too often. We see instances of domestic abuse, child abuse, sexual assault, and neglect; often, there is a lack of action or response from churches and government organizations. All of this is the result of a society that has lost touch with its emotions. It is important to remember that all humans possess both cognitive abilities and emotions, and it is crucial to integrate both into your lives.

This disconnection from emotions is also evident in individuals' lack of compassion and forgiveness, which are emotions that do not stem from cognitive thinking. When individuals are cold-hearted and cause harm or take a life, it is a sign that they have severed the connection to their emotions and have become creatures without feelings.

In the male gender, cognitive thinking is prevalent, while in the female gender, emotions are more dominant. Each gender possesses traits that align with their individual functions. The problem arises when a particular gender, whether male or female, operates primarily at one end of the spectrum.

For example, when a man functions primarily at the cognitive end of the spectrum, he operates with very little emotion, leading him to become a machine-like being, lacking compassion and feelings. Similarly, when a woman operates too much at the emotional end of the spectrum, she becomes a being without reason and understanding.

What is needed for both genders is a balance between cognition and emotion. Men with analytical minds should also learn to think empathetically, while women who are emotionally intuitive should develop the ability to think both emotionally and logically. Striking a balance between the two traits is essential. Many of society's problems lie in the lack of emotional balance.

Young men killing one another is a tragic consequence of a failure to understand and integrate both cognitive thinking and emotions. These individuals lack the knowledge and understanding of the value of human life and the ability to show compassion and empathy towards others.

An example of this balance can be seen in the teachings of Jesus in Matthew, where He advises us to **"turn the other cheek"** when faced with aggression. As cognitive beings, our initial response may be to retaliate, but when we are in balance, we are able to show love and compassion instead. This is a perfect example of how the integration of cognition and emotion leads to a better understanding of the value of human life and the ability to show compassion towards others.

Emotions and cognitive thinking should not operate independently but as a cohesive entity designed to bring stability to humanity. An emotionally balanced individual can respond to situations in a more rational and stable manner, even when the response is driven by emotions.

For example, women tend to be more emotional and may make decisions based on their feelings rather than reason. This may result in impulsive actions such as excessive shopping without a clear reason, leading to financial consequences later on.

Reaching an equilibrium between emotions and cognitive thinking is crucial for true mental development and understanding. It is important for all individuals to strive for emotional balance and integration of both emotions and cognitive thinking to lead a fulfilling life and make sound decisions.

CASSIUS'S THEORY OF EMOTION

The "Cassius Theory of Emotion" is an interesting concept that proposes that stability in individuals is experienced at the median point of cognitive thinking and emotions. This theory suggests that by balancing the cognitive and emotional aspects of our mind, we can achieve a state of equilibrium, resulting in improved decision-making, better relationships, and overall well-being and true success.

I will attempt to explain this in a diagram below:

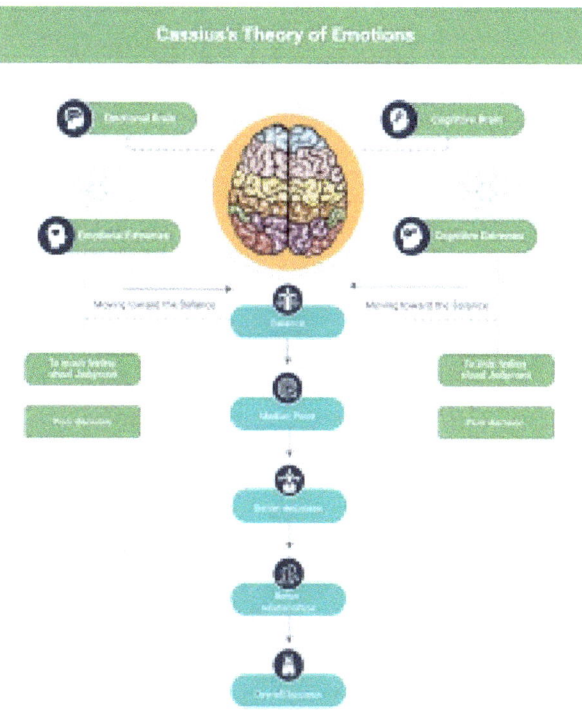

There is a significant amount of scientific research that supports the idea that emotional and cognitive balance is important for overall well-being and decision-making.

One study published in the journal "Emotion" found that people who are able to balance their emotions and cognitive thinking have better emotional regulation and are more resilient in the face of stress. Another study published in the journal "Personality and Social Psychology Review" found that individuals who are able to balance their emotions and cognitive thinking are more likely to make better decisions and have more successful relationships.

Research has also found that cognitive-emotional balance is important in various areas, such as mental health and well-being, relationships, and decision-making. For example, a study published in the journal "Personality and Social Psychology Review" found that people with a balance of cognitive and emotional intelligence tend to have better mental health outcomes and more successful personal relationships. (Lomas, 2012)

Additionally, studies have shown that cognitive-emotional balance is related to better decision-making abilities. A study published in the journal "Emotion" found that people who are able to balance their emotions and cognitive thinking tend to make more rational and effective decisions. (colleagues, 2018)

Achieving true happiness requires finding a balance between cognitive thinking and emotions. The ability to reason and make logical decisions through cognitive thinking is essential, but it must be complemented by the ability to connect with our surroundings and experience emotions. When these two aspects of the mind are in balance, individuals can make sound decisions and have deeper and more meaningful connections with their environment.

THE EVOLUTION OF MEN/ WOMAN

Over time, there has been a shift in the way that women and men relate to emotions and emotions management. Historically, women were seen as more emotionally expressive and in touch with their feelings, while men were seen as more cognitive and focused on logic and reason. However, over the years, this dynamic has changed. Women, who have traditionally been more in touch with their emotions, have now begun to suppress their emotions and adopt more cognitive ways of thinking.

This shift can be attributed to the changes in the societal and family structures. Due to the imbalance in power dynamics and the emotional hurt women have experienced, they have learned to suppress their emotions to survive. This is a result of the societal pressure on women to be strong and independent, which has led to a suppression of their emotional expression.

This change can be seen as an evolutionary process, where women adapt to the changing societal dynamics by becoming more cognitive in their thinking while still maintaining their emotional intelligence.

The evolution of women's relationship with emotions can be seen as an example of Charles Darwin's theory of natural selection. Darwin's theory explains that all creatures are in a constant struggle for self-preservation or survival of the fittest. (Darwin, 1859) In this case, the struggle is not necessarily physical but more of an emotional one. As women have adapted to the changing social dynamics and power imbalances, they have learned to suppress their emotions in order to survive.

This is in line with the philosophy of Baruch Spinoza, who, in his book **"The Ethics of Spinoza,"** states that the foundation of virtue is the endeavor to preserve one's own being and that happiness consists of man's power of preserving his own being. (Spinoza) In this context, preserving one's own being refers to the emotional self-preservation of women in the face of societal pressures and emotional hurt.

Societal changes and power imbalances have forced women to adapt to an environment that is foreign to them. This environment includes the roles of being a single parent, breadwinner, and disciplinary figure in the home. As a result, women are now forced to put their emotions aside in order to assume the artificial role of a father while still remaining a mother. This role requires women to become more cognitive in their way of life.

This evolution is a result of men who have abandoned their natural roles as fathers and have not learned the value of women but used and abused them for their own pleasure.

These changes in the emotional dynamics are having negative effects on society as a whole. Women now have no need for men, not even for sex. They are climbing the corporate ladder and breaking the glass ceiling. Women are now having to act as managers in the offices, fathers, and mothers to their sons and daughters and all the while trying to find time to be a mother and show love in the home. As a result, the family structure is diminished, and society suffers for it in the long run. This is a clear reminder that emotional balance and understanding of each other's role are important for the well-being of society.

On the other hand, men have not progressed much towards the equilibrium point of happiness on the emotional contingent. They have become more and more cognitive in their thinking, and as a result, some are losing their emotional connections not only to their families but also to themselves.

This can be seen in the way that some men allow women to raise their children alone without expressing any concern. This is a clear indication that men have become emotionally detached and have lost touch with their emotions. This action has a negative impact on the next generation as boys grow up wanting to be like their emotionally detached fathers, repeating the same cycle over and over again. This lack of emotional balance and connection not only harms men themselves but also has a ripple effect on society and family structure.

NEW YORK

New York City, with its towering skyscrapers and bustling streets, is a prime example of a metropolis that has transformed into a place where people have become disconnected and mechanical. On a recent visit to attend a United Nations assembly, I took a tour of the city and was struck by the lack of human interaction and connection. Despite the throngs of people on the streets, no one acknowledged my presence or even said hello. The city felt isolated, with each person lost in their own world, going about their business without any sense of community or compassion.

The following day, I took the subway from Manhattan to Brooklyn and was struck by the eerie silence on the train. Despite the cramped quarters, with some passengers standing, no one spoke to each other. It was as if I was riding with a train full of zombies, devoid of emotion and connection. This experience left me concerned that other major cities are becoming or have already become like New York, where people have severed the emotional ties that bind us and become disconnected, robotic beings.

For true emotional growth and understanding of ourselves and others, it is essential to achieve a balance between cognitive and emotional processes. Only by attaining this equilibrium can we fully grasp our identity and connections with others.

UNDERSTANDING YOUR EMOTIONS

It is nearly impossible to accurately identify emotions without observing them manifest through physical expression. As described by Joseph LeDoux, emotions are subjective experiences, a powerful intrusion into our consciousness and a feeling. (Joseph LeDoux)

To gain mastery over our emotions, it is essential to understand them. In his book on ethics, Spinoza identifies three primary emotions: pleasure, pain, and desire. From these three emotions, all other emotions stem, such as love, hate, inclination, aversion, fear, envy, and more.

Given that emotions can only be identified through bodily expression, it is imperative to learn how to control external stimuli that affect our emotions. Understanding how to manage negative emotions and avoid becoming emotionally numb due to past or current experiences is crucial. It is essential to remember that emotions are essential and what makes us human. Without emotions, we would be no different from a sophisticated machine, responding only to reason or logic.

The union of logic and emotion is the mystery that makes a man and a woman complete. With this union, stability in homes and society can be achieved.

Emotions are natural, and it is our responsibility to understand and control them for our well-being and the well-being of those around us.

In a relationship or marriage, men and women bring different perspectives and approaches. For example, when a family moves into a new home, a man may have a more practical and straightforward view of the house, stating something like, "It looks good." On the other hand, a woman may have a more emotional and personal approach, focusing on how to make the house feel like a home by making changes, moving things around, and adding personal touches.

This difference in perspective can be a source of strength for the relationship or marriage. The man's practical approach can provide balance for the woman's emotional approach, and vice versa. Together, they can create a harmonious and functional living space that meets the needs of both partners.

In a similar way, the unique characteristics and perspectives of men and women can bring balance and harmony to a relationship or marriage. By understanding and appreciating each other's strengths and weaknesses, couples can find true happiness and fulfillment. Only at the equilibrium point in their personal lives or in their union can they find true happiness and success.

LOVE

Many philosophers and thinkers have stated that love is one of the strongest emotions, but I would like to challenge this theory. Is love truly an emotion, or is it something deeper? Despite extensive study and analysis by experts in the field, this question remains unresolved until now. This is likely because most philosophers and scientists only examine love at face value, identifying it solely as an emotion based on its observable expressions. However, I posit that love may be a more complex and multi-faceted phenomenon that deserves further exploration and examination.

Love is not simply an emotion but rather the foundation of human existence. It is spiritual in nature, transcending the realm of emotions. When asked, "What is love?" Many people may say it is a feeling or a mutual connection between two individuals. But, in reality, the true nature of love is often misunderstood and difficult to fully grasp.

Love can manifest in many forms: caring, compassion, affection, sensual feelings, and even hatred and rage. Due to the complexity of the concept, the ancient Greeks developed several words for different types of love: storge, phileo, eros, and agape. Storge represents love for material things like a house, car, or pet. Phileo is brotherly love, similar to the meaning of the city Philadelphia, the "City of Brotherly Love." Eros is romantic love, and agape is selfless and unconditional love.

Therefore, Love is a multi-faceted concept that cannot be defined by just one word or one emotion. It encompasses a wide range of feelings and expressions and is an essential part of human existence.

The English language has a limitation in its ability to express the complexities of the concept of love. The four Greek words for love: storge, phileo, eros, and agape, are all translated as simply "love" in English. This causes confusion and lack of clarity in expressing our feelings for animate and inanimate objects. Can we truly love our car with the same intensity as we love our brother or sister? Or can we love God with the same love we have for our house? We say, "I love my job" or "I love my wife," but do these statements truly convey the same meaning?

The problem is that we use the same word to express vastly different feelings and emotions. This limitation in language hinders our ability to fully comprehend and express the nuances of love. It is important to recognize the different forms and expressions of love, rather than using the term generically, to truly understand and appreciate the complexity of this fundamental human experience.

To truly understand the nature of love, we must first recognize its spiritual essence. Love comes from God, and as stated in the Bible, **"God is love"** (I John 4:8). This means that love is not simply an emotion or physical sensation but a spiritual force that emanates from Himself. In fact, the Bible states that whoever does not love does not know God, because **God is love** (I John 4:7-8). Furthermore, it is stated in I John 4:16 that **"God is love. Whoever lives in love lives in God, and God in him."** This passage highlights the deep connection between love and God and how living in love brings one closer to God. Love, in this sense, is not just something we feel or express but something that we embody and live out.

It is crucial to understand that Love is the same Spirit from which God created man. Thus, when we love, we are essentially expressing the very essence of God that resides within us. Love transcends mere emotion or feeling; it is a spiritual force that binds us to God and to each other. This powerful force forms the foundation of human existence and embodies the essence of our being.

Chapter I delves into this concept with greater detail. The Bible states that God created man in His own image and likeness (Genesis 1:26). Given that God is Love, this implies that man's image and likeness are also founded in love. This concept can be better understood through the analogy of a branch that has been severed from a tree. Although the branch is now separate, it retains the same genetic makeup and essence as the tree. In a similar manner, since man originated from God, he embodies the same essence of love that characterizes God.

It is essential to recognize that the love residing within our flesh is often expressed through emotions. Yet, these emotions are merely attempts to manifest love in a physical form. Sex, regarded as the pinnacle of natural pleasure, also represents an effort to express love towards one another. The experience of a sexual orgasm shared between two people can be seen as one of the most profound expressions of love, owing to the deep emotional and physical intimacy involved in such an interaction.

Further, sexual intimacy is often considered to be one of the most intimate forms of connection between two people. It requires a level of vulnerability and trust that allows for a profound expression of love and affection. The physical closeness and release of oxytocin, often referred to as the "cuddle hormone," during sexual orgasm can lead to a sense of bonding and attachment between partners. This can further strengthen the emotional connection between two individuals and deepen their feelings of love for one another. Love cannot be fully understood in the physical realm because the flesh is not capable of comprehending the spiritual nature of love.

To truly understand love, we must understand God, as He is the source of all love. Love is not just an emotional reaction or feeling but rather a spiritual force that emanates from God. It is important not to confuse emotional reactions with love itself. In order to truly understand love, we must connect with God, the source of all love.

One of the most striking aspects of the teachings of Jesus Christ is that He emphasized the importance of love above all else. While on earth, He left us with one central commandment: to love one another. This commandment encompasses all other commandments and teachings, as love encompasses a wide range of virtues and actions. As the Apostle Paul stated, even **"if one has great faith and the ability to prophesy, without love, one is nothing."** (Paul A.) This is because love is essential to our very existence as human beings. Without love, we deny our very humanity.

Emotional development is crucial for human beings, as emotions greatly shape and influence our behavior. It is important to recognize that emotions are not inherently negative, but rather they need to be developed and regulated. Emotions enable us to physically express love to others and are the driving force behind human connections and relationships. They give life and depth to our experiences, and without them, society would be akin to a mechanical dystopia.

As the famous psychologist, Daniel Goleman, once stated, **"Emotional intelligence is the foundation for a host of critical skills—from empathy and self-awareness to self-regulation and relationship management—that are essential for success in life."** (Goleman, 1995.) Emotional development is essential to human flourishing and well-being.

"Love is the only force capable of transforming an enemy into a friend." - Martin Luther King Jr.

Chapter Four
DEVELOPING YOURSELF PHYSICALLY

"Your body is a reflection of your lifestyle choices. Invest in your physical health, and it will pay dividends in all areas of your life."

Unknown

Many individuals fail to grasp the significance of nurturing the physical aspect of their lives. Developing the physical aspect of our lives is paramount as it serves as the foundation for all other areas of our lives. Our physical body serves as the vessel in which we experience and navigate the world around us. Without a healthy and functioning physical body, it becomes challenging to achieve our goals and aspirations. Unfortunately, this area is often neglected and taken for granted by many. It is crucial that we recognize the importance of physical development and make it a priority in our daily lives.

Prioritizing our physical health is vital, which involves regular exercise, a balanced diet, sufficient rest, supplementing with essential vitamins, and finding joy in life. Success in any area, be it finance, politics, religion, or national leadership, hinges on having a well-functioning body.

Neglecting our physical development or neglecting to maintain a healthy body will result in our failure to reach our full potential. To truly achieve success, we must make physical development a priority in our lives.

In pursuit of success, many entrepreneurs and leaders sacrifice their health for the illusion of achievement. They prioritize their goals at the expense of their physical well-being, only to fall short in the end. A healthy body is essential for the enjoyment of any material possessions. We have all known individuals who have amassed great wealth but lack the wealth of good health.

THE GOOSE THAT LAID THE GOLDEN EGG

This reminds me of Aesop's fable, **"The Goose That Laid the Golden Egg."** The story is about a farmer who has nothing to offer his family. One day, as he was checking his barn, he noticed that one of his geese had laid a glittering golden egg. At first, he did not believe it, but as he brushed the egg aside, he said to himself, "I have nothing to lose; I will take it to be appraised." The egg turned out to be pure gold, and the farmer was overjoyed. The next day, the experience repeated itself. Day after day, the farmer would rush to the nest and find another golden egg. He became fabulously wealthy, but his success was short-lived.

With his increasing wealth came greed and impatience. Unable to wait day after day for the golden eggs, the farmer decided to kill the goose and get all the golden eggs at once. But when he opened the goose, he found it empty. There were no golden eggs, and now there was no way to get any more. The farmer had destroyed the goose that produced them and now suffered the loss of his fortune and the very thing that brought it. The moral of the story is that greed and impatience can lead to the destruction of what we value most. Like in the story, many of us fall into this trap of sacrificing our health for success, and in the end, we lose both. (Fables, 2008,)

Many of us can relate to the farmer in Aesop's fable, who sacrificed his goose for the sake of immediate gain. In our daily lives, we often work tirelessly to make a living but forget to live in the process. We neglect the most important aspect of our lives, our physical well-being, in pursuit of success. Physical development is a fundamental component in the formula for success. Without a healthy body, we cannot fully experience the essence of success.

As Mahatma Gandhi once said, **"It is health that is real wealth and not pieces of gold and silver."** (Gandhi M. K., 1948) Many professionals in the corporate world deceive themselves with the illusion of success achieved through material wealth while simultaneously destroying their bodies through poor sleep habits, overwork, improper diet, lack of exercise, drugs, and alcohol.

THE IMPORTANCE OF VITAMINS

As stated in chapter one, the human body is composed of many elements, most of which are acquired through the food we eat. Many of the body's vital nutrients are lost through processed foods. Therefore, it is essential to supplement or replace these lost nutrients. One of the most important ways to do this is by consuming a balanced intake of vitamins. Vitamins are organic substances that are necessary for life. They are essential to the normal functioning of the human body and must be obtained from foods or dietary supplements. Vitamins play such a critical role in human life that it is impossible to sustain life without them. It is important to remember that vitamins cannot replace food and should always be taken with food.

As outlined in chapter one, the human body comprises various elements, most of which are acquired through the food we consume. However, many of these vital nutrients are lost through processed foods.

In order to maintain optimal health, it is necessary to supplement or replace these lost nutrients.

Vitamins are organic compounds that are essential for life. To live a healthy lifestyle, it is important to consume a balanced intake of vitamins. These vital compounds play a crucial role in the normal functioning of the human body and must be obtained from foods or dietary supplements. Without them, it is impossible to sustain life. It is important to understand that vitamins cannot replace food and should only be consumed in conjunction with a balanced diet.

It is important to dispel the myths surrounding vitamins and understand their true role in maintaining optimal health. According to the Vitamin Bible, vitamins are not magic pills and do not provide energy on their own. They are not a substitute for other essential nutrients such as proteins, minerals, fats, carbohydrates, and water, and they do not serve as components of our body structure. Simply taking vitamins without consuming a balanced diet will not lead to optimal health. (Mindell, 2011)

Vitamins play a crucial role in the proper functioning of the body, and a deficiency in even a single vitamin can disrupt the body's normal processes. Dr. T. Quigley, the author of **The National Malnutrition**, states that **"Everyone who has in the past eaten processed sugar, white flour, or canned food has some deficiency disease, the extent of the disease depending on the percentages of such deficient food in the diet."** (Quigley, January 1, 1943)

Furthermore, eating out at restaurants or consuming pre-prepared food can also put a person at risk for vitamin deficiencies. According to the Vitamin Bible, many restaurants reheat or keep food warm under lamps, which can lead to deficiencies in vitamins A, B1, and C. Additionally, for women between the ages of 13 to 40, this type of dining can also lead to deficiencies in calcium and iron. It is important to be aware of these risks and make sure to supplement our diets with vitamins and minerals if we are not consuming a well-balanced diet.

Physical development is more than just exercising, eating a proper meal, or taking vitamins; it is about having an understanding of what you eat and what vitamins and minerals your body needs. It also encompasses an understanding of the importance of minerals, which are essential for optimal health.

Minerals, like vitamins, are essential for the normal functioning of the body. They play a crucial role in energy production, organ function, food utilization, and cell growth. They are needed in addition to carbohydrates, proteins, fats, minerals, vitamins, and water.

However, despite their importance, many of us fail to fully understand the role of vitamins and minerals in our diet. It is important to take the time to learn about the different vitamins and their functions in order to make informed decisions about our nutrition and overall health.

VITAMIN A

Vitamin A is a fat-soluble vitamin that plays a crucial role in maintaining good vision, a healthy immune system, and healthy skin. It is essential for the proper functioning of the eyes, particularly in low-light conditions.

It also helps to maintain the integrity of the skin and mucous membranes, which act as a barrier against infection.

To be properly absorbed by the body, Vitamin A requires fat as well as minerals. It is found in foods such as liver, eggs, butter, and leafy greens. A deficiency in Vitamin A can lead to night blindness and an increased risk of infections. It is important to consume a balanced diet that includes foods rich in Vitamin A or to supplement the diet with Vitamin A supplements if needed.

Vitamin A can be found in a variety of food sources. Some good sources of Vitamin A include:

Fish oils: such as cod liver oil, which is particularly high in Vitamin A.

Liver: particularly beef and chicken liver.

Carrots: which are high in beta-carotene, a precursor to Vitamin A.

Eggs
Milk and dairy products

Yellow fruits: such as apricots and mangoes.

It is important to note that some of these sources can be high in fat and cholesterol, so it is important to consume them in moderation and balance them with various other nutrient-dense foods. Additionally, beta-carotene found in plant-based sources such as carrots, spinach, broccoli, and sweet potato is also converted to Vitamin A in the body. Vitamin A has several important functions in the body, including:

"Vitamin A offers multiple health benefits. It:

Enhances Eye Health: Vitamin A is crucial for optimal eye function, especially in low-light conditions. It preserves the integrity of the retina, the light-sensitive tissue at the rear of the eye. A deficiency in Vitamin A can result in night blindness and an elevated risk of various eye disorders.

Strengthens Immune Defenses: Vitamin A plays a critical role in maintaining a robust immune system. It reinforces the integrity of the skin and mucous membranes, forming a barrier against infections. Additionally, it promotes the production of white blood cells, which effectively combat infections.

In summary, Vitamin A significantly contributes to eye health and reinforces the immune system, aiding the body's defense against infections.

Vitamin A also helps in the removal of aging spots and promotes growth, strong bones, healthy skin, hair, teeth, and gums.

It is important to note that having too much Vitamin A can be harmful and cause toxicity, so it is important to consume the recommended daily intake and not exceed it.

VITAMIN B1 (THIAMINE)

Vitamin B1, also known as thiamine, is a water-soluble vitamin that plays a crucial role in the body's metabolism, particularly in the conversion of glucose into energy. It also supports the proper function of the nervous system and helps to maintain healthy heart function.

Unlike fat-soluble vitamins, water-soluble vitamins like Vitamin B1 are not stored in the body. Any excess is excreted in the urine, which means that it is important to consume enough Vitamin B1 on a daily basis.

Good sources of Vitamin B1 include:

Whole grains: such as wheat germ, oats, and brown rice.

Legumes: such as lentils and black beans.

Meat: particularly pork and beef.

Fish: such as tuna and salmon.

Eggs.

Nuts and seeds.

Deficiency in Vitamin B1 can lead to symptoms such as fatigue, depression, and nerve damage. It is important to consume a balanced diet that includes a variety of foods that are rich in Vitamin B1 or take supplements if needed.

Vitamin B1 has several important functions in the body, including:

Does:

Promote growth: Vitamin B1 plays a crucial role in the body's metabolism, particularly in the conversion of glucose into energy, which is essential for growth.

Aid in digestion, especially of carbohydrates: Vitamin B1 helps in the breakdown and digestion of carbohydrates, which is important for maintaining a healthy digestive system.

Improve mental attitude: Vitamin B1 helps in the proper functioning of the nervous system, which can improve mental attitude.

Keep the nervous system, muscles, and heart functioning normally: Vitamin B1 helps in the proper functioning of the nervous system, muscles, and heart, which is essential for overall health.

Help fight air or seasickness: Vitamin B1 can help in preventing symptoms of air or seasickness.

Aid in the treatment of herpes zoster: Vitamin B1 may help in reducing the symptoms of herpes zoster, a viral infection that causes a painful rash.

It is important to note that it is essential to consume the recommended daily intake of Vitamin B1 and not exceed it. Vitamin B1 supplementation should be done under the guidance of a healthcare professional.

VITAMIN B2 (RIBOFLAVIN)

Vitamin B2, also known as riboflavin, is a water-soluble vitamin that is easily absorbed by the body. Unlike some other vitamins, it is not stored in the body and must be replaced regularly through diet or supplements. Good dietary sources of vitamin B2 include milk, liver, kidney, yeast, cheese, leafy green vegetables, fish, and eggs. Vitamin B2 plays an important role in growth and reproduction and promotes healthy skin, nails, and hair. It also helps to eliminate sour lips, mouth, and tongue and benefits vision, alleviating eye fatigue. Additionally, it functions with other substances in the body to metabolize carbohydrates, fats, and proteins.

Sources: of Vitamin B2 (Riboflavin):

Milk and dairy products such as cheese, yogurt, and cottage cheese.

Liver, kidney, and other organ meats.

Yeast, including nutritional yeast.

Leafy green vegetables such as spinach, broccoli, and kale.

Fish such as salmon and trout.

Eggs.

Fortified cereals, bread, and other grains.

Almonds and other nuts.

Legumes such as peas, lentils, and beans.

Fruits such as avocados and bananas.

It is important to have a well-balanced diet that includes a variety of these foods to ensure adequate intake of Vitamin B2.

Does:

Vitamin B2 plays a vital role in various bodily functions, including:

Aid in growth and reproduction: It helps in the production of red blood cells and the formation of hormones and neurotransmitters that are essential for growth and reproduction.

Promote healthy skin, nails, and hair: It is important for the maintenance of healthy skin, nails, and hair. A deficiency of vitamin B2 can lead to skin disorders such as eczema and seborrheic dermatitis, as well as brittle nails and hair loss.

Help eliminate sour lips, mouth, and tongue: A deficiency of vitamin B2 can cause inflammation of the mouth and tongue, leading to symptoms such as soreness, cracking, and a burning sensation. It also helps to eliminate sour lips.

Benefit vision and alleviate eye fatigue: Vitamin B2 plays a role in the metabolism of vitamin A, which is important for maintaining healthy vision. It also helps to alleviate eye fatigue and prevent cataracts.

Function with other substances to metabolize carbohydrates, fats, and proteins: Vitamin B2 plays an important role in the metabolism of carbohydrates, fats, and proteins. It helps to convert food into energy by facilitating the breakdown of these macronutrients. It also helps to activate enzymes that are involved in these processes.

It is important to have an adequate intake of vitamin B2 to support these functions and avoid deficiency-related issues.

VITAMIN B6 (PYRIDOXINE)

Vitamin B6, also known as pyridoxine, is a water-soluble vitamin that is easily excreted by the body within eight hours of ingestion. Therefore, it must be regularly replenished through diet or supplements to maintain adequate levels in the body.

Vitamin B6 plays an important role in various bodily functions, including:

Necessary for the production of hydrochloric acid and magnesium. This helps in the digestion of proteins and absorption of nutrients from food.

It helps in the formation of red blood cells and the synthesis of neurotransmitters, which are important for healthy brain function.

It plays a role in the formation of collagen, which is important for healthy skin, hair, and nails.

It helps in the metabolism of homocysteine, which is a compound that can increase the risk of heart disease when present at high levels.

It helps in the formation of the hormone's melatonin and serotonin, which are important for regulating sleep and mood.

Good dietary sources of Vitamin B6 include Chicken, fish, pork, beef, potatoes, bananas, chickpeas, and fortified cereals.

It is important to have a well-balanced diet that includes a variety of these foods to ensure adequate intake of Vitamin B6 and to avoid deficiency-related issues.

Source: Vitamin B6 include chicken, fish, pork, beef, potatoes, bananas, chickpeas, fortified cereals, Cantaloupe, cabbage, blackstrap molasses, unmilled rice, eggs, oats, peanuts, walnuts, liver, kidney, wheat germ, wheat bran, and brewer's yeast. It is important to have a well-balanced diet that includes a variety of these foods to ensure adequate intake of Vitamin B6 and to avoid deficiency-related issues. It is worth noting that some of these food items like liver, kidney, and brewer's yeast are also rich in other B vitamins, making them an excellent source of multiple B vitamins.

Does:

Vitamin B6 plays a vital role in various bodily functions, including:

Properly assimilate protein and fat: Vitamin B6 is important for the proper metabolism of protein and fat. It helps the body to properly break down and utilize these macronutrients.

Aid in the conversion of tryptophan to niacin: Vitamin B6 is necessary for the conversion of the essential amino acid tryptophan to niacin (vitamin B3).

Alleviates nausea: Vitamin B6 is commonly used to alleviate nausea and vomiting, especially in pregnant women experiencing morning sickness.

Promote the proper synthesis of anti-aging nucleic acids: Vitamin B6 is essential for the synthesis of nucleic acids, which are the building blocks of DNA and RNA. Help reduce dry mouth and urination problems caused by tricyclic antidepressants: Vitamin B6 has been shown to help alleviate the side effects of tricyclic antidepressants, such as dry mouth and urinary problems.

Reduce night muscle spasms, leg cramps, hand numbness, and certain forms of neuritis in the diuretic: Vitamin B6 helps to regulate nerve function and can help to alleviate symptoms of conditions such as night muscle spasms, leg cramps, hand numbness, and certain forms of neuritis.

Work as a natural diuretic: Vitamin B6 can also act as a natural diuretic, helping to increase urine production and reduce fluid retention in the body.

It is important to have an adequate intake of Vitamin B6 to support these functions and avoid deficiency-related issues

VITAMIN B12 (COBALAMIN)

Vitamin B12, also known as cobalamin, is a water-soluble vitamin that is effective in very small doses. It is unique among vitamins in that it contains essential mineral elements and is mostly supplied by animal products, such as meat, fish, dairy, and eggs.

Vitamin B12 plays an important role in various bodily functions, including:

The formation of red blood cells and DNA synthesis.

Maintaining a healthy nervous system.

Assisting in the metabolism of homocysteine, a compound that can increase the risk of heart disease when present in high levels.

Supporting the production of neurotransmitters, which are important for healthy brain function.

It is important to note that people who follow a vegetarian or vegan diet may be at risk of deficiency since B12 is mostly found in animal products.

Also, people with certain medical conditions, such as pernicious anemia, and those who have had gastrointestinal surgery may have difficulty absorbing B12 and may require B12 supplements.

Source: Liver, beef, pork, eggs, cheese, and kidney are all rich sources of Vitamin B12. In addition, many breakfast cereals, nutritional yeasts, and fortified soy products are also fortified with Vitamin B12. It is important to note that people who follow a vegetarian or vegan diet may be at risk of deficiency since B12 is mostly found in animal products. So, they may consider taking B12 supplements or eating fortified foods.

It is important to have a well-balanced diet that includes various foods to ensure adequate intake of Vitamin B12 and avoid deficiency-related issues.

Vitamin B12 plays a vital role in various bodily functions, including:

Form and regenerate red blood cells, thereby preventing anemia: Vitamin B12 is essential for the formation of red blood cells and helps to prevent anemia.

Does:

Promote growth and increase appetite in children: Vitamin B12 is important for children's growth and development and can help increase appetite.

Increase energy: Vitamin B12 plays a role in the metabolism of carbohydrates, fats, and proteins, which helps to convert food into energy. Maintain a healthy nervous system: Vitamin B12 is important for maintaining a healthy nervous system and is involved in the formation of myelin, the protective coating that surrounds nerve fibers.

Properly utilize fats, carbohydrates, and protein: Vitamin B12 helps to properly utilize fats, carbohydrates, and proteins, which are important for overall health.

Relieve irritability: Vitamin B12 can help to alleviate irritability and other mood-related symptoms.

Improve concentration, memory, and balance: Vitamin B12 can help to improve cognitive function, including concentration, memory, and balance.

BIOTIN (COENZYME R OR VITAMIN H)

Biotin, also known as Vitamin H or coenzyme R, is a water-soluble, sulfur-containing vitamin that is a member of the B-complex family. It plays an important role in various bodily functions, including:

Metabolism of carbohydrates, fats, and proteins: Biotin is required for the proper metabolism of carbohydrates, fats, and proteins and helps convert food into energy.

Maintaining healthy skin, hair, and nails: Biotin is important for maintaining healthy skin, hair, and nails. A deficiency can lead to symptoms such as dry skin, brittle nails, and hair loss.

Supporting nerve function: Biotin is important for maintaining healthy nerve function and may help prevent or alleviate peripheral neuropathy symptoms.

Assisting in the production of certain hormones: Biotin is required to produce certain hormones and helps regulate gene expression.

Good dietary sources of biotin include eggs, dairy products, nuts, seeds, and certain vegetables like sweet potatoes, carrots, and cauliflower.

Sources:

Eggs, particularly the yolks.

Dairy products such as milk and cheese.

Nuts such as almonds and pecans.

Seeds such as sesame and sunflower.

Certain vegetables, such as sweet potatoes, carrots, and cauliflower.

Legumes such as lentils and peas.

Whole grains.

Meat, fish, and poultry.

Yeast and mushrooms.

It is important to have a well-balanced diet that includes a variety of these foods to ensure adequate intake of Biotin. Keep in mind that cooking or processing food can reduce the biotin content. Therefore, it is better to consume them in raw or slightly cooked form.

Does:

Biotin is important for maintaining healthy skin, hair, and nails, and its deficiency can lead to symptoms such as dry skin, brittle nails and hair loss. However, the statement that it specifically "Aid in keeping hair from turning gray" and "Helps in the preventive treatment of baldness" needs more research to confirm. Some studies suggest that biotin may be beneficial in preventing hair loss, but more research is needed to confirm this.

Biotin has been known to:

Ease muscle pains: Some studies suggest that biotin may help to alleviate muscle pain and weakness.

Alleviate eczema and dermatitis: Biotin may be beneficial in the treatment of eczema and dermatitis, as it helps to maintain healthy skin.

It is important to have an adequate intake of Biotin to support these functions and avoid deficiency-related issues. However, it is worth noting that more research is needed to confirm the potential benefits of biotin for hair health, muscle pains, and eczema.

VITAMIN C (ASCORBIC ACID, CEVITAMIN ACID)

Vitamin C, also known as ascorbic acid or cevitamin acid, is a water-soluble vitamin that is important for various bodily functions. Unlike most animals, humans do not have the ability to synthesize their own vitamin C and must obtain it through diet or supplements.

Vitamin C plays an important role in various bodily functions, including:

Formation of collagen: Vitamin C plays a primary role in the formation of collagen, which is important for the growth and repair of body tissue cells, gums, blood vessels, bones, and teeth.

Helps the body's absorption of iron: Vitamin C helps the body to absorb iron from plant-based foods such as fruits, vegetables, and grains.

Preventive for Crib Death or Infant Death Syndrome (SIDS): Vitamin C has been recommended as a preventive for crib death or Infant Death Syndrome (SIDS) as it plays a role in maintaining the health of the nervous system.

Supporting Immune System: Vitamin C has antioxidant properties and helps to support the immune system by fighting off harmful pathogens and supporting the production of white blood cells.

Source: Good dietary sources of Vitamin C include: citrus fruits such as oranges, lemons, and limes, as well as berries, kiwi, papaya, mango, pineapple, guava, bell peppers, spinach, and broccoli.

Does:

Vitamin C plays a vital role in various bodily functions, including:

Heals wounds, burns, and bleeding gums: Vitamin C is important for the formation of collagen, which helps to heal wounds, burns, and bleeding gums.

Help in decreasing blood cholesterol: Vitamin C may help to decrease blood cholesterol levels by increasing the production of bile in the liver.

Aid in preventing many types of viral and bacterial infections and generally potentiate the immune system: Vitamin C has antioxidant properties and helps to support the immune system by fighting off harmful pathogens and supporting the production of white blood cells.

Offer protection against cancer-producing agents: Vitamin C may help to offer protection against cancer-producing agents by neutralizing harmful free radicals.

Act as a natural laxative: Vitamin C may act as a natural laxative by increasing bowel movements and promoting the elimination of waste from the body.

Lowers incident of blood clots in the veins: Vitamin C may help to lower the incidence of blood clots in the veins by promoting the production of collagen, which helps to keep blood vessels strong and flexible.

Aid in the treatment and prevention of the common cold: Vitamin C may help to shorten the duration of the common cold and may also reduce the risk of developing a cold.

Extend life and enable protein cells to hold together: Vitamin C may help to extend life by enabling protein cells to hold together, which helps to maintain the integrity of the body's tissues.

Prevent scurvy: Vitamin C is essential for preventing scurvy, a disease caused by a deficiency of vitamin C that was common among sailors in the past. Scurvy causes symptoms such as tiredness, muscle weakness, joint and muscle pain, and easy bruising.

It is worth noting that Vitamin C is one of the most widely ingested supplements due to its wide range of health benefits. However, it is important to note that excessive intake of Vitamin C can cause adverse effects, such as diarrhea, nausea, and stomach cramps. It is always best to consult a healthcare professional before starting any supplement regimen, especially if you are pregnant or have any pre-existing health conditions.

CALCIUM PANTOTHENATE (PANTOTHENIC ACID, PANTHENOL, VITAMIN B5)

Calcium Pantothenate, also known as Pantothenic acid, Panthenol, or Vitamin B5, is a water-soluble vitamin that is a member of the B-complex family. It plays an important role in various bodily functions, including:

Cell building and normal growth and development: Pantothenic acid is important for the normal growth and development of the body's cells, including those of the central nervous system.

Metabolism: Pantothenic acid helps to convert food into energy and is involved in the metabolism of fats, carbohydrates, and proteins.

Stress relief: Pantothenic acid helps in the production of the hormone cortisol, which plays a role in the body's response to stress.

-Skin health: Pantothenic acid is important for healthy skin and may help to alleviate symptoms of conditions such as acne.

Source: Good dietary sources of Pantothenic acid include meat, fish, poultry, eggs, dairy, whole grains, legumes, and vegetables such as sweet potatoes, broccoli, and mushrooms. Pantothenic acid, also known as Vitamin B5, plays an important role in various bodily functions, including:

Aid in wound healing:

Does:

Pantothenic acid is involved in the formation of red blood cells, which are important for wound healing.

Fights infections by building antibodies: Pantothenic acid is involved in producing antibodies, which help fight off infections.

Treats postoperative shock: Pantothenic acid may help to prevent and treat postoperative shock by supporting the proper function of the adrenal glands.

Prevents Fatigue: Pantothenic acid helps to convert food into energy, which can help to prevent fatigue.

Reduce adverse and toxic effects of many antibiotics: Pantothenic acid may help to reduce the adverse and toxic effects of certain antibiotics by supporting the proper function of the adrenal glands.

CHOLINE

A member of the B- Complex family and a lipotropic (fat emulsifier).

One of the few substances able to penetrate the so-called blood-brain barrier, Choline goes directly into the brain cell to produce a chemical that aids in memory. Seems to emulsify cholesterol so that it does not settle on artery walls or in the gall bladder.

Source: Egg yolks, wheat germ, bran, liver, heart, green leafy vegetables, and yeast.

Does:

Help control cholesterol buildup.

Aid in the sending of nerve impulses, specifically those in the brain used in the formation of memory.

Assist in conquering the problem of memory loss in later years.

Help eliminate poisons and drugs from the body by aiding the Liver.

Aid in the treatment of Alzheimer's disease.

VITAMIN D (SUNSHINE VITAMIN)

Vitamin D, also known as the "sunshine vitamin," is a fat-soluble vitamin that is primarily acquired through sunlight or diet. Ultraviolet rays from the sun act on the oils in the skin to produce vitamin D, which is then absorbed into the body. However, it is important to note that after a suntan, vitamin D production through the skin stops.

Vitamin D plays an important role in various bodily functions, including:

Bone health: Vitamin D helps the body to absorb calcium and phosphorus, which are essential for maintaining strong and healthy bones.

Immune system: Vitamin D helps support the immune system by promoting the production of white blood cells and fighting harmful pathogens.

Cardiovascular health: Vitamin D may help to lower the risk of cardiovascular disease by promoting the proper function of the cardiovascular system.

Mood and mental health: Vitamin D may help to improve mood and mental health by promoting the production of neurotransmitters such as serotonin and dopamine.

Source:

Good dietary sources of Vitamin D include fatty fish, egg yolks, and mushrooms. However, it is important to note that many people may not get enough Vitamin D from diet alone, especially during the winter months or for people who spend most of their time indoors. In these cases, supplementation or spending time in the sun may be necessary. Soluble fats are acquired through sunlight or diet. Ultraviolet sunrays act on the oils of the skin to produce this vitamin, which is absorbed into the body.

Does:

Vitamin D does play a role in properly utilizing calcium and phosphorus, which are necessary for strong bones and teeth. It helps the body to absorb these minerals from the diet and aids in their deposit into the bones. Additionally, taking vitamin D with vitamins A and C can aid in the prevention of colds, as vitamin D helps to boost the immune system. It also aids in the assimilation of vitamin A, which is important for maintaining healthy vision, skin, and immune function.

VITAMIN E

Vitamin E, also known as Tocopherol, is a fat-soluble vitamin that acts as an antioxidant in the body. It helps to protect cells from damage caused by free radicals and supports the immune system. It also helps in maintaining healthy skin, eyes, and blood vessels.

Food sources of vitamin E include nuts, seeds, and leafy greens. It is also available in supplement form.

MINERAL TABLE

Name	Natural source	What it does
Calcium	Milk, cheeses, soybean, peanuts.	Strong Bones, Healthy Heart.
Chlorine	Table Salt, kelp, Olives.	Helps digestion & alertness.
Chromium	Chicken, corn oil, wheat germ clams.	Prevent low blood pressure.
Cobalt	Meat, Kidney, liver, oysters.	Staff off anemia.
Copper	Dried Bean, Peas, prunes, and most Seafood.	Helps convert Iron into hemoglobin and keeps the energy up.
Fluorine	Fluoridated Drinking Water. Seafood and Te.a	Reduce Tooth decay and strengthens bones.
Iodine	Onions, all Seafood, kelp	Burn excess fat, Improve Mental alacrity.
Iron	Pork liver, beef kidney, red meat, egg yolk, oyster, nuts, oatmeal, asparagus.	Prevent fatigue, good skin tone, promote resistance to disease, and prevent iron deficiency.
Magnesium	Whole-grain cereals, nuts.	Helps prevent osteoporosis, improves memory, Helps in Muscles reflexes.
Manganese	Whole grains. Dark-green leafy vegetables.	Helps prevent anemia and promote a healthy body.

Molybdenum	Fish, poultry, meat, eggs, nuts, and seeds.	Lessen the pain of arthritis. Promote healthy gums.
Phosphorus	Citrus fruits, cantaloupe, green vegetables, tomatoes, potatoes.	Aid in clear thinking, dispose of body wastes, reduce blood pressure.
Potassium	Citrus fruits, cantaloupe, green vegetables, tomatoes, potatoes, and bananas.	Aid in clear thinking, dispose of body wastes, and reduce blood pressure.
Selenium	Seafood, kidney, onions, tomatoes, broccoli, and bran.	Keeps you looking youthful, Alleviating hot flashes & distress from menopause. Fights cancer and helps prevent dandruff.
Sodium	Salt, shellfish, carrots, beets, bacon, kidney.	Helps nerves & muscles function, and heat stroke.
Sulfur	Lean Beef, dried beans, fish, cabbage.	Tone up the skin and keeps hair looking healthy. Fight bacterial infections.
Vanadium	Fish.	Aid in preventing heart attacks.
Zinc	Meat, liver, seafood, oysters, pumpkin seeds, eggs.	Speed up healing. Remove white spots on the face. Help avoid a prostate problem. Helps decrease calcium deposit and increase mental alertness.
Water	Juices, fruits, and vegetables.	Help prevent constipation. Keeps the body functioning properly.

In this book, I aim to provide a comprehensive guide on the essential vitamins and minerals needed for optimal health and well-being. The information provided serves as a reference for readers to understand the various benefits and attributes associated with consuming these nutrients. It is crucial to remember that vitamins and minerals play a vital role in maintaining overall health and physical fitness. They contribute to proper growth and development, support a healthy immune system, and are necessary for the smooth functioning of various bodily processes. For instance, Vitamin D and Calcium are crucial for maintaining strong bones, Vitamin C helps in the production of collagen and strengthens the immune system, and Vitamin E acts as an antioxidant to protect cells from harm. Incorporating a daily vitamin supplement into your diet can help boost your overall system and improve your body's performance.

PROSTATE CANCER

Prostate cancer is a serious and prevalent form of cancer that affects the prostate gland, a small organ located in men that surrounds the urethra and produces semen. This cancer is the most common type of cancer among older men, and its incidence increases with age. Studies have shown that diet plays a significant role in the development of prostate cancer. Research has found that a diet high in calcium, vitamin D, and other essential vitamins and minerals may decrease the risk of prostate cancer. (Capiello, 2012) Additionally, taking supplements containing these nutrients may also help to reduce the risk; however, it is crucial to consult with a healthcare professional before starting any supplement regimen.

Prostate cancer is a significant health concern for men over the age of 45 years, and it is essential that men understand the disease and how to prevent or treat it.

Prostate cancer is a dangerous form of cancer that develops in the prostate gland, a vital organ that plays a crucial role in the proper functioning of the male reproductive tract. According to the American Cancer Society, prostate cancer is the most common cancer among American men, affecting about one in nine men during their lifetime. (Society, Cancer Facts & Figures 2022, 2022) While this disease is most prevalent among older men, with the incidence increasing with age, it is important to note that prostate cancer can also occur in younger men. The disease often develops without symptoms, which is why it is crucial for young men to undergo regular check-ups.

Prostate cancer is a life-threatening disease that can be effectively managed if detected early. It is essential that we take care of our health and not neglect the importance of regular check-ups and screenings. Studies have shown that early detection and treatment can significantly improve the survival rate of prostate cancer patients. Despite the high incidence of prostate cancer, many men are still unaware of the function and location of the prostate gland. According to a survey conducted by the Prostate Cancer Foundation, only 30% of men could correctly identify the prostate on a diagram. This highlights the importance of educating men about the disease and the need for regular check-ups (Foundation, 2016).

The prostate is a small, walnut-shaped gland situated below the bladder and in front of the rectum. It plays a crucial role in the reproductive system by producing fluids and enzymes that constitute around one-third of the semen during ejaculation. The sperm, which is produced in the testicles, is transported through the vas deferens, a tube that passes through the prostate and receives contributions from it before reaching the urethra. The urethra is the tube inside the penis that carries both urine and semen out of the body. The seminal vesicles, which are glands located behind and slightly above the prostate, also contribute to the semen during ejaculation. In addition to its reproductive functions, the prostate also plays a role in urine control.

The seminal vesicles, in addition to the prostate, also play a crucial role in the reproductive system by secreting fluids that are added to the semen during ejaculation. However, due to the close proximity and direct physical connection between the seminal vesicles and the prostate, it is possible for cancer to spread from the prostate to the seminal vesicles or the prostate capsule (a fibrous membrane that surrounds the prostate). This can make it difficult for surgery to completely remove the cancer. A doctor can perform a physical examination of the prostate through a rectal examination, which allows the doctor to feel the contour of the prostate. A healthy prostate should have a smooth and firm texture but should not be too hard.

While the exact causes of prostate cancer are not fully understood, researchers have identified several risk factors associated with the disease. One known risk factor is family history, with a higher probability of developing prostate cancer in men who have a father or brother with the disease. Another significant risk factor is age, with men over the age of 65 accounting for more than 75% of all reported cases of prostate cancer.

PROSTATE CANCER IN AFRICAN AMERICAN MEN

African American men have a disproportionately high incidence of prostate cancer worldwide. According to data from the National Cancer Institute, African American men are at an increased risk of being diagnosed with prostate cancer and dying from the disease, with a two-fold higher incidence and two-and-a-half to three-fold higher mortality rate compared to other racial groups. (Society, Cancer Facts & Figures for African Americans 2019-2021, 2019)

Several factors contribute to this increased risk, including environmental and socioeconomic factors. Studies have found that exposure to certain toxins, such as pesticides and heavy metals, may increase the risk of prostate cancer in African American men. Additionally, research has also linked air pollution and certain occupational exposures to an increased risk of prostate cancer. Furthermore, research from **"Social Determinants of Health Among African-American Men"** shows that poverty, lack of access to healthcare, and limited access to healthy food options can contribute to the high rates of prostate cancer among African American men. (Perron, 2016)

African American men are also more likely to have more advanced prostate cancer at the time of diagnosis and are less likely to receive appropriate treatment, which can contribute to poorer outcomes. These disparities in diagnosis and treatment may be due to a lack of access to healthcare, a lack of awareness about the disease and the importance of early detection, and cultural barriers.

Research also suggests that African American men may have a different genetic makeup and biology of prostate cancer, which may affect their risk of developing and dying from the disease. (Rebbeck, 2017)

While the **"Guide to Surviving Prostate Cancer"** provides useful information for patients and their families, it is important to remember that it is not a scientific publication, and its information should be verified with credible sources. The book recommends that African American men discuss their risk of prostate cancer with their healthcare provider and consider starting regular screenings at an earlier age than other men. Additionally, the book suggests that African American men should educate themselves about the disease and its risk factors and take an active role in their healthcare.

PROSTATE CANCER IN WHITE MEN

According to **"The Cancer Complexity: Exploring Advanced Prostate Cancer" and "Leukemia: A Personal Experience,"** prostate cancer is the most common cancer among American men. (Denmeade, 2000) The American Journal of Medicine states that about one in nine men will be diagnosed with prostate cancer during their lifetime. Specifically, the incidence rate for white men is approximately 12.4%, according to the American Cancer Society. (Etzioni, 2008) The likelihood of a white man developing prostate cancer increases with age, with men over the age of 65 having the highest risk. Furthermore, the American Cancer Society states that the incidence rate for prostate cancer among white men is slightly higher than for

African American men and Asian/Pacific Islander men and significantly higher than for Hispanic men and American Indian/ Alaska Native men. (Society, Society, American Cancer, 2022) Additionally, it is important to note that while age and race are significant risk factors for prostate cancer, other factors such as family history and genetics also play a role.

Men with a family history of prostate cancer, particularly if a first-degree relative (father or brother) has been diagnosed, are at an increased risk of developing the disease. Certain genetic mutations, such as those in the BRCA1 and BRCA2 genes, have been linked to an increased risk of prostate cancer. These genetic mutations are more common in certain populations, such as Ashkenazi Jewish men.

Case in point, Black Africans have a low incidence of prostate cancer when compared to the high rates in African Americans. (Rebbeck TR, 207) Also, research shows that The Asian population has a low risk of prostate cancer. For instance, Japanese men have an incidence of prostate cancer that is 40 times lower than African American men.

However, when Asians immigrate to the United States, their incidence of prostate cancer rises. It is possible that differences in the environment or the types of food people eat may help to explain these observations, but that remains to be proven.

It is not my intention to go in-depth about prostate and treatments. My position is to raise awareness among men about the disease so that the proper steps can be taken to address this problem. I do recommend that all men consult their doctor or check the Internet for more information.

Remember, knowledge is power. When you have knowledge of something, you have the power to act. Act now!

PROSTATE CANCER IN ASIAN MEN

The incidence of prostate cancer among Asian men is lower compared to men of other racial/ethnic groups. However, the incidence of prostate cancer in Asian men has been increasing in recent years. According to data from Dr. Patrick **"Walsh's Guide to Surviving Prostate Cancer",** the incidence of prostate cancer among Asian men is generally lower than among men of other racial/ethnic groups, with an average age-adjusted incidence rate of approximately 22 cases per 100,000 men. However, this rate is rising, particularly in certain Asian countries such as Japan, South Korea, and China. (Walsh P. C., 2012)

One study published in the Journal of Medicine found that the incidence of prostate cancer among men in Japan increased by approximately 2.5% per year between 1975 and 2004 (Shimizu). Another study, also published in the Journal of Medicine, found that the incidence of prostate cancer among men in South Korea increased by approximately 6.3% per year between 1993 and 2007. Similarly, a study from China found that the incidence of prostate cancer among men in China increased by approximately 4.2% per year between 1993 and 2008. (Sakamoto H, 2008)

The cause of the increasing incidence of prostate cancer among Asian men is not well understood. However, several factors have been proposed as possible explanations. One possible explanation is that the increasing incidence of prostate cancer among Asian men is due to changes in lifestyle and dietary habits. For example, as more Asian men adopt a Western-style diet, which is high in red and processed meats and low in fruits and vegetables, they may be at increased risk of developing prostate cancer. Another possible explanation is that the increasing incidence of prostate cancer among Asian men is due to exposure to environmental and occupational toxins such as pesticides and other chemicals.

Another explanation could be the increasing rate of screening for prostate cancer which may lead to the detection of more cases.

Overall, the incidence of prostate cancer among Asian men is rising, and more research is needed to understand the causes of this trend. However, it is important to note that the overall incidence of prostate cancer among Asian men remains lower than among men of other racial/ethnic groups and that prevention and early detection strategies, such as regular screenings and healthy lifestyle choices, can help to reduce the risk of prostate cancer in this population.

PROSTATE CANCER IN LATINO MEN

Prostate cancer among Latino men is lower compared to men of other racial/ethnic groups. However, the incidence of prostate cancer in Latino men has been increasing in recent years. According to data from Dr. Patrick **Walsh's Guide to Surviving Prostate Cancer,** the incidence of prostate cancer among Latino men is generally lower than among men of other racial/ethnic groups, with an average age-adjusted incidence rate of approximately 96 cases per 100,000 men. However, this rate varies widely depending on the specific country of origin and the population's socioeconomic status. (Walsh P. C., 2007)

A study published in the Journal of Medicine found that the incidence of prostate cancer among Latino men in the United States is higher than among Latino men in their countries of origin. The study found that the incidence of prostate cancer among U.S.-born Latino men is approximately 126 cases per 100,000 men, compared to a rate of approximately 66 cases per 100,000 men among foreign-born Latino men. Additionally, the study found that the incidence of prostate cancer among U.S.-born Latino men is higher among those who have a lower socioeconomic status. (Gomez, 2008)

The cause of the increasing incidence of prostate cancer among Latino men is not well understood. However, several factors have been proposed as possible explanations. One possible explanation is that the increasing incidence of prostate cancer among Latino men is due to changes in lifestyle and dietary habits. For example, as more Latino men adopt a Western-style diet, which is high in red and processed meats and low in fruits and vegetables, they may be at increased risk of developing prostate cancer. Another possible explanation is that the increasing incidence of prostate cancer among Latino men is due to exposure to environmental and occupational toxins such as pesticides and other chemicals.

Another possible explanation is the lack of access to healthcare and cultural and language barriers that make it difficult for Latino men to access the healthcare system, leading to late detection and diagnosis of prostate cancer.

Overall, it is clear that the incidence of prostate cancer among Latino men is rising, and more research is needed to understand the causes of this trend. However, it is important to note that the overall incidence of prostate cancer among Latino men remains lower than among men of other racial/ethnic groups and that prevention and early detection strategies, such as regular screenings and healthy lifestyle choices, can help to reduce the risk of prostate cancer in this population.

BREAST CANCER

Breast cancer is a disease that is affecting more and more women around the world today. According to the American Journal of Medicine, breast cancer is the leading cause of cancer deaths among women between the ages of 40 and 59. In fact, it is the leading cancer among American women and is second only to lung cancer in cancer deaths. However, according to the American Cancer Society, in 2020, an estimated 276,480 women in the United States were expected to be diagnosed with invasive breast cancer, and 42,170 were expected to die from the disease. (Medicine, 2015 Aug)

It is important to note that, like most cancers, breast cancer cannot be prevented completely. However, as research continues to advance, doctors and medical professionals are able to better understand the causes of the disease and develop ways to reduce a woman's risk of developing it.

Regular breast self-examination, annual clinical exams, and annual mammograms (for women over 40 years) are recommended as a way to help prevent and lower the risk of breast cancer. Additionally, women who have a family history of the disease or other risk factors, such as age at first menstrual period or age at first live birth, should take additional steps to reduce their chances of developing the disease.

It is also worth noting that men can develop breast cancer as well, although it is less common. According to the American Cancer Society, about 2,620 men will be diagnosed with breast cancer, and about 540 will die from the disease in the United States in 2021. (Society, Breast Cancer in Men: , 2021)

Breast cancer is a disease that affects a significant number of women globally, and it is essential to raise awareness of the disease and its risk factors. Regular breast self-examination, annual clinical exams, and annual mammograms are highly recommended and can help reduce the risk of breast cancer. Additionally, women with a family history of the disease or other risk factors should take additional steps to reduce their chances of developing the disease. It is also important to note that men can also develop breast cancer.

BREAST CANCER AMONG WHITE WOMEN

According to the American Journal of Medicine, breast cancer is the most common cancer among women in the United States, and it disproportionately affects white women. In 2020, it was estimated that about 123,810 cases of invasive breast cancer were diagnosed in white women, representing about 45% of all new invasive breast cancer cases in the US. Additionally, it is estimated that about 42,170 white women died from breast cancer in 2020.

However, according to the American Cancer Society, breast cancer is the most commonly diagnosed cancer among women in the US, regardless of race or ethnicity, with an estimated 276,480 new cases expected in 2020. Among racial/ethnic groups, non-Hispanic white women have the highest incidence of breast cancer, but the mortality rates are highest among Black women. In 2020, it was estimated that about 42,170 women in the US died from breast cancer. (Society., Breast Cancer Facts & Figures, 2020-2021)

Fortunately, recent studies show that the incidence of breast cancer among white women has been decreasing in recent years, likely due to a combination of factors such as increased awareness and access to screening and treatment advances. However, breast cancer is still a significant health problem among white women, and it is important to continue to raise awareness and educate the public on the risk factors, early detection, and treatment options for the disease.

It is also worth noting that although breast cancer incidence rates have been decreasing, breast cancer death rates have been decreasing at a slower pace; this could be due to socio-economic factors, access to healthcare, and other factors that may impact the outcomes of the disease. Additionally, research has shown that breast cancer disparities exist among white women, with higher rates of breast cancer incidence and mortality among certain subpopulations such as older white women, those with lower income and education, and those living in rural areas.

As a note, breast cancer remains a significant health problem among white women in the United States, and it is important to continue to raise awareness and educate the public on the risk factors, early detection, and treatment options for the disease. Additionally, research should continue to focus on reducing disparities in breast cancer outcomes among different subpopulations of white women.

BREAST CANCER AMONG BLACK WOMEN

According to the American Journal of Medicine, breast cancer is a significant health problem among Black women in the United States. In 2020, it was estimated that about 30,700 cases of invasive breast cancer were diagnosed in Black women, representing about 11% of all new invasive breast cancer cases in the US. Additionally, it is estimated that about 6,830 Black women died from breast cancer in 2020. (figures, 2021-2022)

Recent studies have shown that breast cancer incidence rates among Black women are lower compared to White women; however, the death rate is higher. This is likely due to a combination of factors such as delayed diagnosis, lack of access to appropriate treatment, and socioeconomic disparities, which are more pronounced among Black women compared to white women.

Research also shows that Black women are more likely to be diagnosed with triple-negative breast cancer, a type of breast cancer that is more aggressive and difficult to treat than other types of breast cancer. Additionally, Black women are more likely to be diagnosed with breast cancer at a younger age and at more advanced stages of the disease, which further complicates treatment and increases the risk of death. (Oncology)

In comparison, white women had an estimated 123,810 cases of invasive breast cancer in 2020, representing 45% of all invasive breast cancer cases in the US and 42,170 deaths.

In conclusion, breast cancer is a significant health problem among Black women in the United States, and it is important to continue to raise awareness and educate the public on the risk factors, early detection, and treatment options for the disease. Additionally, research should continue to focus on reducing disparities in breast cancer outcomes among Black women, particularly in terms of access to appropriate treatment and early diagnosis, compared to white women.

BREAST CANCER AMONG ASIAN WOMEN

According to the American Journal of Medicine, breast cancer is a significant health problem among Asian women in the United States. In 2020, it was estimated that about 42,870 cases of invasive breast cancer were diagnosed in Asian women, representing about 15% of all new invasive breast cancer cases in the US. Additionally, it is estimated that about 8,660 Asian women died from breast cancer in 2020. (DeSantis, 2020)

Recent studies have shown that breast cancer incidence rates among Asian women are lower compared to white and Black women. However, Asian women tend to be diagnosed at a later stage than white and Black women, which may result in a higher mortality rate among this group. It is also worth noting that breast cancer incidence rates vary among different subpopulations of Asian women, with higher rates among certain subpopulations such as Japanese and Filipino women.

Additionally, research shows that Asian women are more likely to be diagnosed with ER-negative breast cancer, a type of breast cancer that is more difficult to treat than other types of breast cancer. (Chen, 2015) (Society., Breast cancer facts & figures 2019-2020. Atlanta:, (2020))

In conclusion, breast cancer is a significant health problem among Asian women in the United States, and it is important to continue to raise awareness and educate the public on the risk factors, early detection, and treatment options for the disease. Additionally, research should continue to focus on reducing disparities in breast cancer outcomes among Asian women, particularly in terms of access to appropriate treatment and early diagnosis, compared to white and Black women.

BREAST CANCER AMONG LATIN WOMEN

According to the American Journal of Medicine, Latinas have a lower incidence of breast cancer than non-Latina white women; however, they have a higher mortality rate from the disease. This disparity can be attributed to several factors, such as:

Latinas are more likely to be diagnosed with later-stage breast cancer, which may contribute to the higher mortality rate.

Cultural and linguistic barriers and lack of access to healthcare may play a role in this disparity.

Latinas are more likely to have certain genetic risk factors for breast cancer, such as mutations in the BRCA1 and BRCA2 genes. (John, 2017)

It is crucial for Latinas to be aware of their breast cancer risk and to receive regular screenings. To address this issue, the following actions can be taken:

Increase access to healthcare and breast cancer education for Latinas.

Culturally sensitive outreach and support.

Targeted interventions to reduce these disparities.

In comparison to Black women, Latinas have a lower incidence of breast cancer but a similar mortality rate. Cultural and socio-economic factors have been identified as key contributors to the disparities seen in breast cancer outcomes among Latinas and Black women. It highlights the need for targeted interventions to reduce these disparities.

FACTS ABOUT BREAST CANCER

- Out of the 252,710 women diagnosed with Breast Cancer, 40,810 will die annually.
- All women, regardless of age or race, are at risk of developing Breast Cancer.
- The older a woman gets, the higher her chances are of developing the cancer.
- Approximately 80% of the women with breast cancer are over age 50.
- Half of all cancer cases in the US occur in women 65 years and older.
- Young women can also develop breast cancer, and men can also be diagnosed with the disease.

It is important to understand that early detection is crucial in controlling and managing breast cancer. Regular self-exams and physician check-ups can greatly increase the chances of detecting breast cancer at an early stage when it is most treatable. Women are encouraged to be aware of their bodies, perform regular self-exams, and consult their physicians for regular check-ups to detect any potential signs of breast cancer.

STROKE

Medical research has found that stroke is one of the most preventable medical illnesses. This means that with proper care and attention to one's health, it is possible to greatly reduce the risk of having a stroke. Unfortunately, many people, particularly those who are 60 years or older, do not take this risk seriously enough and fail to take the necessary steps to protect their health. It is crucial that individuals in this age group understand the importance of being vigilant about their health and take the necessary precautions to reduce their risk of having a stroke. This may include making lifestyle changes such as eating a healthy diet, exercising regularly, and avoiding smoking and excessive alcohol consumption. It is also important to work closely with a healthcare provider to monitor and manage any underlying health conditions, such as high blood pressure or diabetes, that may increase the risk of stroke.

When dealing with stroke, prevention is crucial. Even with modern treatments available, it remains important to minimize stroke risk by identifying and managing potential risk factors.

It is crucial to have a conversation with your healthcare provider and discuss the following risk factors:

Age - As you get older, your risk for stroke increases. It is important to be aware of this risk and take steps to reduce it, particularly after age 35, when the risk doubles with each decade.

High blood pressure - High blood pressure is a leading cause of stroke and affects nearly 70% of stroke victims.

Irregular heartbeat - Conditions such as atrial fibrillation, which causes an irregular heartbeat, can increase the risk of stroke. If diagnosed and treated, the risk of stroke can be reduced by as much as 70%.

Atherosclerosis and heart disease - The buildup of cholesterol in the arteries can lead to both stroke and heart attack.

Smoking - Not only does smoking increase the risk of stroke, but it can also accelerate the buildup of cholesterol in the arteries.

Diabetes - Diabetes can make it harder for the body to process fat, increasing the risk of heart problems and stroke.

Race - African Americans have a higher risk of stroke, although the reasons for this are not fully understood.

Use of birth control pills - While stroke is uncommon in young women, the use of birth control pills in combination with other risk factors, such as smoking, can increase the risk of stroke.

It is important to consult with a doctor to evaluate the risk factors that may be applicable to you and to develop a plan for reducing your risk of stroke.

It is essential to prevent strokes, and individuals can take various steps to lower their risk. Adopting healthy lifestyle choices stands out as one of the most effective methods for stroke prevention.

Some steps that can be taken include:

- **Maintaining a healthy weight:** Following a low-fat diet can help to keep weight in check and reduce the risk of stroke.

- **Quitting smoking:** Smoking is a major risk factor for stroke, and quitting smoking can greatly reduce this risk.

- **Regular screenings:** Regular screenings for blood pressure, cholesterol, and blood sugar, as recommended by a doctor, can help to identify any potential health issues that may increase the risk of stroke.

- **Taking medication as prescribed:** If you are taking medication, particularly for high blood pressure, it is essential to take it exactly as directed. This can help to effectively manage any underlying health conditions that may increase the risk of stroke.

It is important to keep in mind that these steps, especially lifestyle changes, are lifelong commitments that must be made a part of one's daily routine. It is also important to work closely with a healthcare provider to develop a personalized plan for preventing stroke and to regularly monitor any underlying health conditions.

SYMPTOMS OF STROKE

The symptoms of a stroke can vary depending on which part of the brain is affected. Some common symptoms include:

- **Sudden onset of numbness, weakness, or clumsiness on one or both sides of the body.**
- **Double vision, severe dizziness, or unsteadiness.**
- **Loss of vision in one or both eyes or loss of speech.**
- **Difficulty speaking or problems with language.**
- **A sudden severe headache that rapidly reaches maximal intensity.**

Symptoms may also vary depending on which hemisphere of the brain is affected. For example, if the stroke occurs in the back of the brain where vision is controlled, the only symptom may be a loss of vision. In contrast, if the stroke occurs in the hemisphere that controls strength and sensation on the opposite side of the body, paralysis, and loss of sensation may be the symptoms.

It is important to note that some patients may not be aware of or may deny obvious weakness or paralysis. If you suspect that you or someone else is experiencing a stroke, it is essential to seek immediate medical attention by calling 911 or going to the nearest hospital. Time is of the essence in treating a stroke, and early intervention can improve the chances of recovery.

STROKE & RACE

Some studies have found that certain ethnic and racial groups have a higher risk of stroke than others. For example, African Americans have a higher risk of stroke than whites, and this risk is especially high for African American women. Studies have shown that African Americans are more likely to have high blood pressure, which is a major risk factor for stroke and are also more likely to have hypertension at a younger age. Other factors that may contribute to the higher stroke risk in African Americans include diabetes, obesity, and a higher prevalence of smoking. (Prevention, https://www.cdc.gov/stroke/facts.htm, (2021))

Other racial and ethnic groups, such as Asian Americans and Hispanic Americans, also have a higher risk of stroke compared to non-Hispanic whites. The reasons for this increased risk vary among different groups and may be related to genetics, lifestyle factors, or socio-economic status.

It is important to note that while certain groups may have a higher risk of stroke, stroke can affect anyone, and it is important to be aware of the risk factors, make lifestyle changes, and work with a healthcare provider to develop a plan to prevent stroke.

EXERCISE ROUTINE

Physical development is a lifelong journey. Embrace it, challenge it, and discover the incredible potential of your own body." – Unknown

Exercise is an essential part of maintaining a healthy lifestyle and achieving true success in all areas of life. Regular physical activity not only improves physical health but also has a positive impact on mental and emotional well-being. It is a powerful tool for preventing chronic diseases such as cancer, high blood pressure, and stroke. In this book, we will explore the benefits of exercise, the importance of developing a weekly exercise routine, and how to make exercise a sustainable part of your lifestyle.

Exercise offers numerous advantages, notably its role in preventing chronic illnesses. Consistent physical activity is proven to lower the risk of conditions like cancer, hypertension, stroke, and other chronic diseases. This benefit stems from exercise's ability to enhance cardiovascular health, bolster the immune system, and balance hormones that might lead to chronic illnesses. Moreover, exercise aids in weight management and blood sugar regulation, further contributing to the prevention of chronic diseases.

Exercise also has a positive impact on mental and emotional well-being. It is well known that physical activity can help to reduce stress, anxiety, and depression. Regular exercise helps to release endorphins, which are the body's natural feel-good chemicals and can help to improve mood, reduce feelings of stress, and promote relaxation. Additionally, exercise can also improve sleep quality, which can further enhance mental and emotional well-being.

Developing a weekly exercise routine is key to making exercise a sustainable part of your lifestyle. It is important to set specific goals and make a plan to achieve them. The Centers for Disease Control and Prevention (CDC) recommends that adults aim for at least 150 minutes of moderate-intensity or 75 minutes of vigorous-intensity aerobic activity per week or a combination of both. Additionally, adults should also aim for at least two days of muscle-strengthening activities per week. To make sure you are meeting these guidelines, it is important to have a weekly exercise routine that includes a combination of cardio and strength training.

When creating your exercise routine, it is important to keep in mind that variety is key. Mixing up your routine will help to keep things interesting and prevent boredom. This could include a combination of different types of cardio, such as running, cycling, swimming, or dancing. Strength training can include weightlifting, bodyweight exercises, or resistance band exercises. Additionally, it is important to include flexibility and balance exercises to improve overall mobility and stability.

To make exercise a sustainable part of your lifestyle, finding activities you enjoy is important. This could include joining a sports team, taking a dance class, or going for a hike. It is also important to set realistic and achievable goals and to celebrate your progress along the way. Finding a workout buddy or joining a fitness community can also provide accountability, motivation, and support.

It is important to remember that exercise is an essential part of maintaining a healthy lifestyle and achieving true success in all areas of life. Engaging in regular physical activity is key to preventing chronic diseases, enhancing mental and emotional health, and fostering overall well-being. Establishing a weekly workout regimen that incorporates cardiovascular and strength training, as well as exercises for flexibility and balance, is crucial for integrating exercise sustainably into your lifestyle.

Remember to find activities that you enjoy, set realistic and achievable goals, and celebrate your progress along the way.

I have created a seven-day workout routine for you as a guide, but please keep in mind that it can be adjusted to suit your preferences and fitness level.

Monday

30 minutes of cardio.
20 minutes of strength training.
10 minutes of stretching.

Tuesday

40 minutes of yoga or Pilates.
15 minutes of core exercises.

Wednesday

30 minutes of cardio.
20 minutes of strength training.
10 minutes of stretching.

Thursday

30 minutes of cardio.
20 minutes of strength training.
10 minutes of stretching.

Friday

45 minutes of hiking or outdoor activity.
15 minutes of yoga or stretching.

Saturday

Rest day.

Sunday

Rest day.

Monday	Tuesday	Wednesday	Thursday	Friday	Saturday	Sunday
30min cardio	40min yoga or Pilates	30min cardio	30min cardio	45min hiking or outdoor	Rest Day	Rest Day
20min strength training	15min core exercises	20min strength training	20min strength training	15min yoga or stretching		
10min stretching		10min stretching	10min stretching			

Please note that this is a sample exercise routine and should be adjusted based on individual fitness levels and goals. It is also important to consult a doctor before starting any new exercise routine, especially if you have any pre-existing health conditions. Additionally, it is crucial to listen to your body and give it the proper rest it needs to recover and avoid injury. Remember, regular exercise not only improves physical health but also mental well-being, making it an essential component of a healthy lifestyle.

RESTROUTINE

In my previous book, **"A New Start in Business"**, I briefly touched on the topic of rest. Here, we will dive a little deeper into the subject and explore the importance of rest for maintaining a healthy lifestyle and achieving true success.

First and foremost, it is important to understand that rest is just as important as exercise and proper nutrition in maintaining overall health. Studies have shown that a lack of rest can lead to a variety of health problems, including obesity, diabetes, heart disease, and even certain cancers. Additionally, a lack of rest can also lead to mental health issues such as depression and anxiety.

One of the main reasons why rest is so important is because it allows the body to repair and rejuvenate itself. During sleep, the body is able to repair damaged tissues, replenish energy stores, and release hormones that are necessary for growth and development. Additionally, sleep is also important for the brain, as it allows for the consolidation of memories and the formation of new neural connections.

Rest also plays a crucial role in enhancing mental and emotional health. Getting enough rest is vital for preserving cognitive function and can also uplift mood while diminishing stress and anxiety. Research indicates that well-rested individuals tend to be more productive, alert, and focused during the day.

Research has also shown that getting enough rest is essential for maintaining a healthy weight. Studies have found that people who do not get enough rest are more likely to be overweight or obese. This is because a lack of rest can lead to hormonal imbalances that can increase appetite, particularly for high-calorie foods. Additionally, a lack of rest can also lead to an increased risk of developing type 2 diabetes. (Prevention, Sleep and Chronic Disease., (2017))

Lastly, rest is very important for overall longevity and quality of life. Studies have found that people who get enough rest are more likely to live longer and healthier lives and to have a better quality of life overall.

REST, FROM A RELIGIOUS PERSPECTIVE.

The importance of rest is recognized in many religions, including Judaism, Christianity, Islam, and others. In the Torah, the commandment to rest on the Sabbath is given as a way to honor God and to allow the body and mind to rejuvenate. The Tanakh, the Hebrew Bible, also emphasizes the importance of rest and the need for balance in life. Similarly, in the Quran, the importance of rest and balance is emphasized in the concept of the "middle way" or "moderation" in all things. The Bible also mentions the importance of rest and the need for balance in life.

Different religions may have different views on rest, but many religious traditions place a strong emphasis on the importance of rest and the role it plays in achieving spiritual well-being.

For example, **in Christianity,** the concept of the Sabbath is a day of rest and worship that is observed on Sundays. The Sabbath is seen as a time for rest and reflection and is considered a sacred day in the Christian faith.

In Judaism, the Sabbath is also considered a day of rest and worship and is observed from sundown on Friday to sundown on Saturday. The Sabbath is seen as a time for rest, reflection, and spiritual renewal.

Islam also has a strong emphasis on rest and the importance of taking time for rest and worship. The Five Pillars of Islam include the duty of Muslims to perform daily prayers, which serve as a reminder to take time for rest and reflection.

In Buddhism, the concept of mindfulness is central to the belief system, and mindfulness meditation is a common practice that is used to achieve inner peace and rest.

In Hinduism, the practice of yoga is often used as a way to achieve inner peace and rest through physical and mental exercises.

Overall, many religious traditions place a strong emphasis on the importance of rest and promote practices such as worship, meditation, and reflection as ways to achieve spiritual well-being and inner peace. **If you do not rest, you will rest in Peace.**

Taking care of your physical well-being is crucial for achieving success in all areas of your life. This chapter delved into the importance of nourishing your body with essential vitamins and minerals, as well as providing a comprehensive overview of the most common diseases that affect different ethnic and racial groups. We also examined who is most at risk for these diseases and effective ways to prevent them.

It is important to note that prevention is key when it comes to maintaining good health. As the famous quote by Benjamin Franklin states, **"An ounce of prevention is worth a pound of cure."** By taking proactive steps to protect your health and prevent disease, you can increase your chances of living a long and fulfilling life. This includes making healthy lifestyle choices such as eating a balanced diet, getting regular exercise, and avoiding smoking and excessive alcohol consumption. Additionally, it is essential to work with a healthcare provider to develop a personalized plan for maintaining optimal health.

Exercise is a crucial component of maintaining a healthy body, and it is recommended that adults get at least 150 minutes of moderate-intensity or 75 minutes of vigorous-intensity aerobic activity per week or a combination of both. It is also important to include muscle-strengthening exercises at least twice a week. Proper rest is also essential for physical well-being. Adults should aim for 7-9 hours of sleep per night, and it is recommended to avoid using electronic devices for at least an hour before bedtime.

Maintaining a healthy physical body is essential for achieving success in any form, and by following the guidelines discussed in this chapter, including regular exercise and proper rest, you can take steps to improve your physical well-being and prevent disease.

Remember, investing in your physical health is an investment in your overall well-being and success in all areas of your life.

> *"A sound mind in a sound body is a short but full description of a happy state in this world."*
>
> -John Locke

Chapter Five
DEVELOPING YOURSELF SOCIALLY

"Treat yourself as you are, and you will remain as you are. Treat yourself as you could be, and you will become what you should be."

Ralph Waldo Emerson

INTRODUCTION

THE IMPORTANCE OF SOCIAL DEVELOPMENT IN OVERALL SUCCESS AND WELL-BEING

Social development is crucial for overall success and well-being for a number of reasons. Firstly, it plays a vital role in building and maintaining relationships. People who have good social skills are able to communicate effectively, understand and empathize with others, and build strong connections with those around them. These relationships can be instrumental in personal and professional success, as well as in overall happiness and fulfillment.

Secondly, social development is closely tied to mental health. People with good social skills are better able to cope with stress and manage their emotions, which in turn leads to better mental health outcomes. Additionally, social connections provide a sense of belonging and support, which is essential for overall well-being.

Finally, social development is important for personal growth and development. By learning and practicing social skills, people are able to take on new opportunities, face new challenges, and grow as individuals. Social development is not only about what we can do for others but also about how we can better ourselves as well.

Social development refers to the process of acquiring and honing social skills and abilities, such as communication, empathy, and cooperation. It encompasses the growth of personal relationships, the development of a sense of self and identity, and the ability to navigate and function within society.

Social development begins in early childhood and continues throughout the lifespan. During childhood, children learn how to interact with others and form relationships. They learn how to communicate, share, and take turns. They also learn how to express their emotions and regulate their behavior. As children grow and develop, they learn more complex social skills, such as empathy and perspective-taking. They also begin to develop a sense of self and identity, which includes understanding their own feelings, values, and beliefs.

Social development is a key component of overall success and well-being. Strong social skills allow individuals to form healthy and fulfilling relationships, which can provide support, companionship, and a sense of belonging. The ability to communicate effectively and empathize with others also enables individuals to navigate and succeed in a variety of social and professional settings.

Furthermore, social development also plays a crucial role in personal and professional success. It allows individuals to build and maintain networks, which can provide valuable opportunities and resources. Additionally, social skills are highly valued by employers and can be a major factor in career advancement. For example, individuals who are able to effectively communicate and collaborate with others are more likely to be successful in leadership positions.

However, it is also worth mentioning that social development is not just about acquiring new skills and abilities; it is also about putting them into practice in real-life situations. Therefore, it is important to have opportunities to practice and apply social skills in diverse settings.

This can include volunteering, joining clubs or organizations, participating in community events, or even traveling to different cultures.

Moreover, social development is not just about the individual; it is also about the society they are part of. This can include having access to quality education and healthcare, as well as having a supportive and inclusive community.

Social development is a critical aspect of overall success and well-being. It encompasses the growth of personal relationships, the development of a sense of self and identity, and the ability to navigate and function within society. Strong social skills allow individuals to form healthy and fulfilling relationships, succeed in a variety of social and professional settings and build and maintain networks. It is important to have opportunities to practice and apply social skills in diverse settings and to have a society that promotes and facilitates social development.

Social development focuses on empowering individuals and communities by creating opportunities for them to realize their full potential. It involves dismantling obstacles and offering support and resources to those in greatest need. This approach goes beyond merely tackling poverty; it is about enabling people to become self-reliant and attain their aspirations.

The process of social development is not just a set of policies and programs but a continuous movement towards progress and improvement. It involves increasing awareness and understanding, leading to better organization and more efficient use of resources.

This results in a society that is more dynamic, productive, and inclusive.

Social development is a process of social change that requires a strong driving force and the necessary resources to support it. This includes not only financial resources but also technology and infrastructure. It also requires overcoming the obstacles that prevent change from happening, such as entrenched societal beliefs and lack of political will.

Social development centers on enabling individuals and communities to realize their maximum potential and attain success. It is an ongoing journey of societal transformation that demands a robust impetus, adequate resources, and the surmounting of challenges to foster a more inclusive and vibrant society.

Social development is a key component of overall success and well-being. Strong social skills allow individuals to form healthy and fulfilling relationships, which can provide support, companionship, and a sense of belonging.

As society grows and changes, it goes through well-defined stages of development. To meet challenges and take advantage of opportunities, society must be able to organize its resources effectively. Social development is a vital component of this progression since it enables individuals to cultivate the competencies and aptitudes necessary for engaging with others and thriving in a communal setting.

Additionally, social development is not just about the individual; it is also about the society they are part of. Therefore, it is important to have a society that promotes and facilitates social development. This can include having access to quality education and healthcare, as well as having a supportive and inclusive community.

Having good social skills is important for making friends and having a higher level of satisfaction in life. It is essential for communication, negotiation, and understanding others. However, sometimes we might face situations where we lack assertiveness, or our actions might come across as rude or hurtful to others. In those cases, it is important to know how to improve social skills to avoid slowing down in work and social life and maintain good self-esteem and mental health.

According to leading social psychologist, Dr. Susan Krauss Whitbourne, in her book **"Social Psychology,"** having good social skills can lead to better mental health, greater job success, and stronger relationships. She states that social skills are essential for navigating the complex social world and that individuals who lack them often struggle with building and maintaining relationships. (Whitbourne, (2019))

For instance, studies have shown that people with better social skills are more likely to interact positively with others, which leads to greater job satisfaction, better performance evaluations, and higher earnings. Additionally, research has also shown that people with strong social skills tend to be happier, have a greater sense of well-being, and have lower rates of depression and anxiety.

To improve your social skills, Dr. Whitbourne recommends building self-awareness, practicing active listening, and developing effective communication skills. This can be done through various methods, such as attending social skills workshops, practicing with friends and family, or seeking out therapy.

It is important to remember that social skills are always a work in progress, and it will take time to develop them. However, with effort and dedication, it is possible to improve your social skills and enjoy the many benefits that come with it.

Let us talk about what social skills are.

WHAT ARE SOCIAL SKILLS?

Social skills are the abilities that help us initiate, build, and sustain meaningful connections—whether we are chatting with a neighbor, collaborating on a team project, or leading a community group. They cover both verbal elements (what we say and how we say it) and non-verbal cues (facial expressions, posture, eye contact, tone, and timing). Think of them as the "software" that lets your inner thoughts interface smoothly with the outside world.

Like socializing a puppy, early and consistent interaction shapes how comfortably we navigate future encounters. Children who practice sharing toys, taking turns, and reading body language accumulate a reserve of social experience, making adult interactions feel natural rather than intimidating. Yet—even with a solid upbringing—social skills can stall without ongoing attention and growth.

UNDERSTANDING SOCIAL SKILLS:

When people hear the phrase social skills, they usually picture easy small talk, making friends quickly, or earning respect at work. Those are outcomes; beneath them lie teachable micro-skills:

Core Skill	*Everyday Example*	*Why It Matters*
Active Listening	Nodding, paraphrasing, asking clarifying questions	Signals respect, prevents miscommunication
Empathy	Noticing a friend's slumped shoulders and asking how they're doing	Builds trust and emotional safety
Assertiveness	Stating opinions firmly but kindly, using "I" statements	Protects boundaries without aggression
Adaptability	Adjusting tone in a quiet library vs. a lively party	Helps you blend into diverse settings
Conflict Resolution	Finding win–win compromises, focusing on issues not personalities	Keeps relationships intact under stress

These skills do not come equally or automatically to everyone. People with social anxiety may find eye contact daunting; introverts might prefer solitude and be misinterpreted as aloof. Cultural norms can further complicate things—what signals confidence in one culture might be viewed as brash in another. And neurodivergent individuals (e.g., those on the autism spectrum) may process social cues differently, needing intentional strategies to decode unspoken rules.

GROWING YOUR SOCIAL TOOLKIT

The encouraging news is that social skills behave more like muscles than fixed traits: they strengthen with use and atrophy with neglect. Here are practical ways to develop them:

1. **Deliberate Practice** – Choose one micro-skill a week (e.g., maintaining eye contact for two extra seconds) and track your progress.
2. **Role-Play & Feedback** – Practice tricky conversations with a trusted friend or coach who can point out blind spots.
3. **Micro-Exposures** – Start tiny: greet the barista by name, compliment a colleague's idea in a meeting, or join a short community event.
4. **Reflect & Adjust** – After social encounters, jot down what worked, what felt awkward, and one tweak for next time.
5. **Study Models** – Observe someone skilled at rapport. Note their tone, pacing, humor, and how they transition topics. Imitate, then adapt to your style.

WHY IT ALL MATTERS

Strong social skills multiply the value of every other asset you possess—education, talent, even positive attitude. They open doors to mentorships, collaborations, and friendships that enrich both career and personal life. Equally important, they contribute to mental well-being: people who communicate effectively report lower stress and stronger support networks.

So whether you are an exuberant extrovert, a thoughtful introvert, or somewhere between, view social competence as a lifelong craft. Each interaction—successful or awkward—is raw material for refinement. Invest in that craft, and you will find conversations flow smoother, conflicts resolve quicker, and relationships run deeper—fueling success in every arena of life.

IMPORTANCE OF IMPROVING SOCIAL SKILLS

Regardless of the circumstances, it is important to have guidance when it comes to improving social skills. Research in social psychology has shown that social skills play a crucial role in determining an individual's well-being and overall success in life. (Cacioppo, (2009))

Social skills are essential for building and maintaining relationships in both personal and professional settings. While some people may naturally possess strong social skills, others may need to work on improving them. By understanding the importance of social skills and utilizing the guidance and principles provided by social psychology research, individuals can work towards improving their social skills and ultimately lead a more fulfilling life.

THE ADVANTAGES OF HAVING STRONG SOCIAL ABILITIES

The importance of developing and maintaining strong social skills cannot be overstated. They are crucial for both mental and physical health and have a significant impact on our overall well-being.

According to research, individuals with strong social bonds have lower rates of anxiety and depression and a higher sense of self-worth, empathy, and cooperation. (Hawkley, 2010). In fact, studies dating back to 1988 have shown that a lack of social connections can be more detrimental to health than risk factors such as obesity, smoking, and high blood pressure. Other research also suggests that social isolation is linked to a 50% greater risk of dementia as one age. (House, 1988)

Moreover, developing strong social skills also leads to increased social capital - the benefits gained from belonging to a social group. This can include access to resources, support networks, and opportunities for personal growth and development.

Investing time and effort in improving your social skills can have a profound impact on your overall well-being and quality of life. It is essential for individuals to strive for strong social connections and to develop strong social skills.

I will emphasize the benefits of having strong social skills in a list below:
- Lower rates of anxiety and depression.
- Greater sense of self-worth, empathy, and cooperation.
- Improved physical health, including a lower risk of chronic diseases.
- Reduced risk of dementia as one age.
- Increased social capital, which can include benefits such as networking

opportunities and access to resources.

Social capital, defined as the sum of all the benefits that come from belonging to a social group, has become increasingly important in today's digital age. With the rise of social media platforms, individuals now have access to a vast network of people and resources that can be used to their advantage. However, with this newfound access comes a set of advantages and disadvantages.

ADVANTAGES OF SOCIAL CAPITAL IN THE SOCIAL MEDIA AGE

Social media has turned once-local networks into global webs of relationships, radically expanding the reach and impact of social capital—the value we derive from the people and communities we know. Below are the key advantages this new landscape offers and why they matter.

1. Increased Networking Opportunities

Platforms such as LinkedIn, X (formerly Twitter), and niche Facebook or Discord groups remove geographic barriers, letting a software engineer in Kenya brainstorm with a designer in Brazil or a mentor in Boston. The result is a vast reservoir of weak ties—acquaintances who, research shows, often provide the most transformative job leads, referrals, and fresh ideas.

2. Greater Access to Resources

From open-source code libraries on GitHub to free university courses on YouTube and Coursera, social media acts as a real-time directory of tools, funding calls, scholarships, and how-to threads. A quick hashtag search (#grants, #remotejobs) can surface opportunities that once required insider knowledge or expensive gatekeepers.

3. Seamless Communication & Collaboration

Group chats, cloud documents, and virtual whiteboards mean project teams can iterate around the clock. Time-zone diversity—once a hurdle—now shortens delivery cycles as work "follows the sun." Small businesses use Instagram DMs to finalize orders; researchers coordinate multi-site studies in Slack; nonprofits rally volunteers via WhatsApp.

4. Heightened Sense of Community

Shared-interest spaces—book-tok, running subreddits, maker channels—offer belonging even when physical proximity is impossible. For many, these micro-communities become emotional lifelines, providing encouragement, accountability, and a safe venue to exchange knowledge without judgment.

5. Greater Representation & Visibility

Historically marginalized voices can bypass traditional media filters, telling their own stories in their own style. Viral threads spotlight systemic issues; creator funds help under-represented entrepreneurs launch products; hashtags like #BlackBirdersWeek and #DisabledAndCute amplify narratives once overlooked in mainstream outlets.

6. Rapid Learning & Innovation Loops

Tutorial videos, live Q&A sessions, and open feedback cycles accelerate skill acquisition. A developer posts beta code, receives bug reports overnight, and releases an improved version the next morning. This iterative energy drives faster breakthroughs in everything from sustainable fashion to citizen science.

7. Grass-Roots Mobilization

Hashtags can morph into movements—raising disaster-relief funds, organizing protests, or crowd-sourcing medical bills within hours. Because messages spread peer-to-peer, mobilization feels personal, urgent, and inclusive, unlocking collective power that traditional hierarchies often suppress.

Bottom Line: Social media multiplies social capital by widening networks, lowering information barriers, and amplifying voices. When used intentionally—with respect for privacy, authenticity, and digital well-being—these platforms transform casual connections into rich reservoirs of opportunity, collaboration, and communal strength.

DISADVANTAGES OF SOCIAL CAPITAL IN THE SOCIAL MEDIA AGE

Disconnection from reality: Spending excessive time on social media can lead to a disconnection from reality, resulting in feelings of loneliness and isolation.

Cyberbullying and harassment: Social media platforms can also be used to bully and harass others, leading to emotional distress and mental health issues.

Spread of misinformation: Social media can be used to spread false information and conspiracy theories, leading to confusion and mistrust.

Invasion of privacy: Social media platforms can also lead to an invasion of privacy, as personal information and data are often shared online.

Increased pressure to conform: Social media can also create pressure to conform to societal norms and expectations, leading to feelings of inadequacy and low self-esteem.

BENEFITS OF SOCIAL CAPITAL

WHAT IS THE NEED FOR SOCIAL CAPITAL AMONG DIFFERENT DEMOGRAPHICS?

Social capital is the sum of all the benefits that come from belonging to a social group. It is the value that is derived from social connections, networks, and relationships. The need for social capital among different demographics varies depending on the individual's circumstances and goals.

For example, individuals from marginalized communities may have a greater need for social capital to access resources and opportunities that are not readily available to them. Similarly, those who are new to a community or city may benefit from social capital to form connections and build a support system.

In the business world, social capital is crucial for entrepreneurs and professionals to gain access to funding, customers, and industry connections. Social capital can also be important for those looking to advance their careers, as it can provide opportunities for mentorship, networking, and professional development.

In the age of social media, social capital can be both an advantage and a disadvantage. On the one hand, social media platforms have made it easier than ever to connect with people and build networks. However, the abundance of online connections can also dilute the quality and value of one's social capital. Social capital is crucial in the modern gig economy. It can earn you greater pay, get you access to more exciting projects, and be the deciding factor in your next job application.

UNDERSTANDING SOCIAL DEVELOPMENT: DEFINING SOCIAL DEVELOPMENT AND HOW IT RELATES TO OVERALL GROWTH AND CHANGE IN SOCIETY.

Social Development, as described in the book "Social Development" by Ross D. Parke, Glenn I. Roisman, et al., refers to the ways in which individuals grow and change in their understanding of and interactions with others in society. This growth and change are a fundamental aspect of overall development and can have a profound impact on a person's life and well-being.

According to the authors, social development encompasses a wide range of skills and abilities, including emotional regulation, empathy, communication, and prosocial behavior. These skills and abilities develop gradually over time, influenced by factors such as genetics, environment, and experience. As individuals grow and mature, they become better equipped to navigate social situations and form positive relationships with others. (Parke, 2010)

One key aspect of social development is the formation of attachment relationships, which are close and emotionally significant relationships with others. These relationships provide a sense of security and comfort and serve as a foundation for later social and emotional development. For example, secure attachments with caregivers in childhood have been linked to better social skills and relationships in adulthood.

In addition to attachment relationships, social development is also influenced by a person's experiences and interactions with others. This can include things like socialization, peer relationships, and exposure to diverse perspectives and cultures. These experiences can shape an individual's understanding of themselves and others, as well as their attitudes and beliefs about the world.

Finally, the authors highlight the importance of considering social development in the context of larger societal trends and changes. This includes understanding the ways in which cultural norms and values influence individual behavior and relationships, as well as the impact of technology and other forms of social media on social connections and communication.

Overall, social development is a complex and dynamic process that plays a central role in overall growth and change in society. By understanding the factors that influence social development and the ways in which it is intertwined with other aspects of development, we can gain a deeper appreciation for the role it plays in shaping our lives and the world around us.

UNDERSTANDING HOW SOCIETY GROWS: EXPLORING SOCIAL DEVELOPMENT STAGES

The book **"Leadership for a Better World: Understanding the Social Change Model of Leadership Development"** by Susan R. Komives outlines the stages of social development as a key component of leadership development.

According to the authors, social development is a well-defined process that individuals can navigate to become more effective leaders, agents of change and experience true success.

The first stage of social development, as described by the NCLP, is the stage of **Self-Awareness.** At this stage, individuals begin to understand their own beliefs, values, and biases and how they impact their interactions with others. This self-awareness helps individuals understand their own role in society and lays the foundation for more effective leadership.

The second stage is **Skill Development,** where individuals focus on building the skills necessary for leadership and social change. This includes skills such as communication, conflict resolution, and teamwork, as well as a deeper understanding of systems and structures of power and oppression.

The third stage is **Action,** where individuals use their skills and understanding to act towards creating positive social change. This can involve engaging in advocacy, community organizing, and other forms of activism, as well as working to create more inclusive and equitable communities and systems.

Finally, the fourth stage is **Reflection and Renewal,** where individuals reflect on their experiences and continue to grow and develop as leaders. This includes ongoing self-reflection, as well as seeking feedback and learning opportunities to continue to improve and evolve as leaders.

Throughout these stages, individuals are challenged to critically examine their own experiences and beliefs and to seek out diverse perspectives and experiences.

This leads to a greater understanding of the complexities of social change and the role that individuals can play in creating a better world.

The stages of social development described in the book **"Leadership for a Better World: Understanding the Social Change Model of Leadership Development"** provides a roadmap for individuals seeking to become more effective leaders and agents of change. By navigating these stages and continually growing and evolving as leaders, individuals can play a critical role in creating a better world for all. (Komives, 2018)

LEARNING SOCIAL SKILLS: HOW EDUCATION, HEALTH, AND COMMUNITY HELP

Acquiring and practicing social skills is a crucial aspect of personal and social development that can have a significant impact on an individual's overall well-being and success. Education, healthcare, and community organizations play a vital role in assisting individuals in developing and honing these skills.

Education is a crucial aspect of social skill development, particularly in the early years of childhood. Through structured educational programs, such as preschool and elementary school, children can learn vital social skills, including communication, cooperation, and empathy. Additionally, teachers can create a supportive and inclusive learning environment that helps children feel confident and secure as they navigate social interactions.

Healthcare providers also have a role to play in promoting social skill development, especially for individuals with social or developmental challenges. For instance, occupational therapists and speech therapists can work with children and adults to improve their communication and interaction skills. Mental health professionals can also help individuals develop coping strategies for managing social anxiety and other mental health conditions that affect social interactions.

Community organizations and initiatives also play a crucial role in promoting social skill development. For example, community centers and youth programs can provide opportunities for children and youth to engage in positive social interactions and develop important life skills. Volunteer programs, such as mentorship programs, can offer individuals opportunities to practice their social skills and build meaningful relationships with others.

Furthermore, social skills can be honed and developed through extracurricular activities, such as sports teams, clubs, and community service organizations. These activities provide opportunities for individuals to interact with others who share similar interests, practice teamwork, and learn how to resolve conflicts in a positive and constructive manner.

Moreover, the family plays a critical role in shaping an individual's social skills. A supportive and nurturing family environment can help children develop healthy self-esteem and social skills, such as empathy and communication. On the other hand, an abusive or neglectful family environment can have the opposite effect, hindering an individual's social and emotional development.

The rise of technology is significantly influencing the development of social skills, especially among younger generations raised in an era of ubiquitous digital media and social networking platforms. While these technologies provide chances for online interaction and honing digital communication skills, they can also negatively affect social growth, leading to issues like social isolation and a decrease in direct, in-person interactions.

The road to success can only be realized with the acquisition and practice of social skills, which is a complex process influenced by many factors, including education, healthcare, community organizations, extracurricular activities, family relationships, and technology. By providing individuals with supportive and inclusive environments and opportunities for skill-building, we can help them develop the social skills necessary for success and happiness in life.

"USING SOCIAL SKILLS IN REAL LIFE: OPPORTUNITIES EVERYWHERE!

The real-life application of social skills is an important factor in determining true success. Opportunities to practice and apply these skills in diverse settings, such as volunteering, clubs, and community events, can have a profound impact on an individual's personal and professional growth.

Volunteering provides an opportunity to put social skills into practice by interacting with people from different backgrounds and cultures. By working together to achieve a common goal, volunteers can develop teamwork, cooperation, and communication skills. Additionally, volunteering can help individuals build confidence and self-esteem by giving them a sense of purpose and the feeling of making a positive impact on their community.

Joining clubs and organizations also provides opportunities for individuals to practice and apply their social skills. By participating in group activities and events, individuals can develop their leadership, negotiation, and interpersonal skills. In addition, by working with a diverse group of people, individuals can learn to appreciate and respect different perspectives and cultures, which is essential for building strong relationships and working effectively in diverse settings.

Community events, such as festivals and fairs, provide opportunities for individuals to practice social skills in a fun and engaging environment. These events bring people together to celebrate and engage in shared experiences, providing a platform for individuals to practice their communication and social skills. Additionally, community events often provide opportunities for individuals to build relationships with others and create a sense of community, which can lead to a greater sense of well-being and happiness.

In conclusion, real-life opportunities to practice and apply social skills in diverse settings, such as volunteering, clubs, and community events, play a critical role in determining true success. These experiences provide individuals with the opportunity to grow and develop their social skills in real-world situations, which is essential for building strong relationships, working effectively in diverse environments, and achieving personal and professional success.

SOCIAL DEVELOPMENT'S EFFECT ON CONFIDENCE, HAPPINESS AND MENTAL HEALTH: HOW IT CAN HELP OR HURT, AND HOW TO BUILD BETTER SOCIAL SKILLS

Social development has a significant impact on an individual's self-esteem and mental health. Self-esteem is a person's overall evaluation of their own worth, and it is closely linked to their experiences in social interactions and relationships. Positive social interactions and relationships can build self-esteem and lead to increased confidence and resilience, while negative experiences can erode self-esteem and contribute to feelings of low self-worth.

Mental health is also closely connected to social development. Social skills, such as effective communication, conflict resolution, and empathy, are critical to maintaining healthy relationships and reducing stress and anxiety.

Conversely, poor social skills can lead to conflict, stress, and anxiety, which can negatively impact mental health.

It is important to focus on improving social skills to avoid negative effects on self-esteem and mental health. This can be achieved through education, practice, and feedback. Formal education, such as social skills training programs and workshops, can provide individuals with the knowledge and skills needed to effectively navigate social interactions. Practicing these skills in real-life settings, such as volunteering, clubs, and community events, can help individuals gain confidence and improve their social skills.

In addition to formal education and practice, receiving feedback from others can be incredibly valuable in improving social skills. Receiving feedback can help individuals identify areas for improvement and provide them with the tools they need to develop their skills further.

Social development has a significant impact on an individual's self-esteem and mental health. Positive social experiences and relationships can build self-esteem and promote mental health, while negative experiences can erode self-esteem and negatively impact mental health. Improving social skills through education, practice, and feedback is a key factor in avoiding negative effects and promoting positive self-esteem and mental health.

THE SIGNIFICANCE OF SOCIAL DEVELOPMENT AND IMPROVING SOCIAL SKILLS.

Understanding social development is essential for understanding overall growth and change in society. Social development is the process of improving the well-being and quality of life for individuals and communities through the promotion of social and economic progress. It involves addressing issues such as poverty, inequality, and social exclusion and working towards a more just and equitable society.

Social development is not just about improving the lives of individuals but also about creating a more cohesive and functioning society. When people have access to education, healthcare, and economic opportunities, they are more likely to be productive members of society, contribute to their communities, and have better lives. This, in turn, leads to a more stable, prosperous, and inclusive society.

Furthermore, social development plays a crucial role in addressing social issues that affect the entire society, such as discrimination, inequality, and crime. By addressing these issues, social development can lead to a more harmonious and peaceful society where people can live and work together in a more productive and fulfilling way.

In addition, social development is closely connected to economic development. A society with a high level of social development is more likely to have a strong economy with a high standard of living and low levels of poverty. The two are mutually reinforcing and addressing one will help improve the other.

Social development is a vital aspect of overall growth and change in society. It promotes social and economic progress, leads to a more cohesive and functioning society, addresses social issues, and is connected to economic development.

Understanding social development is essential for understanding the complex dynamics of society and working towards a more just and equitable future.

OVERCOMING FEAR AND SOCIAL ANXIETY

The fear of social interaction and the related experience of social anxiety can be debilitating for some individuals, affecting their social development, self-esteem, and overall well-being. However, both the Bible and ancient Chinese philosophy offer guidance for overcoming fear and social anxiety.

In the Bible, there are many passages that encourage individuals to overcome fear and trust in God's love and protection. For example, Isaiah 41:10 states, **"So do not fear, for I am with you; do not be dismayed, for I am your God. I will strengthen you and help you; I will uphold you with my righteous right hand."** This passage and others like it offer comfort and encouragement to individuals who are struggling with fear and anxiety, reminding them that they are not alone and that they have the strength and support they need to overcome their challenges.

Similarly, ancient Chinese philosophy provides insight into the nature of fear and anxiety and offers guidance for overcoming these emotions. For example, the Chinese philosopher Lao Tzu wrote in the Tao Te Ching, **"Nature does not hurry, yet everything is accomplished."** (Tzu.) This quote reminds individuals that the natural world operates in its own time and pace and that the same should be true for our inner selves. By letting go of the need to control and rushing to accomplish, individuals can reduce stress and anxiety and cultivate a more relaxed and centered approach to life.

Another important concept from Chinese philosophy is the idea of **"finding stillness in movement"** or **"calm in action."** This idea is based on the concept of balance and harmony in life, and it encourages individuals to focus on the present moment rather than dwelling on past experiences or worrying about the future. Individuals can reduce anxiety and overcome fear by learning to find calm amid activity.

Whether through a focus on trusting in God's love and protection, embracing the natural pace of life, or finding stillness in movement, these teachings provide individuals with the tools and insights they need to develop the social skills and confidence they need to succeed and thrive in life.

TRUE FEAR VS. PHYSICAL FEAR

True fear and physical fear are two distinct experiences that impact individuals in different ways. True fear is a psychological experience that arises from the perception of an imminent threat or danger. It is an adaptive response that helps individuals prepare for potential danger and navigate challenging situations. Physical fear, on the other hand, is a physiological experience that is triggered by an actual physical threat or danger. It is characterized by physical responses such as increased heart rate, sweating, and muscle tension.

In his teachings, Xunzi, a disciple of Confucius, offers a profound insight relevant to overcoming fear: **"Not seeing is not as good as seeing, seeing is not as good as knowing, knowing is not as good as acting; true learning continues until it is put into action."** This quote highlights his belief that understanding, awareness, and action are crucial in overcoming challenges, including fears. Xunzi emphasized that it is not enough to be aware of our fears; we must actively work to understand and confront them.

This process involves a steady progression from ignorance to knowledge and, ultimately, to action. According to Xunzi, such perseverance and dedication are essential for overcoming the obstacles that fear presents in our lives. He advocated for a pragmatic approach, where theoretical knowledge is transformed into practical application, illustrating that true wisdom lies in the ability to apply what one has learned, especially in the face of fear and uncertainty.

Another Chinese philosopher, Lao Tzu, wrote in the "Tao Te Ching" that fear can be both a source of strength and a weakness. Lao Tzu stated, **"Knowing others is wisdom; knowing yourself is enlightenment."** He believed that individuals who understand their own fears and limitations have the capacity to overcome them and live a fulfilled life. Lao Tzu also emphasized the importance of letting go of fear and living in the present moment.

In the Bible, the book of Proverbs encourages individuals to overcome fear by having faith in God. Proverbs 3:5-6 states, **"Trust in the Lord with all your heart and lean not on your own understanding; in all your ways submit to him, and he will make your paths straight."** This passage suggests that by relying on God, individuals can overcome fear and live a life of purpose and peace.

It is important to remember that true fear and physical fear are distinct experiences that impact individuals differently. Overcoming fear and anxiety requires a deep understanding of one's own fears and limitations, as well as a willingness to face and overcome them. Confucius, Lao Tzu, and the Bible all provide guidance and inspiration for individuals who seek to overcome fear and live a fulfilled life.

SOCIAL ANXIETY

Social anxiety disorder—often called social phobia—is more than simple shyness; it is a persistent, sometimes crippling fear of being watched, judged, or humiliated in everyday interactions. The condition typically emerges in early adolescence, just when peer approval feels most critical, and can narrow a person's world for years if left unaddressed.

How It Manifests

- **Physical cues:** racing heart, sweating, trembling, upset stomach, shaky voice—sometimes triggered merely by imagining a social encounter.
- **Emotional cues:** days of intense worry leading up to an event, replaying perceived mistakes afterward, and harsh self-criticism.
- **Behavioral cues:** avoiding class presentations, skipping social invitations, steering clear of dating, or choosing jobs with minimal face-to-face contact.

Seemingly routine tasks—ordering coffee, using a public restroom, or working out at a gym—can feel like high-stakes performances. Continual avoidance shrinks opportunity, erodes self-esteem, and feeds isolation or depression.

DAY-TO-DAY IMPACT

Life Area	*Common Consequence*
School / Work	Declining leadership roles, limiting networking, under-participating in meetings
Relationships	Difficulty initiating friendships or romantic connections; misreading neutral cues as rejection
Health	Chronic stress, disrupted sleep, and higher risk of self-medicating with alcohol or drugs
Personal Growth	Missed travel, public-speaking, or community-service opportunities that broaden horizons

Core Paths to Improvement

1. Cognitive Behavioral Therapy (CBT)

Considered the gold standard, CBT helps people challenge catastrophic thoughts ("Everyone will notice I'm nervous") and gradually face feared situations so confidence can grow (Barlow, 2017).

2. Skills & Lifestyle Strategies

- **Relaxation techniques**—deep breathing, progressive muscle relaxation—to calm the body's alarm system.
- Social-skills workshops for eye contact, small talk, and assertiveness in a low-pressure environment.
- Consistent exercise, balanced sleep, and nutrient-dense meals, all of which stabilize mood chemistry.

3. Peer & Support Networks

Online or in-person groups provide reassurance that others share the struggle, plus a safe space to practice new skills.

Professional Guidance Note

In some cases, a licensed physician or psychiatrist may decide that medication—such as selective serotonin reuptake inhibitors (SSRIs) or certain beta-blockers—can help manage physical symptoms and support therapeutic progress. Any decision about medication must be made solely between an individual and a qualified healthcare professional. This book is informational and does not offer medical advice.

Moving Forward

If you suspect social anxiety is steering your decisions, reach out for help early. Telehealth appointments can ease first-session jitters, and celebrating small wins (asking one question in class, greeting a coworker) builds steady momentum. Social anxiety disorder is highly treatable; with consistent support and practice, people learn to replace catastrophic "what-ifs" with balanced perspectives and reclaim the full range of relationships, opportunities, and everyday joys.

PHYSICAL FEAR EQUALS SOCIAL ANXIETY

Physical fear and social anxiety are two separate entities, although they are often intertwined. Physical fear is a normal and instinctual response to dangerous or life-threatening situations, while social anxiety is an excessive fear of social situations and interaction with others.

Physical fear is a survival mechanism that has evolved to help us protect ourselves from harm. It is a response to real or perceived danger, such as the fear of heights, fear of animals, or fear of public speaking. It is a normal and natural reaction to a stressful situation and is necessary for our survival.

On the other hand, social anxiety is not a survival mechanism and is not necessary for our survival. It is a psychological disorder that involves excessive and persistent fear of social situations and the scrutiny of others. It can be a debilitating condition that can prevent an individual from participating in everyday activities, such as socializing, public speaking, and dating.

To overcome social anxiety, it is important to understand that it is not a reflection of who you are but rather a condition that can be treated. A combination of therapy and medication, such as cognitive-behavioral therapy (CBT) and selective serotonin reuptake inhibitors (SSRIs), have been shown to be effective in treating social anxiety.

Additionally, self-help techniques, such as exposure therapy, deep breathing exercises, sound therapy and mindfulness, can also be helpful in managing social anxiety. It is also important to understand that overcoming social anxiety takes time and effort, but with the right support and treatment, it is possible to lead a fulfilling life. (Health, (2021))

By seeking help from a mental health professional, practicing self-help techniques, and being patient and persistent, individuals with social anxiety can overcome their fears and lead fulfilling lives.

SITUATIONS THAT TRIGGER ANXIETY

Anxiety is a normal human emotion that becomes problematic when it becomes excessive, persistent, and interferes with daily life. It is a response to stress and fear that is often triggered by specific situations or events. Here are ten common triggers of anxiety:

- Stress at work or school.
- Health concerns.
- Financial worries.
- Relationship problems.
- Public speaking.
- Test-taking or exams.
- Crowds or busy public places.
- Time pressure or deadlines.
- Changes in routine or schedule.
- Personal failures or perceived shortcomings.

It is important to note that triggers can vary from person to person and that what triggers anxiety for one person may not affect another in the same way. Additionally, some people may have anxiety even without a specific trigger, which is known as 'generalized anxiety disorder.'

SIGNS AND SYMPTOMS

Social anxiety disorder is a persistent and intense fear of being judged or evaluated by others in social or performance situations. This fear can be so severe that it interferes with daily activities, self-confidence, relationships, and job or school performance. The signs and symptoms of social anxiety disorder are as follows:

EMOTIONAL SIGNS:

- Self-consciousness and anxiety in everyday social situations.
- Distressed about upcoming social events.
- Fear of being watched by others.
- Constant worry about making mistakes.

PHYSICAL SYMPTOMS:

- Rapid heartbeat.
- Sweating.
- Shaking.
- Rapid breathing.
- Nausea.
- Feeling exhausted.
- Avoiding eye contact.
- Blushing.

BEHAVIORAL SIGNS:

- Reliance on alcohol in social situations.
- Avoiding attention by staying quiet at social events.
- Avoiding social events altogether.

CAUSES

Social anxiety disorder typically develops at a specific point in an individual's life and can become more pronounced over time. It is often rooted in experiences during childhood, such as being emotionally or physically abused by peers or parents. These negative experiences can become ingrained in the individual's subconscious, leading to anxiety in similar situations later in life.

OTHER POSSIBLE CAUSES OF SOCIAL ANXIETY DISORDER INCLUDE:

- Heredity and family factors.
- Negative social experiences.
- Psychological factors.
- Unfortunate events.

It is important to note that while these causes can contribute to the development of social anxiety disorder, they can also be addressed and treated with proper care and support.

TREATMENT

Managing social anxiety through treatment is crucial for attaining genuine success in life. This condition, which can severely limit a person's capacity to partake in social interactions and fully enjoy life, can be mitigated with proper treatment. Such intervention assists individuals in controlling their anxiety symptoms, enhancing their confidence and self-esteem, and acquiring techniques to effectively navigate social scenarios.

There are several effective treatment options for social anxiety; cognitive-behavioral therapy, exposure therapy, and medication are included. Cognitive-behavioral therapy focuses on changing negative thoughts and behaviors associated with social anxiety, while exposure therapy helps individuals gradually face their fears in a controlled and safe environment. (Furmark, 2002)

Ultimately, the goal of treatment is to help individuals overcome their fears and participate in the joyous activities of life. Success in treatment can be measured by an individual's improved ability to engage in social situations, increased self-esteem and confidence, and overall quality of life. With the right treatment and support, individuals can achieve true success and live a fulfilling life free of the constraints of social anxiety.

10 POSSIBLE CURES WE CAN HAVE AND HOW BEST WE CAN MANAGE SOCIAL PHOBIA.

- **Cognitive-behavioral therapy (CBT):** This type of therapy helps individuals change negative thought patterns and behaviors associated with social anxiety.

- **Exposure therapy:** This therapy involves gradually exposing individuals to the situations they fear in a controlled and safe environment.

- **Mindfulness and relaxation techniques:** Practices such as deep breathing, meditation, and yoga can help individuals manage stress and anxiety.

- **Group therapy:** Talking with others who have social anxiety can be a helpful and supportive experience.

- **Social skills training:** This type of therapy helps individuals develop and practice social skills to improve their ability to engage in social situations.

- **Lifestyle changes:** Simple changes, such as getting regular exercise, eating a balanced diet, and getting enough sleep, can help manage symptoms of anxiety.

- **Acceptance and commitment therapy (ACT):** This type of therapy helps individuals learn to accept their thoughts and feelings without judgment and focus on their values and goals.

- **Eye Movement Desensitization and Reprocessing (EMDR):** This therapy uses eye movements to process and resolve past traumas that may contribute to anxiety symptoms.

- **Laughter therapy:** Laughter can help reduce stress and anxiety and improve overall mood. Engaging in activities that bring joy and laughter can be helpful for managing social anxiety.

It is essential to recognize that various treatments are more effective for different individuals, and finding the appropriate method may require time. Equally important is to garner support from friends and family and collaborate with a mental health professional to devise a personalized treatment strategy.

FREEDOM FROM FEAR

FREEDOM FROM FEAR

"The journey of a thousand miles begins with one step." - Lao Tzu

Freedom from fear refers to the state of being free from the negative emotions and mental distress that come from fear and anxiety. For individuals with social anxiety, the fear of being judged or embarrassed in social situations can greatly impact their quality of life. However, with the right tools and support, freedom from fear is achievable.

"It does not matter how slowly you go as long as you do not stop." - Confucius.

One of the key steps in achieving freedom from fear is seeking professional help. A mental health professional can help individuals understand the root causes of their anxiety and develop a treatment plan to manage their symptoms. This may include therapy, medication, and lifestyle changes.

"The man who asks a question is a fool for a minute; the man who does not is a fool for life." - Confucius.

Another important aspect of achieving freedom from fear is learning to recognize and challenge negative thoughts and beliefs. Negative thoughts can perpetuate anxiety, so it is important to learn how to identify and reframe these thoughts in a more positive and realistic manner.

"The best time to plant a tree was 20 years ago. The second best time is now." - Chinese Proverb.

Developing healthy coping skills and relaxation techniques, such as mindfulness, deep breathing, and exercise, can help individuals manage stress and anxiety. Engaging in activities that bring joy and fulfillment can also be a helpful way to reduce fear and improve overall well-being.

"The man who moves a mountain begins by carrying away small stones." - Confucius.

Ultimately, achieving freedom from fear requires a combination of self-awareness, support, and the right tools and techniques. With the right approach, individuals with social anxiety can learn to manage their symptoms, build confidence and self-esteem, and enjoy a fulfilling and joyful life free from the constraints of fear.

SOCIAL SKILL AND ITS ADVANTAGES TO YOUR CAREER

Social skills are an essential aspect of life and can have a significant impact on one's personal and professional life. In the workplace, strong social skills can lead to improved relationships with coworkers, better communication, and greater opportunities for advancement.

One of the key advantages of having good social skills in the workplace is the ability to build and maintain positive relationships with coworkers. This can lead to a more positive and supportive work environment, which can increase job satisfaction and overall well-being. Good social skills can also help individuals network and build connections within the industry, which can open opportunities for advancement and growth.

Effective communication is another important aspect of social skills in the workplace. Individuals with strong social skills can communicate clearly and effectively, which can lead to improved productivity, more successful negotiations and collaboration, and better problem-solving. Good communication skills can also help individuals build trust and credibility, which can have a positive impact on their professional reputation.

In addition to these benefits, social skills can also impact one's salary and opportunities for advancement. For example, individuals with strong social skills are often better at networking, which can lead to new job opportunities and higher salaries. They may also be more likely to be considered for promotions and leadership positions due to their ability to work well with others and communicate effectively.

Social skills are an asset in the workplace and can have a significant impact on one's career success. By building strong relationships, communicating effectively, and demonstrating leadership and collaboration skills, individuals with good social skills can open new opportunities for advancement and achieve greater success in their careers.

SOCIAL SKILLS AND EFFECTIVE COMMUNICATION

The ability to communicate effectively with others is a critical component of one's social skillset. With strong communication skills, individuals can articulate their thoughts and opinions clearly, ensuring their message is understood by those they interact with. This is particularly important in leadership roles, where leaders need to be able to explain tasks and goals in a simple and concise manner.

Communication is the cornerstone of all relationships, as it allows individuals to share information and gain a deeper understanding of one another. However, it is essential to note that much of communication is nonverbal. While a person may not express their dissatisfaction verbally, their body language may indicate otherwise, such as through crossed arms, avoiding eye contact, or positioning their feet towards the door. As a result, it is crucial to be aware of both your own body language and that of others to avoid misunderstandings.

To be an effective communicator, one should speak in a direct and straightforward manner, using language that is easily understood. They should be assertive in expressing their views and opinions but also open to feedback and suggestions from others. Effective communicators make eye contact, use positive language, and listen attentively to what others have to say.

Some key traits of effective communicators include being active contributors to the workplace, being relied upon by others, being forthright with their beliefs, having a unique communication style, and being able to simplify complicated topics. Effective communication is critical in both personal and professional settings, as it enables individuals to form stronger relationships, collaborate effectively with others, and achieve shared goals. By infusing good body language into your interactions, you can further enhance your communication skills and the impact of your message.

WHAT IS AN EFFECTIVE COMMUNICATOR?

An effective communicator is someone who can express their thoughts, ideas, and opinions in a clear, concise, and assertive manner, using language that is easily understood by others. They are not just effective speakers but also active listeners, who make eye contact, show empathy, and use affirmative language when engaging with others.

SOME KEY TRAITS THAT DEFINE AN EFFECTIVE COMMUNICATOR INCLUDE:

- **Active contribution to the workplace:** Effective communicators play a crucial role in the smooth functioning of an organization. They have a clear understanding of the company's goals and are skilled at communicating with their coworkers. They are also open to receiving feedback and guidance.

- **Rely on by others:** Good communicators are often seen as trusted advisors and are often the first individuals that others turn to for guidance. This is because they communicate truthfully and listen attentively, building trust and respect with those around them.

- **Clear expression of opinions:** Effective communicators are not afraid to express their opinions and views, but they do so in a firm yet respectful manner. They are aware of the significance of being straightforward in their beliefs and ideas and are able to provide clear and concise feedback.

- **Unique communication style:** To be an exceptional communicator, one must have a distinctive communication style that makes their input memorable. This may involve speech inflections, nonverbal cues, and the use of humor or personal anecdotes.

- **Ability to simplify complex topics:** Effective communicators should be able to convey complex ideas in a manner that is easily understood by the majority of people. Whether they are breaking down a poem for literature students or demystifying search engine optimization for non-technical stakeholders, effective communicators have the skill to make complex subjects understandable for their audience.

- **Assertiveness and receptiveness:** Effective communicators are assertive in expressing their views and opinions, but they are also receptive to the suggestions of others. This balance allows for productive and respectful conversations, even when opinions differ.

- **Eye contact and affirmative language:** Strong communicators make eye contact when speaking and listening and use affirmative language such as "I hear you" and "I understand your concerns." This demonstrates that they are engaged and present in the conversation.

For personal and professional success, effective communication is a vital social skill that can greatly improve relationships and increase one's value as a team member. By honing their communication skills, individuals can contribute to the achievement of organizational goals, fostering cooperation and collaboration in the workplace.

Effective communication can strengthen connections, deepen understanding, and enhance the ability to convey thoughts and ideas clearly, making it an essential component of personal and professional success.

By embodying these traits, effective communicators can build stronger relationships, become more valuable members of their teams, and help organizations achieve their goals.

WHY IS EFFECTIVE COMMUNICATION IMPORTANT?

Effective communication is important for numerous reasons, as it can greatly impact personal and professional relationships, as well as the success of organizations. Communication is the foundation for all relationships, and by being able to communicate effectively, one can deepen their relationships, foster mutual understanding and build trust. In a professional setting, effective communication can lead to better teamwork and collaboration, as team members are able to express their thoughts and ideas clearly and comprehend the contributions of others.

Moreover, effective communication is vital for successful decision-making and problem-solving, as it allows individuals and teams to fully understand a situation and make informed choices. Additionally, clear and concise communication helps to avoid misunderstandings, reduces conflicts, and promotes a positive work environment.

Effective communication skills also benefit one's career, as they make one a more effective leader and valuable team member. Good communicators are often sought after by organizations, as they can explain complex ideas in simple terms, listen attentively, and contribute to the workplace in a meaningful way. Effective communication skills can also help individuals to stand out, as they can communicate their ideas in a memorable and distinct manner, making them an asset to any organization.

Effective communication is crucial for building and maintaining relationships, promoting teamwork, making informed decisions, avoiding conflicts and fostering a positive work environment, and advancing one's career.

HOW TO BE AN EFFECTIVE COMMUNICATOR

To be an effective communicator, one can draw upon the teachings of Dale Carnegie's book "How to Win Friends and Influence People" and Eckhart **Tolle's "The Power of Now."**

According to Carnegie, effective communication requires an understanding of the other person's point of view. This can be achieved by actively listening and showing empathy and respect towards the speaker. Carnegie also emphasizes the importance of speaking in a clear and concise manner, using language that is easily understood, and avoiding criticism and negativity. (Carnegie, 1936)

In **"The Power of Now,"** Tolle advocates for mindfulness and being present in the moment as key components of effective communication. He suggests letting go of distractions, such as our own thoughts and emotions, to truly listen and be fully engaged in the conversation. (Tolle, 1997)

Both Carnegie and Tolle emphasize the importance of being authentic and genuine in our communication, avoiding pretentiousness and insincerity. By combining these teachings and incorporating active listening, empathy, clarity, mindfulness, and authenticity, one can become an effective communicator and strengthen personal and professional relationships.

Effective communication is a crucial aspect of personal and professional success, and there are several ways to improve your communication skills using the principles from both **"How to Win Friends and Influence People"** by Dale Carnegie and **"The Power of Now"** by Eckhart Tolle. From **"How to Win Friends and Influence People,"** you can learn to be a better listener and to show genuine interest in others. Carnegie suggests that you should become genuinely interested in other people, listen to them with attention, and ask questions that show you are interested in what they have to say. This not only helps you to build rapport with others but also demonstrates your respect for their opinions and ideas.

In addition, Carnegie emphasizes the importance of speaking in terms that others can relate to and of avoiding criticism, complaining, and arguments. He suggests that you should seek to understand the other person's perspective and present your own ideas in a way that appeals to their interests and concerns.

From **"The Power of Now,"** you can learn to be present and mindful in your communication. Tolle emphasizes that the state of your mind directly influences the quality of your communication. If you are thinking about the past or worrying about the future, you will not be fully present at the moment, and your communication will be less effective. To be an effective communicator, Tolle suggests that you need to cultivate mindfulness, which means being aware of what is happening in the present moment without judgment or distraction.

Tolle also emphasizes the importance of being authentic and genuine in your communication. He suggests that you should communicate from a place of truth rather than trying to impress or manipulate others. When you communicate authentically, you will be more confident, and your communication will be more effective.

By combining the principles from **"How to Win Friends and Influence People"** and **"The Power of Now,"** you can become a more effective communicator, building stronger relationships and improving your personal and professional success.

LEE KUAN YEW

Lee Kuan Yew's book, **"From Third World to First: The Singapore Story 1965-2000,"** provides valuable insights into the role of effective communication in building a successful nation. Lee Kuan Yew, the former Prime Minister of Singapore, was known for his visionary leadership and effective communication skills. His ability to communicate effectively with his citizens, government officials, and the international community played a critical role in the development of Singapore.

In his book, Lee Kuan Yew emphasizes the importance of clear, concise, and persuasive communication in shaping public opinion and policy. He writes about how he used effective communication strategies to explain complex policies to the public, thus gaining their support and buy-in. He also highlights the role of communication in creating a sense of national unity and purpose.

Furthermore, Lee Kuan Yew emphasizes the importance of active listening in effective communication. He writes about how he would listen to the concerns of his citizens and adjust policies accordingly. This approach not only helped him to build trust and credibility with the public, but it also helped to ensure that policies were based on the needs and desires of the citizens. (Lee, 2000)

The success of Singapore is a testament to the importance of effective communication in shaping the future of a nation. Lee Kuan Yew's approach to communication set a strong foundation for the country's economic and social development. His lessons on the power of effective communication continue to inspire leaders around the world and serve as a model for success.

In contrast, countries with poor communication can experience negative effects such as a lack of trust and cooperation between different levels of government, businesses, and the general public. Confusion and misunderstandings can lead to decreased productivity and effectiveness, hindering a country's ability to move forward and achieve its goals.

Additionally, ineffective communication can also lead to social and political unrest, as the people may not understand the reasons behind government decisions or may feel ignored and unheard.

Therefore, as demonstrated by Lee Kuan Yew's leadership in Singapore, effective communication is crucial for a country's success and progress. It helps build trust, cooperation, and understanding among the different stakeholders and contributes to a more harmonious and prosperous society.

HOW YOU CAN IMPROVE YOUR COMMUNICATION ABILITIES

Active Listening: Effective communication starts with active listening, which involves giving your full attention to the person speaking and truly understanding their message. This can be done by maintaining eye contact, asking clarifying questions, and avoiding distractions while they are speaking.

Clarity: Ensure that your message is clear and concise. Use simple language, avoid ambiguity, and be direct. Ensure that the person you are communicating with fully understands your message by checking for their comprehension.

Empathy: Empathy is key to effective communication. It means putting yourself in the other person's shoes, understanding their perspective, and showing compassion and understanding. This helps build trust and rapport and makes the other person feel heard and valued.

Body Language: Your body language can communicate as much, if not more, than your words. Pay attention to your posture, gestures, and facial expressions, and use them to reinforce your message. Make sure that your body language is open and inviting, as opposed to closed or intimidating.

Confidence: Confidence is a crucial aspect of effective communication. Speak clearly and assertively, but also be open to feedback and willing to listen. Confidence builds credibility and helps you effectively convey your message to others.

CONFLICT RESOLUTION

Good social skills play a crucial role in conflict resolution as they allow individuals to interact with others in a productive and effective manner. This leads to better understanding and improved relationships, reducing the likelihood of conflicts arising in the first place.

Conflict is an inevitable part of any human interaction and can occur in personal or professional settings. When conflict does arise, it is important to handle it in a way that leads to a positive outcome for all parties involved.

This is where the importance of good social skills comes into play.

Individuals with strong social skills are able to effectively listen to and understand others, express their own views and opinions in a clear and concise manner, and engage in open and honest dialogue. This allows them to identify the root cause of the conflict, negotiate a solution that addresses the needs of all parties, and move forward in a positive and productive manner.

According to the book **"High Conflict: Why We Get Trapped and How We Get Out,"** effective conflict resolution requires an understanding of the different types of conflict and the skills needed to address them. In the book, the authors highlight the importance of empathy, active listening, and effective communication in resolving conflicts. (Ripley, 2021)

Similarly, **"The Handbook of Conflict Resolution: Theory and Practice"** provides a comprehensive overview of the theories and techniques used in conflict resolution, including effective communication and negotiation skills. The authors stress the importance of understanding the needs and motivations of all parties involved and using empathetic and non-judgmental language to build rapport and resolve conflicts. (Folger, 2014)

Strong social skills and adept conflict resolution are intricately connected and crucial for fostering and sustaining healthy relationships, both personally and professionally. By refining these abilities, individuals can ensure that conflicts are settled constructively and positively, resulting in enhanced relationships and beneficial outcomes for everyone involved.

WHY IS CONFLICT RESOLUTION IMPORTANT?

Conflict resolution is an important aspect of human interaction, and it plays a critical role in overall success. As stated earlier, conflicts can arise in personal and professional relationships and can take many forms, such as disagreements, misunderstandings, and personality clashes. These conflicts can be destructive to relationships and can impede progress if left unresolved.

Therefore, it is crucial to have good conflict resolution skills to avoid prolonged or escalated conflict and maintain positive relationships. Good conflict resolution skills help individuals and organizations find mutually beneficial solutions to problems, reducing stress and improving relationships.

When conflicts are resolved effectively, it leads to better collaboration, improved communication, and increased trust.

Conflict resolution also helps to maintain a healthy work environment. A workplace that is free from conflict and tension is more productive, and employees are more likely to be motivated and engaged in their work. On the other hand, a workplace filled with unresolved conflicts can lead to low morale, decreased productivity, and increased absenteeism.

Overall, conflict resolution is a vital component of good social skills, and it is a critical factor in success. It helps individuals and organizations achieve their goals and maintain positive relationships, and it contributes to a healthy and productive work environment.

SOCIAL ISOLATION

SOCIAL ISOLATION: ITS NEGATIVE AND POSITIVE EFFECTS

Social isolation is a phenomenon that refers to a lack of social interaction or limited interaction with others. It is a growing concern in today's society, where people are increasingly disconnected from each other due to technology, work, and other life demands. Social isolation can have both negative and positive effects, and it is important to understand them to determine how to approach the issue.

The negative effects of social isolation are numerous and can be quite devastating. For one, social isolation increases the risk of depression and anxiety. This is because human beings are social animals and require interaction with others in order to thrive. Without this interaction, people can become lonely and isolated, leading to feelings of depression and anxiety. Additionally, social isolation can have a negative impact on physical health. This is because people who are isolated are more likely to have poor nutrition and lack physical activity, both of which can have a detrimental effect on overall health. Furthermore, social isolation can increase the risk of cognitive decline and dementia, particularly in older individuals.

Another negative effect of social isolation is a decreased sense of purpose and meaning. When people are isolated, they may feel that their life lacks direction and that their contributions to society are insignificant. This can lead to feelings of hopelessness and a lack of motivation to pursue their goals and aspirations. Finally, social isolation can make it difficult for people to form and maintain relationships. This is due to the fact that individuals experiencing isolation often face challenges in trusting others and may have difficulty in establishing significant connections with people.

However, social isolation can also have positive effects. For example, social isolation can increase focus and productivity, allowing for personal and professional growth. When people are isolated, they can devote their full attention to a task or project, leading to improved performance and outcomes. Additionally, social isolation can improve mental health by reducing stress and allowing for introspection and self-reflection. This can lead to a greater sense of well-being and a deeper understanding of oneself.

Social isolation can also increase creativity and independent thinking. When people are isolated, they are free to think and reflect on their own, leading to new insights and ideas. Furthermore, social isolation can increase appreciation for close relationships and social interaction. People who have experienced social isolation may appreciate the importance of social interaction and may be more likely to seek out meaningful relationships with others.

In conclusion, social isolation can have both negative and positive effects. While it is important to understand the potential downsides of social isolation, it is also important to recognize its positive aspects. The key is to balance one's need for solitude with their need for social interaction and support. By doing so, individuals can reap the benefits of social isolation while avoiding its negative effects.

SOCIAL ISOLATION AND THE EFFECT OF THE COVID-19 EPIDEMIC

The COVID-19 pandemic has had a profound impact on social isolation, affecting individuals and communities worldwide. The measures taken to curb the spread of the virus, such as lockdowns, quarantines, and physical distancing, have resulted in decreased in-person interactions and a significant increase in time spent alone.

One of the most notable effects of the COVID-19 epidemic on social isolation has been an increase in feelings of loneliness and depression. The restrictions on physical interaction and the closure of social gathering places have resulted in a decrease in social support, leading to feelings of isolation and a lack of emotional connection with others. This has also had a negative impact on mental health, with a rise in cases of depression and anxiety being reported.

The COVID-19 epidemic has also placed a strain on families and relationships. With people spending more time at home and with limited opportunities for social interaction, this has led to increased stress and tension within families, particularly in households where multiple people are living in close quarters.

Vulnerable populations, such as the elderly and individuals with disabilities, have been particularly affected by the epidemic. These individuals were already at a higher risk of social isolation before the pandemic, and the restrictions on physical interaction have further exacerbated their feelings of loneliness and isolation.

However, the COVID-19 epidemic has also led to increased creativity and innovation in finding new ways to connect with others. This has included an increase in virtual social gatherings, such as video calls and online games, as well as increased community outreach and support.

The COVID-19 pandemic has significantly influenced social isolation, bringing both adverse and beneficial effects. While actions to contain the virus have heightened feelings of loneliness and depression in numerous people, they've also spurred greater innovation and creativity in developing new methods of connecting with others. Society must maintain a balance between fostering and strengthening social ties and implementing essential measures to halt the virus's spread.

WHAT EFFECT DOES SOCIAL ISOLATION HAVE ON MENTAL HEALTH?

Social isolation is a growing concern in our society, with increasing numbers of people experiencing feelings of loneliness and disconnection from others.

This lack of social interaction and support can have a profound impact on mental health, leading to a range of negative outcomes.

One of the most well-known effects of social isolation on mental health is an increased risk of depression. Studies have shown that individuals who experience chronic feelings of loneliness and isolation are more likely to develop depression compared to those who have strong social connections. This is because social interaction provides a sense of validation and belonging, which is critical for maintaining good mental health.

In addition to depression, social isolation can also increase the risk of anxiety disorders. Loneliness and isolation can lead to feelings of uncertainty and insecurity, which can trigger anxiety symptoms. This can make it difficult for individuals to manage their anxiety, leading to a cycle of increased anxiety and further social isolation.

Social isolation can also have a negative impact on overall cognitive function and brain health. Studies have shown that social interaction and connection are critical for maintaining brain function and that social isolation can lead to decreased cognitive function and an increased risk of cognitive decline.

It is important to note that social isolation can affect individuals of all ages, but it is particularly concerning for the elderly population. Older adults are at a higher risk of experiencing social isolation, and this can lead to a decline in physical health, increased risk of chronic diseases, and increased risk of death.

On the positive side, there is a range of interventions that can help individuals overcome feelings of social isolation and improve their mental health. This can include participating in community events, joining social clubs or groups, volunteering, and participating in online communities. In addition, therapy and counseling can also be helpful in managing symptoms of depression and anxiety.

Social isolation can have a profound impact on mental health, leading to a range of negative outcomes such as depression, anxiety, and decreased cognitive function. However, with the right interventions and support, individuals can overcome feelings of social isolation and improve their mental health.

It is important for society to prioritize measures that support and enhance social connections, to ensure that everyone has access to the social support they need to maintain good mental health.

SIX NEGATIVE CONSEQUENCES OF SOCIAL ISOLATION

Social isolation refers to the lack of social connections and interactions with others. It can have serious negative consequences on an individual's physical and mental health. Here are six consequences of social isolation:

- **Physical Health Issues:** Social isolation has been linked to a variety of physical health problems, including cardiovascular disease, weakened immune system, and increased risk of stroke and other chronic conditions.
- **Mental Health Concerns:** Isolation can lead to feelings of depression, anxiety, and loneliness, which can have a negative impact on an individual's mental health. It can also contribute to the development of cognitive decline, memory problems, and an increased risk of dementia.
- **Decreased Life Satisfaction:** Social isolation can lead to a decline in overall life satisfaction and a sense of purposelessness. It can also result in a lack of motivation and decreased energy levels.
- **Difficulty in Coping with Stress:** Without the support of friends, family, and community, individuals who are isolated may have a harder time coping with stress, leading to increased levels of anxiety and depression.
- **Increased Substance Abuse:** Social isolation can increase the risk of substance abuse, as individuals may turn to drugs or alcohol as a way to cope with feelings of loneliness and depression.
- **Higher Risk of Mortality:** Studies have shown that social isolation can increase the risk of death, as individuals who are isolated are more likely to engage in unhealthy behaviors and have less access to health resources and support.

In conclusion, social isolation can have far-reaching consequences on an individual's physical and mental health, and it is important to prioritize building and maintaining social connections and support networks.

SIX STRATEGIES FOR OVERCOMING SOCIAL ISOLATION

Social isolation can be a difficult and challenging experience, but there are strategies that individuals can use to overcome it. Here are six strategies for overcoming social isolation:

- **Building Strong Relationships:** Focus on building strong, meaningful relationships with family members, friends, and others in your community. This can involve actively reaching out to others, participating in activities you enjoy, and trying to be there for others when they need support.
- Joining Community Groups: Join community groups and organizations that align with your interests and values. This can be a great way to meet new people and connect with others who share similar experiences.
- **Engaging in Hobbies and Interests:** Pursuing hobbies and interests can be a great way to meet new people, as well as provide a sense of purpose and fulfillment.
- **Volunteering:** Volunteering can provide opportunities to connect with others while also giving back to the community.
- **Utilizing Technology:** Utilize technology, such as video conferencing or social media, to stay connected with friends and family who are not physically present.
- **Seeking Professional Help:** If feelings of isolation persist, it may be helpful to seek professional help from a mental health provider. A mental health professional can provide support, guidance, and resources to help individuals overcome social isolation and improve their overall well-being.

Overcoming social isolation requires a proactive and intentional approach. By utilizing these strategies, individuals can build and strengthen their social connections, improve their physical and mental health, and live a more fulfilling life. Loneliness may be crippling. Nonetheless, there are straightforward steps you can take to disrupt the cycle of social isolation.

CONCLUSION

Social development is a crucial aspect of personal growth and success in life. It refers to the process of acquiring and refining social skills, such as communication, empathy, and relationship building, that enable individuals to interact effectively with others. Social development is linked to overall success in several ways.

Firstly, it allows individuals to form strong relationships with others, including family, friends, and colleagues, which can provide support and opportunities for personal growth.

Secondly, strong social skills are essential in the workplace, as they help to build trust, foster collaboration, and lead to professional advancement.

Finally, social development is also related to emotional intelligence, which is critical for personal well-being, happiness, and resilience in the face of life's challenges.

In conclusion, social development plays a vital role in an individual's success and overall satisfaction with life. Whether it is building strong relationships, excelling in the workplace, or maintaining personal well-being, social development is an ongoing process that requires ongoing effort and attention. Individuals who invest time and energy into developing their social skills will reap the rewards in the form of a more fulfilling life and greater success in all areas.

Chapter Six
DEVELOPING YOURSELF ECONOMICALLY

"Being rich is having money; being wealthy is having time."

Margaret Bonann

INTRODUCTION

The concept of economic development is crucial for individuals looking to secure their financial future and achieve their goals. Regardless of your current financial situation, developing yourself economically is a journey that requires effort, discipline, and a willingness to learn and grow. This chapter aims to provide a comprehensive overview of the different aspects of economic development and guide you in your journey towards financial stability and success.

We will begin by understanding your current financial situation and setting some realistic financial goals. This is followed by a discussion on budgeting and saving, which are the foundation of any successful financial plan. We will also delve into the world of investing and explore different types of investments that can help you build wealth over time. In addition, we will discuss entrepreneurship, real estate investing, and other ways to create passive income streams. Finally, we will address the importance of managing debt and avoiding debt traps, which can impede your financial progress.

Through this chapter, you will gain a deeper understanding of how to develop yourself economically and take control of your financial future. The key is to remain committed, educate yourself, and be proactive in your financial decision-making.

IMPORTANCE OF ECONOMIC DEVELOPMENT

Economic development is crucial for individuals and societies as it provides the means for individuals to improve their quality of life and achieve their goals. It is not just about accumulating wealth but rather a holistic approach to financial stability and well-being. Economic development involves improving one's financial literacy, making informed investment decisions, managing debt effectively, and creating multiple streams of income.

Furthermore, economic growth carries broader consequences for society at large. A flourishing economy results in job creation, enhanced consumer expenditure, and more investment in local areas. Consequently, this contributes to overall economic expansion and raises living standards. Additionally, individuals who are economically prosperous are better equipped to contribute to their communities and assist those who are less fortunate.

Moreover, economic development provides individuals with a sense of security and independence. It allows individuals to be self-sufficient and less reliant on government assistance or handouts. This, in turn, empowers individuals to take control of their own financial future and achieve their personal and financial goals.

Economic development is an ongoing process that requires effort, discipline, and a willingness to learn and grow. It is a key factor in improving the quality of life for individuals and societies and should be a priority for anyone looking to secure their financial future.

In addition to providing individuals with financial stability and independence, economic development also has wider implications for society as a whole. For example, a thriving economy leads to increased consumer spending, which stimulates business growth and job creation. This, in turn, leads to higher tax revenues for the government, which can be used to fund essential public services and infrastructure development.

Moreover, economic development encourages entrepreneurship and innovation, as individuals with financial resources are more likely to take risks and start new businesses. This drives innovation and competition, which can lead to improved products, services, and technologies, benefiting consumers and society as a whole.

In addition, economically developed individuals are more likely to invest in their local communities and support those in need. This can be through philanthropy, volunteering, or providing employment opportunities. This not only helps to improve the standard of living for those in need but also strengthens the social fabric of the community.

Furthermore, economic development helps to reduce poverty and inequality, which are key challenges facing many societies today. By providing individuals with financial stability and independence, it helps to break the cycle of poverty and enables people to improve their standard of living. This, in turn, leads to a more equitable distribution of wealth and greater social stability.

The importance of economic development cannot be overstated. It is a key factor in improving the quality of life for individuals and societies and has far-reaching implications for economic growth, job creation, innovation, and community development.

THE PURPOSE OF THE CHAPTER

The purpose of this chapter on Developing Yourself Economically is to provide a comprehensive overview of the different aspects of economic development and guide individuals on their journey towards financial stability and success. The chapter is designed to educate individuals on the key principles of budgeting, saving, investing, and building wealth, as well as managing debt effectively.

The chapter is aimed at individuals of all financial backgrounds, from those just starting out on their financial journey to those looking to take their financial skills to the next level. The focus is on providing practical and actionable advice that individuals can use to improve their financial situation and achieve their goals.

The chapter will cover a range of topics, including understanding your current financial situation and setting financial goals, budgeting, and saving, investing, building wealth through entrepreneurship and real estate, and managing debt efficiently. Through these topics, individuals will gain a deeper understanding of how to develop themselves economically and take control of their financial future.

The purpose of this chapter is to provide individuals with the tools and knowledge they need to achieve their financial goals and build a secure financial future. By educating individuals on the principles of economic development, it aims to empower them to make informed financial decisions and achieve financial stability and success.

UNDERSTANDING YOUR FINANCIAL SITUATION

Understanding your financial situation is the first step towards developing yourself economically. It involves taking an honest and objective look at your current financial situation and identifying areas that need improvement. This includes evaluating your income, expenses, debts, and assets.

Income: Your income is the money you receive from all sources, including employment, investments, and passive income streams. Understanding your income is crucial for budgeting and planning for your financial future. Make a list of all your income sources and calculate your average monthly income.

Expenses: Your expenses are the money you spend each month to meet your needs and wants. To understand your expenses, keep a record of all your spending for a month and categorize it into essential and non-essential expenses. This will help you identify areas where you can cut back on spending and redirect the savings towards your financial goals.

Debts: Your debts are the amounts you owe to lenders, including credit card debts, student loans, and mortgages. Understanding your debt levels is important for managing your finances effectively. Make a list of all your debts, including the interest rate, payment due date, and minimum payment amount.

Assets: Your assets are the things you own that have monetary value, such as cash, investments, property, and jewelry. Understanding your assets is important for creating wealth and building a strong financial foundation. Make a list of all your assets and their current market value.

Once you have a clear picture of your financial situation, you can use this information to set realistic financial goals and develop a plan to achieve them. This involves prioritizing your financial goals, creating a budget, and making smart financial decisions.

Understanding your financial situation is an essential step in the journey towards economic development. It helps you to identify areas for improvement and provides a foundation for setting realistic financial goals and making informed financial decisions. By taking control of your financial situation, you can achieve financial stability and success.

ASSESSMENT OF CURRENT FINANCIAL STATUS

Assessing your current financial status is an essential step in understanding your financial situation and making informed decisions about your money. While evaluating income, expenses, debts, and assets is important, it is also important to take a holistic view of your financial status and consider the following:

Emotional connection to money: Our emotions play a significant role in our financial decisions. It is important to assess how you feel about money and identify any negative beliefs or behaviors that may be impacting your financial situation. By addressing your emotional relationship with money, you can break down limiting beliefs and create a positive, empowered relationship with your finances. The emotional connection to money is a complex and often overlooked aspect of our financial situation. Our emotions play a significant role in shaping our relationship with money, and it is important to understand and address them to achieve financial success.

Fear of scarcity: Many people have a fear of not having enough money and live in a state of constant worry about their finances. This fear can lead to impulsive spending, hoarding, and an inability to make sound financial decisions. Understanding and addressing this fear can help to create a more positive and empowered relationship with money.

Shame and guilt: Some people may feel ashamed or guilty about their financial situation, which can lead to a negative relationship with money. Shame and guilt can also prevent individuals from seeking help or making positive changes in their financial situation. It is important to recognize and address these emotions to create a more positive and productive relationship with money.

The desire for security: The desire for financial security is a common emotional connection to money. People may feel that having enough money will bring them security and peace of mind. While financial security is important, it is important to recognize that true financial security comes from making informed decisions and developing good money habits rather than solely from having a large amount of money.

Understanding and addressing the emotional connection to money is a crucial aspect of developing yourself economically. By recognizing and addressing negative emotions, such as fear, shame, guilt, and desire for security, individuals can create a positive and empowered relationship with their finances, which can lead to better financial decision-making and greater financial success.

Financial values and priorities: Your values and priorities shape your financial decisions. To assess your current financial status, it is important to identify your core financial values and the priorities you have for your money. This will help you to align your spending and saving habits with your values and priorities and make decisions that align with what truly matters to you. Financial values and priorities are an important aspect of personal finance, as they shape the way we think about and handle our money. Understanding and aligning your financial values and priorities with your spending and saving habits can help to ensure financial success and satisfaction.

Identifying financial values: Your financial values are the beliefs and principles that guide your financial decisions. They may include values such as security, independence, generosity, or simplicity. Identifying your financial values can help you to make informed decisions about your money that align with what truly matters to you.

Setting financial priorities: Once you have identified your financial values, you can use them to set financial priorities. For example, if security is a core value, you may prioritize saving for an emergency fund or paying off debt. If independence is a priority, you may prioritize investing for retirement or starting a business.

Aligning spending and saving with values and priorities: Aligning your spending and saving habits with your values and priorities can help you to make informed decisions about your money and ensure that you are spending your money on what truly matters to you. For example, if simplicity is a value, you may prioritize reducing expenses and living below your means rather than constantly striving for material possessions.

Financial values and priorities significantly influence our approach to money and overall financial well-being. Recognizing and harmonizing these values and priorities with your spending and saving behaviors enables you to make well-informed financial decisions. By doing so, you ensure that your financial activities reflect and support what is genuinely important in your life.

Current and future goals: Your financial goals can have a significant impact on your financial status. To assess your current financial status, it is important to identify both short-term and long-term financial goals and determine if your current spending and saving habits are in line with achieving these goals.

Current and future goals are critical aspects of personal finance and play a crucial role in shaping our financial decisions and overall financial success. Understanding and setting achievable financial goals can help us to stay focused and motivated and ensure that we are making the most of our resources.

Setting achievable financial goals: Setting achievable financial goals involves determining what you want to achieve financially and developing a plan to achieve them. Goals may include short-term goals, such as paying off debt or building an emergency fund, or long-term goals, such as saving for a down payment on a house or retirement. It is important to set specific, measurable, attainable, relevant, and time-bound (SMART) goals to increase the chances of success. (Doran, 1981)

Prioritizing goals: Once you have set your financial goals, it is important to prioritize them based on their importance and urgency. For example, you may prioritize paying off high-interest debt before saving for a down payment on a house. By prioritizing your goals, you can ensure that you are using your resources effectively to achieve what is most important to you.

Developing a plan: Achieving financial goals requires a plan of action. This may involve creating a budget, reducing expenses, increasing income, or a combination of these strategies. It is important to regularly review your progress and adjust your plan as necessary.

Current and future financial goals play a critical role in shaping our financial success. By setting achievable goals, prioritizing them, and developing a plan of action, individuals can ensure that they are using their resources effectively to achieve what is most important to them. This can lead to greater financial security and peace of mind and ensure that they are on track to achieving their financial aspirations.

Lifestyle: Your lifestyle can have a significant impact on your financial situation. Assessing your current financial status should include an evaluation of your current lifestyle and the associated costs. This can help you identify areas where you can make changes to reduce expenses and align your lifestyle with your financial goals.

Personal lifestyle is a crucial element of personal finance, greatly influencing our financial health. The decisions we make regarding aspects like housing, transportation, food, and entertainment expenditures are key factors in shaping our overall financial status.

Understanding your lifestyle: Understanding your current lifestyle and how it affects your financial situation is an important first step in managing your finances. This involves evaluating your current spending habits, identifying areas where you can reduce expenses, and determining how you want to allocate your resources in the future.

Setting a budget: Setting a budget is a crucial step in managing your finances and ensuring that your lifestyle choices align with your financial values and priorities. A budget helps you to track your spending, prioritize expenses, and ensure that you are living within your means.

Making adjustments: Making adjustments to your lifestyle can help you to achieve your financial goals and ensure that you are making the most of your resources. This may involve reducing expenses, increasing income, or a combination of these strategies. For example, if you have a goal to save for a down payment on a house, you may need to adjust your spending on entertainment and dining out.

Our lifestyle choices play a critical role in shaping our financial well-being. By understanding our current lifestyle, setting a budget, and adjusting where necessary, individuals can ensure that their spending aligns with their financial values and priorities and that they are making the most of their resources. This can lead to greater financial security and peace of mind and ensure that they are on track to achieving their financial aspirations.

While it is important to assess your current financial status by evaluating income, expenses, debts, and assets, it is also important to take a holistic view and consider the emotional, values-based, goal-oriented, and lifestyle aspects of your finances. This will give you a more comprehensive understanding of your financial situation and enable you to make informed decisions about your money.

SETTING FINANCIAL GOALS

Setting financial goals is a critical aspect of personal finance, as it helps individuals to stay focused and motivated and ensures that they are making the most of their resources. Financial goals can range from short-term goals, such as paying off debt or building an emergency fund, to long-term goals, such as saving for a down payment on a house or retirement.

Benefits of setting financial goals: Setting financial goals can bring many benefits, including increased motivation, a clearer focus on what is important, and a greater sense of control over your finances. By setting goals, individuals can ensure that they are making the most of their resources and working towards what is most important to them.

How to set financial goals: Setting financial goals involves determining what you want to achieve financially and developing a plan to achieve them. This process can involve several steps, including:

Identifying your values and priorities: This involves understanding what is most important to you and what you value most in life. This can help you to determine what financial goals are most important to you. Identifying your values and priorities is a critical step in personal finance, as it helps to ensure that your spending aligns with what is most important to you as stated earlier. Our values and priorities can influence our spending habits and determine how we allocate our resources.

Why it is important: Understanding what is most important to you can help you to make informed decisions about your finances and ensure that your spending aligns with your priorities. This can lead to a greater sense of satisfaction and well-being and reduce the stress and anxiety associated with managing money.

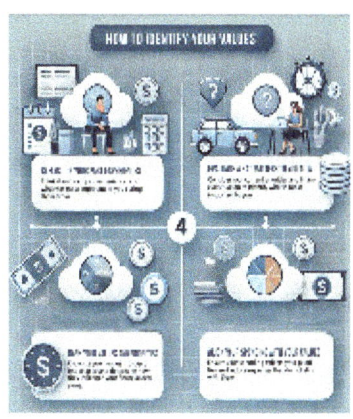

HOW TO IDENTIFY YOUR VALUES AND PRIORITIES:

Identifying your values and priorities can involve several steps, including:

- **Reflecting on your past experiences:** This involves thinking about your past experiences and what was most important to you during those times. This can help you to determine what is most important to you in life.

- **Evaluating your current situation:** This involves considering your current financial situation and what is most important to you now.
- **Prioritizing your values and goals:** This involves ranking your values and goals in order of importance and determining which are most important to you.
- **Aligning your spending with your values and priorities:** This involves ensuring that your spending aligns with what is most important to you and reducing spending on things that are less important.

Recognizing your values and priorities plays a crucial role in personal finance, ensuring that your spending matches what truly matters to you. By reflecting on past experiences, assessing their current circumstances, prioritizing their values and goals, and aligning their spending accordingly, individuals can maximize their resources and work effectively towards what matters most to them.

This can lead to greater financial security and peace of mind and ensure that they are on track to achieving their financial aspirations.

Evaluating your current financial situation: This information can help you to determine what financial goals are achievable and what changes you need to make to achieve them.

Evaluating your current financial situation is an essential step in personal finance, as it provides an understanding of your current financial status and enables you to make informed decisions about your finances. This involves understanding your income, expenses, debts, and assets and using this information to develop a comprehensive picture of your financial situation.

Why it is important: Evaluating your current financial situation is important because it provides a baseline for your financial goals and helps you to identify areas where you may need to make changes. This can help you to make informed decisions about your finances and reduce the stress and anxiety associated with managing money.

How to evaluate your current financial situation: Evaluating your current financial situation can involve several steps, including:

Tracking your income: This involves understanding your sources of income and the amount of money you earn each month.

Tracking your expenses: This involves understanding your monthly expenses and where your money is going. This can be done by creating a budget or using financial tracking software.

Evaluating your debt: This involves understanding your current debts, such as credit card debt, student loans, and mortgages, and determining what your monthly payments are.

Assessing your assets: This involves understanding your assets, such as savings, investments, and property, and determining their value.

Evaluating your net worth: This involves subtracting your debts from your assets to determine your net worth or the overall value of your financial situation.

Evaluating your current financial situation is an important step in personal finance, as it provides a comprehensive understanding of your current financial status. Individuals can ensure that they are making the most of their resources and working towards what is most important to them by tracking their income, expenses, debts, and assets and evaluating their net worth. This can lead to greater financial security and peace of mind and ensure that they are on track to achieving their financial aspirations.

(SMART) GOALS

Setting specific, measurable, attainable, relevant, and time-bound (SMART) goals: This involves setting specific and achievable financial goals that are relevant to your values and priorities. Setting SMART goals can increase the chances of success. (Doran, 1981)

Setting specific, measurable, attainable, relevant, and time-bound (SMART), goals is a critical step in personal finance, as it helps to ensure that your financial goals are clear, attainable, and trackable.

SMART goals are a useful tool for ensuring that your financial goals are well-defined and that you have a clear plan for achieving them.

Why it is important: Setting SMART goals is important because it helps to ensure that your financial goals are clear, realistic, achievable, and measurable. This can help to reduce the stress and anxiety associated with managing money and increase the likelihood that you will achieve your financial aspirations.

WHAT ARE SMART GOALS? SMART GOALS ARE DEFINED AS FOLLOWS:

Specific: Your goals should be clear and well-defined, outlining exactly what you want to achieve.

Measurable: Your goals should be measurable, and you should be able to track your progress towards achieving them.

Attainable: Your goals should be achievable, and you should have the resources and ability to reach them.

Relevant: Your goals should be relevant to your life and what is most important to you.

Time-bound: Your goals should have a clear deadline, and you should be able to track your progress towards achieving them within a specific timeframe.

How to set SMART goals: Setting SMART goals can involve several steps, including:

Identifying your financial goals: This involves determining what you want to achieve financially, such as paying off debt, saving for a down payment on a house, or building an emergency fund.

Making your goals specific: This involves making your financial goals clear and well-defined and outlining exactly what you want to achieve.

Making your goals measurable: This involves determining how you will measure your progress towards achieving your goals and setting milestones or deadlines.

Making your goals attainable: This involves ensuring that your financial goals are achievable and that you have the resources and ability to reach them.

Making your goals relevant: This involves ensuring that your financial goals are relevant to your life and what is most important to you.

Making your goals time-bound: This involves setting a deadline for achieving your financial goals and tracking your progress towards achieving them within a specific timeframe.

By using the SMART framework, individuals can increase the likelihood that they will achieve their financial aspirations and reduce the stress and anxiety associated with managing money.

Developing a plan of action: This involves developing a plan to achieve your financial goals. This may involve creating a budget, reducing expenses, increasing income, or a combination of these strategies.

Developing a plan of action is an important step in personal finance, as it helps to ensure that you have a clear strategy for achieving your financial goals. A well-structured plan of action can help to simplify the process of managing your finances and increase your chances of success.

Why it is important: Developing a plan of action is important because it provides a roadmap for achieving your financial goals. It helps to ensure that you have a clear strategy in place and that you are taking the necessary steps to reach your financial aspirations.

What is a plan of action? A plan of action is a detailed plan that outlines the steps you need to take to achieve your financial goals. It should include specific and measurable goals, as well as a timeline for achieving those goals.

How to develop a plan of action: Developing a plan of action can involve several steps, including:

Identifying your financial goals: This involves determining what you want to achieve financially, such as paying off debt, saving for a down payment on a house, or building an emergency fund.

Evaluating your current financial situation: This involves reviewing your current financial situation, including your income, expenses, and debts.

Setting specific, measurable, attainable, relevant, and time-bound (SMART) goals: This involves using the SMART framework to set clear, achievable financial goals.

Identifying your values and priorities: This involves determining what is most important to you and ensuring that your financial goals align with your values and priorities.

Developing a budget: This involves creating a budget that considers your income, expenses, and debt repayment plan.

Creating a savings plan: This involves determining how much you need to save each month to reach your financial goals and creating a savings plan that works for you.

Monitoring your progress: This involves tracking your progress towards achieving your financial goals and adjusting as necessary.

Formulating a strategic approach is vital in personal finance, as it serves as a guiding blueprint in reaching your financial objectives. Adhering to a meticulously crafted strategy enables individuals to amplify their prospects of prosperity, while minimizing the apprehensions and tension linked to financial management.

In conclusion, setting financial goals is a crucial step in managing personal finances. By identifying your values and priorities, evaluating your current financial situation, setting SMART goals, and developing a plan of action, individuals can ensure that they are making the most of their resources and working towards what is most important to them. This can lead to greater financial security and peace of mind and ensure that they are on track to achieving their financial aspirations.

PLANNING FOR THE FUTURE: CRAFTING A FINANCIAL BLUEPRINT

Establishing financial benchmarks is an essential initiative in cultivating financial steadiness and safeguarding one's future. It empowers individuals to strategically channel their financial resources towards defined aims, including retirement savings, home acquisition, debt elimination, or amplifying their safety net fund. By delineating financial objectives, individuals can devise a clear trajectory for their financial journey, aspiring towards a fortified financial status.

To inaugurate financial planning, individuals should scrutinize their present financial landscape, encompassing income streams, expenditure patterns, existing debts, and assets. This analysis will be the cornerstone for goal formulation, assisting individuals in pinpointing their fiscal strengths and areas needing improvement.

Subsequently, it is vital to pinpoint personal values and priorities, thereby establishing what holds paramount financial significance. This could entail evaluating present and impending financial requisites, like funding a child's education or assisting aging parents.

With a clear perception of their financial condition and priorities, individuals can then forge specific, measurable, attainable, relevant, and time-bound (SMART) objectives. These are delineated targets accompanied by a definitive timeline and a blueprint for realization. An exemplar of a SMART financial goal could be accruing a $10,000 nest egg for a home down payment within a span of three years.

Beyond the creation of SMART objectives, individuals should carve out a tactical blueprint to accomplish their aspirations. This strategy could encompass budget formulation, curtailing expenditures, augmenting income, or venturing into financial instruments.

Undoubtedly, crafting financial benchmarks is a seminal stride towards attaining financial stability and safeguard. By dedicating time to evaluate their fiscal landscape, pinpoint values and priorities, and construct SMART objectives, individuals pave the path towards a fortified financial tomorrow.

During this process, it is imperative to maintain a realistic outlook and foresee potential hurdles or impediments. This preparation could mean foreseeing unforeseen expenditures like medical emergencies or shifts in employment status. Crafting a well-thought contingency plan will aid individuals in maneuvering through these challenges while keeping their financial objectives in sight.

Moreover, a periodic revisitation and evaluation of financial goals are essential to ensure their continued relevance and feasibility. Life's dynamics can alter, necessitating adjustments to financial plans accordingly. Through consistent surveillance and goal modification, individuals remain aligned with their trajectory, fostering continual progress towards financial accomplishment.

Accountability stands as a pivotal element in goal setting. Engaging the guidance of a financial consultant or sharing ambitions with a reliable friend or family member can foster motivation and support. This external accountability acts as a catalyst, encouraging steadfast commitment to financial objectives.

In the grand scheme of things, patience and perseverance hold the key to achieving financial objectives. Attaining financial equilibrium and safety is a gradual process, often marked by slow progression. Nonetheless, with undeterred focus and dedication, individuals can steadily work towards securing a robust financial future.

In summation, delineating financial goals is a critical phase in achieving financial equilibrium and protection. Through meticulous evaluation of one's financial status, recognizing personal values and priorities, crafting SMART goals, and forming an actionable plan, individuals are well-placed to realize their financial dreams. Regular reassessment, a sense of accountability, and sustained effort are vital components in steering individuals towards the fulfillment of their financial aspirations.

BUDGETING AND SAVING

Budgeting and saving are critical components of a sound financial plan. Budgeting involves determining how much money is coming in and going out each month and allocating funds in a way that allows individuals to achieve their financial goals. A budget should be realistic and flexible, allowing for adjustments as circumstances change.

Saving is the act of setting aside a portion of one's income for future use, such as for emergencies, retirement, or the purchase of a major item. Regular savings, even small amounts, can help individuals build an emergency fund, which can provide a safety net in the event of unexpected expenses.

There are a variety of savings options available, including traditional savings accounts, money market accounts, certificates of deposit (CDs), and individual retirement accounts (IRAs). Each has its own benefits and risks, and individuals should consider their financial goals and risk tolerance when choosing a savings option.

To be successful at budgeting and saving, individuals should make saving a priority and be mindful of spending. This may involve reducing discretionary spending, such as eating out or entertainment, and looking for ways to cut costs. It is also important to regularly monitor spending and adjust the budget as needed.

Having a budget and regularly saving can help individuals take control of their finances and achieve their financial goals. By allocating their funds in a thoughtful and responsible manner, individuals can work towards a more secure financial future.

Budgeting and saving are key components of a sound financial plan. By determining how much money is coming in and going out each month and setting aside a portion of income for future use, individuals can work towards financial stability and security. Regular monitoring, reducing discretionary spending, and making saving a priority are also important factors in successful budgeting and saving.

When creating a budget, it is important to have a clear understanding of your income and expenses. This can be done by tracking your spending for a month and categorizing it into different categories such as housing, food, transportation, etc. Once you have a clear picture of your spending habits, you can create a budget that reflects your income and expenses.

50/30/20 RULE

A common budget model is the **50/30/20** rule, which suggests that 50% of your income should go towards necessities, 30% towards wants, and 20% towards savings and debt repayment. (Warren, 2006)

Necessities include things like housing, food, transportation, and utilities. It is important to prioritize these expenses, as they are necessary for daily life.

Wants, on the other hand, include things like entertainment, dining out, and travel. While these expenses are not necessary, they are still an important part of a balanced budget.

Finally, 20% of your income should be set aside for savings and debt repayment. This includes building an emergency fund, contributing to retirement savings, and paying off any outstanding debts.

It is important to keep in mind that everyone's financial situation is different, and the **50/30/20** rule may not work for everyone. The goal of creating a budget is to understand your spending habits and adjust as needed in order to achieve your financial goals.

Here is an example of how the **50/30/20** rule might look for someone with a monthly income of $4,000:

- **Necessities:** $2,000 (50% of income)
- **Wants:** $1,200 (30% of income)
- **Savings and debt repayment:** $800 (20% of income)

Of course, this is just an example, and individuals should adjust their budgets to reflect their unique financial situation. Regularly reviewing and adjusting your budget can help ensure that you stay on track to achieving your financial goals.

THE STUART RULE
40/30/20/10

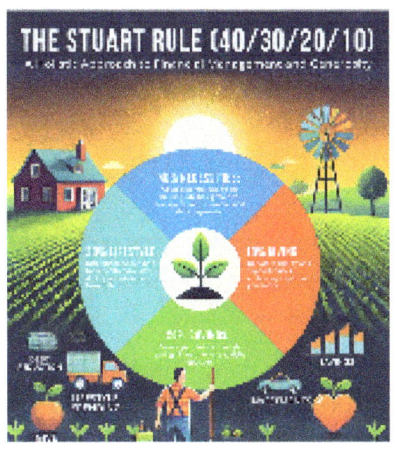

While I like **the rule** by (Warren) I would offer an amendment to the rule the big (10).

Introducing the Stuart Rule: A Holistic Approach to Financial Management and Generosity.

The Stuart Rule is a budgeting guideline that encourages individuals to allocate their income in a balanced and purposeful manner. Derived from the wisdom of Jesus' words, **"Give and it shall be given to you,"** this rule encompasses four essential components: 40/30/20/10. Each part represents a distinct financial priority, fostering not only financial stability but also a culture of giving and generosity.

1. 40% - Necessities: Forty percent of your income should be dedicated to covering essential expenses. This includes housing, utilities, groceries, transportation, insurance, and any necessary loan or debt payments. Just as a farmer must tend to the basics of his crop, meeting these needs ensures your financial well-being.

2. 30% - Lifestyle and Discretionary Spending: Allocate 30% of your income to discretionary spending, allowing for a comfortable and enjoyable life. This category covers non-essential expenses like dining out, entertainment, travel, and personal indulgences. It is essential to strike a balance between financial responsibility and enjoyment.

3. 20% - Savings and Debt Repayment: Twenty percent of your income should be dedicated to securing your financial future. This includes contributions to your emergency fund, retirement accounts, investments, and paying down debts like credit cards, loans, or mortgages. Remember, just as a farmer stores seeds for future harvests, this portion of your income secures your long-term financial stability.

4. 10% - Sowing Seeds (Giving to Charity/Poor): The final component of the Stuart Rule is a unique emphasis on giving. Allocate 10% of your income to charitable donations and acts of kindness. This reflects the biblical principle of giving, as exemplified by Jesus' teachings. Just as a farmer who sows seeds reaps a harvest, your generosity can yield blessings and enrich

the lives of others. This portion is your opportunity to make a positive impact on your community and the world.

The Stuart Rule encourages a holistic approach to financial management, emphasizing not only personal financial security but also the power of generosity. By giving to those in need, you create a cycle of abundance, as echoed in the biblical principle: "Give and it shall be given to you" (Luke 6:38). This rule reflects a balance between personal responsibility and compassion for others, ensuring a fulfilling and purpose-driven financial life.

Creating a Budget

Budgeting is a crucial aspect of personal finance management and can help individuals better understand their spending habits, prioritize expenses, and achieve their financial goals. Here are some steps to creating a budget:

Track your spending: Keep track of all your expenses for a month, including both fixed expenses (such as rent and utilities) and variable expenses (such as groceries and entertainment).

Categorize expenses: Organize your expenses into different categories, such as housing, food, transportation, entertainment, etc.

Determine your income: Make sure to include all sources of income, including your salary, any side hustles, and any other sources of passive income.

Identify areas where you can cut back: Look for areas where you can reduce spending, such as dining out, subscriptions, or impulse purchases.

Allocate your budge the amended rule: For the Stuart Rule, prioritize and distribute your budget according to your financial objectives. In contrast to the conventional 50/30/20 budgeting model, the Stuart Rule prescribes a new approach to budgeting, where 40% is dedicated to essentials, 30% to discretionary spending, 20% to savings and debt management, and 10% to charitable giving, aligning your finances with your values and goals.

Set up a system to track your spending: Use a spreadsheet, app, or paper-based system to track your spending and stick to your budget.

Regularly review and adjust your budget: Regularly review your budget to see how you are tracking and make adjustments as needed.

Remember, creating a budget is not a one-time process but an ongoing effort to understand your spending habits and adjust as needed. By having a clear understanding of your income and expenses, you can take control of your finances and work towards achieving your financial goals.

BUILDING AN EMERGENCY FUND

An emergency fund is a savings account specifically set aside for unexpected expenses or emergencies, such as job loss, medical bills, or car repairs. Building an emergency fund is an important step towards financial stability and peace of mind. Here are some tips for building an emergency fund:

- **Determine your emergency fund goal:** A commonly recommended emergency fund goal is to save three to six months' worth of living expenses.
- Set up an emergency fund account: Choose a savings account specifically for your emergency fund and set up automatic transfers to make saving easier.
- **Prioritize saving for your emergency fund:** Make building an emergency fund a priority and consider reducing other expenses or finding ways to increase your income to free up funds to put towards your emergency fund.
- **Be disciplined:** Avoid dipping into your emergency fund for non-emergency expenses, as this will undermine your efforts to build it.
- **Review and adjust your emergency fund goal:** Regularly review your emergency fund goal to ensure it still aligns with your needs and adjust as necessary.

Having an emergency fund can give you peace of mind and financial stability in case of unexpected events. It is a key component of a comprehensive personal finance strategy and can help you avoid going into debt during difficult times.

The importance of building an emergency fund is a crucial step in ensuring financial stability and security. Here are some more reasons why it is important:

Protection against unexpected events: Emergencies happen, and they can have a significant impact on your finances. An emergency fund provides a cushion against unexpected expenses, such as a sudden job loss, medical bills, or home repairs, so you can focus on solving the problem instead of worrying about how you will pay for it.

- **Avoiding debt:** Without an emergency fund, it is easy to turn to high-interest credit card debt or loans to cover unexpected expenses. This can lead to a cycle of debt that can be difficult to break out of and can also negatively impact your credit score. An emergency fund helps you to avoid going into debt and maintain control of your finances.

- **Maintaining financial stability:** Having an emergency fund gives you a sense of financial stability and peace of mind, knowing that you are prepared for unexpected events. This can reduce stress and anxiety and allow you to focus on other financial goals, such as saving for retirement or paying down debt.

- **Flexibility:** An emergency fund provides flexibility in your financial planning. Instead of feeling pressured to take on a side job or make drastic cuts to your budget when an emergency arises, you have the peace of mind in the awareness that you have a safety net in place.

- **Building good habits:** Building an emergency fund requires discipline and commitment and can help you to establish good financial habits. By setting aside money each month, you are building a habit of savings that can have a positive impact on your finances in the long term.

To sum it up, building an emergency fund is an important step in achieving financial stability and security. It can provide peace of mind during unexpected events, help you avoid debt, and provide a foundation for reaching your long-term financial goals.

STRATEGIES FOR SAVING MONEY

Saving money can be a challenge, but there are many strategies that can help you build a robust savings account. Here are some tips for saving money:

- **Create a budget:** A budget can help you identify areas where you can reduce spending and prioritize saving.
- Automate your savings: Set up automatic transfers from your checking account to your savings account to make saving a habit.
- **Reduce expenses:** Look for areas where you can reduce spending, such as cutting back on eating out, reducing your grocery bill, or finding ways to save on bills like utilities or insurance.
- **Increase your income:** Consider taking on a side job, selling items you no longer need, or finding other ways to increase your income.
- **Save windfalls:** When you receive a bonus, tax refund, or other windfalls, put most of it into your savings account.
- **Make saving a priority:** Consider your savings a non-negotiable expense and make it a priority, just like you would with your rent or utilities.
- **Delay gratification:** Challenge yourself to put off purchases until you have saved enough money to pay for them in cash.

Saving money takes discipline and a commitment to making it a priority, but by following these strategies, you can build a robust savings account and achieve your financial goals.

In addition to the strategies mentioned above, there are a few other tactics you can use to save money and build wealth:

- **Cut back on unnecessary subscriptions:** Monthly subscriptions for services like streaming platforms, gyms, or premium phone services can add up quickly. Assess your subscriptions and cancel those you do not need.
- **Shop for sales and use coupons:** Taking advantage of sales and using coupons can help you save money on groceries and other household items.
- **Live below your means:** Avoid lifestyle inflation and maintain a frugal lifestyle, even if your income increases.
- **Invest in your future:** Consider contributing to a retirement account or

investing in a taxable investment account to help grow your wealth over time.

- **Be mindful of debt:** High levels of debt can make it difficult to save money, so focus on paying down debt and avoiding taking on new debt whenever possible.
- **Stay disciplined:** Stick to your savings plan, even if you experience setbacks or face temptations to spend money.

By combining these strategies with a budget and automatic savings, you can make significant progress towards building a strong financial future. Remember, saving money is a marathon, not a sprint, so be patient and persistent in your efforts.

INVESTING

Investing is an important aspect of personal finance, as it allows you to grow your wealth over time. There are several key considerations to keep in mind when it comes to investing:

Start early: the earlier you start investing, the more time your money has to grow. This is due to the power of compounding, which is when interest on your investments earns interest, leading to exponential growth over time.

- **Diversify your portfolio:** Do not put all your eggs in one basket. Spread your investments across different asset classes, such as stocks, bonds, real estate, and commodities, to reduce risk.
- **Know your risk tolerance:** Your investment portfolio should reflect your risk tolerance or how much risk you are comfortable taking on. If you are risk-averse, consider investments that are lower risk, such as bonds. If you are more willing to take risks, you might choose investments with a higher potential for growth, such as stocks.
- **Do your research:** Before making any investment, research the company or asset you are considering and understand its potential for growth. This will help you make informed decisions and reduce your risk.
- **Work with a professional:** If you are new to investing or want to ensure you are making informed decisions, consider working with a financial advisor who can help guide you through the process.
- **Be patient:** Investing is a long-term strategy, and it is important to keep this in mind when making investment decisions. Do not let short-term market fluctuations discourage you from staying the course.

By following these tips and regularly monitoring your investments, you can make the most of your money and build wealth over time. It is important to remember that investing carries risk, and there is no guarantee of success, so it is essential to be informed and mindful of your investment decisions.

In addition to the above strategies, it is important to be mindful of the costs associated with investing, such as fees and taxes. Some investment products carry high fees that can eat into your returns, so it is important to be aware of these costs and consider low-cost alternatives when possible.

Another important consideration is to understand the different types of investments, such as individual stocks, mutual funds, exchange-traded funds (ETFs), and more.

Each type of investment has its own risks and benefits, so it is important to research and understand the options available to you before making any decisions.

It is also important to have a well-diversified portfolio. This means investing in a mix of different assets, such as stocks, bonds, and real estate, as well as different types of stocks and bonds. This will help to reduce your overall risk and provide more stability for your portfolio.

Another important aspect of investing is to regularly review and adjust your portfolio as needed. Your financial goals, risk tolerance, and other personal circumstances may change over time, so it is important to review your investments regularly to ensure they're still aligned with your overall financial strategy.

Finally, it is important to understand the importance of time in investing. The longer you have to invest, the more time your money has to grow, so it is essential to start investing as early as possible. With discipline, patience, and a well-diversified portfolio, you can build wealth and reach your financial goals over time.

UNDERSTANDING THE STOCK MARKET

The stock market is a marketplace where shares of publicly traded companies are bought and sold. It is an important part of the financial system, as it allows companies to raise capital by issuing and selling shares of stock, and it provides individuals and institutions with the opportunity to invest in those companies and potentially earn a return on their investment.

In order to understand the stock market, it is essential to understand what stocks are and how they work. A stock represents a share in the ownership of a company, and when you buy a stock, you become a partial owner of that company. As the company grows and earns profits, the value of the stock is likely to rise, allowing you to sell your shares for a profit.

Another important concept in the stock market is the stock price, which is determined by supply and demand. The price of a stock is the amount that investors are willing to pay for it at a given time, and it can fluctuate based on various factors, such as company performance, economic conditions, and investor sentiment.

There are several stock exchanges around the world, including the New York Stock Exchange (NYSE) and the NASDAQ, where stocks can be bought and sold. It is important to understand the different types of stocks, including common and preferred stocks, as well as the different investment strategies, such as growth, value, and dividend investing.

I will elaborate on these two types of Stocks. There are two main types of stocks: common stocks and preferred stocks.

common stocks

Common stocks are the most common type of stock and represent ownership in a company. As a common shareholder, you have a right to vote on important company decisions, such as electing directors and approving mergers and acquisitions. Additionally, common shareholders are entitled to a portion of the company's profits in the form of dividends if the company chooses to pay them. The value of common stock is determined by supply and demand and can fluctuate based on various factors, such as the company's financial performance and market conditions.

Preferred stocks

Preferred stocks are different types of security that have some characteristics of both stocks and bonds. Preferred shareholders have a higher claim on the company's assets and earnings than common shareholders, but they typically do not have voting rights. Preferred stocks also have a fixed dividend, which means that the company is obligated to pay a specified dividend each year. Preferred stocks are generally considered to be less risky than common stocks, as they have a more predictable dividend income, but they also have less potential for growth.

When considering which type of stock to invest in, it is important to understand your financial goals and risk tolerance. Common stocks have the potential for higher returns but also higher volatility, while preferred stocks offer more stability but lower returns. A well-diversified portfolio that includes both common and preferred stocks can help to balance risk and reward.

It is also important to consider other factors, such as the company's financial performance, management, and industry trends, before making an investment decision. As with any investment, it is essential to educate yourself on the stock market and seek the advice of a professional if necessary.

Investing in the stock market can be risky, as the value of your investments can fluctuate based on various factors. However, with a well-diversified portfolio and a long-term investment horizon, it can be a valuable way to grow your wealth and reach your financial goals.

Understanding the function of stock market experts, like stockbrokers, financial advisors, and analysts, is vital, as they offer insights and guidance on stock market investments. Prior to investing, educating oneself about the stock market, clarifying your financial objectives and risk appetite, and consulting a professional when needed, is crucial.

In addition to common and preferred stocks, there are other types of investments that are traded in the stock market, including futures, options, commodities, and exchange-traded funds (ETFs).

Futures

Futures contracts are financial instruments that enable the buying or selling of a specified asset, like a commodity, at a pre-agreed price and date in the future. These contracts are pivotal for companies looking to hedge against market price volatility, but they also present opportunities for individual investors seeking speculative investments. Futures allow for the speculation on the future value of underlying assets, including commodities and securities, and are actively traded on exchanges by a diverse array of market participants such as producers, processors, speculators, and hedgers.

The primary function of futures is to facilitate price risk management. This is achieved by locking in future prices for underlying assets. For instance, a farmer may sell a futures contract for their soybean crop to secure a fixed price ahead of the harvest, thereby mitigating the risk associated with potential price decreases. Conversely, a speculator might purchase a soybean futures contract anticipating a profit from a future price rise.

However, it is crucial to acknowledge that futures are high-risk investments, primarily due to their inherent leverage and the practice of trading on margin. This complexity requires investors to have a thorough understanding of market dynamics and the intricate mechanics of futures trading to minimize the risk of substantial losses. Consequently, seeking professional financial advice is highly recommended for anyone considering investing in futures, to ensure informed and prudent decision-making.

Commodities

Commodities, such as grains, soybeans, gold, and oil, are raw materials or primary products that are traded in the market. Commodities are often subject to fluctuations in supply and demand, and their prices can be influenced by various factors, such as weather patterns, geopolitical events, and economic conditions.

Commodities are basic goods or raw materials that are used in the production of other goods and services. Examples of commodities include crude oil, gold, silver, copper, wheat, corn, soybeans, coffee, and cotton. Commodities are traded on commodity exchanges, where they are bought and sold based on their current market price.

Investing in commodities can provide a way to diversify an investment portfolio, as the prices of commodities are often not directly tied to the stock market. Commodities can serve as a hedge against inflation, as their prices tend to increase when the cost of living goes up. Additionally, commodities can offer an opportunity for profit through price appreciation, as their prices are influenced by various factors such as supply and demand, geopolitical events, and weather patterns.

However, investing in commodities is not without risks. Commodity prices can be volatile, and unexpected events such as natural disasters, changes in government regulations, and fluctuations in currency values can impact the price of commodities. Additionally, investing in commodities requires a good understanding of the underlying markets and an awareness of the potential for price fluctuations.

Overall, commodities can be a good investment option for individuals who are looking to diversify their portfolio and are willing to take on additional risk. It is important to seek professional advice and to understand the potential risks and rewards before investing in commodities.

Options

Options are contracts that give you the right, but not the obligation, to buy or sell a stock at a predetermined price and date. Options can be used for a variety of purposes, such as hedging against market volatility or generating income through option premiums.

Options can be used for a variety of purposes, including hedging against market risk, generating income, and speculating on market movements.

There are two main types of options: call options and put options. A call option gives the buyer the right to purchase an underlying asset at a specified price, while a put option gives the buyer the right to sell the underlying asset at a specified price.

For example, let us say an individual believes that the price of a particular stock is going to increase. The individual could purchase a call option on that stock, which would give them the right to buy the stock at a specified price (the strike price) within a specified time frame. If the stock's price does indeed increase, the individual could exercise their option and purchase the stock at the lower strike price and then sell it at the higher market price for a profit.

On the other hand, if an individual believes that the price of a particular stock is going to decrease, they could purchase a put option on that stock. This would give them the right to sell the stock at the specified strike price within a specified time frame, regardless of whether the stock's price has decreased or not.

Options can be a valuable tool for individuals who have a good understanding of the underlying markets and the potential risks and rewards involved. However, options trading is not suitable for everyone and can be risky but as stated always consulted your financial advisor for in-dept advise.

Exchange-traded.

Exchange-traded funds (ETFs) are investment products that track an underlying asset or group of assets, typically stocks, bonds, commodities, or a combination thereof. ETFs are traded on stock exchanges, and like individual stocks, their price can fluctuate throughout the trading day. They offer investors a convenient and cost-effective way to diversify their portfolios.

ETFs are different from mutual funds in several ways. Unlike mutual funds, ETFs are traded on stock exchanges, and their prices change throughout the day in response to market conditions. Also, ETFs typically have lower expense ratios than mutual funds, making them a more cost-effective option for investors. Additionally,

ETFs offer greater flexibility and tax efficiency compared to mutual funds, as they allow investors to buy and sell shares throughout the trading day and can also be used to implement various investment strategies.

There are various types of ETFs available, such as sector-specific ETFs, international and emerging market ETFs, and bond ETFs, among others. Investors can choose an ETF that aligns with their investment goals and risk tolerance. For example, a conservative investor may choose a bond ETF, while a more aggressive investor may choose an ETF that invests in high-growth technology companies.

In conclusion, ETFs provide a convenient and cost-effective way for investors to diversify their portfolios and participate in the stock market. They offer greater flexibility and tax efficiency compared to other investment products, making them an attractive option for many investors.

Each of these investment types has its own unique risks and rewards, and it is important to understand the characteristics of each before making an investment decision. It is also important to consider factors such as your financial goals, risk tolerance, and investment time horizon before making an investment decision.

As with any investment, it is essential to educate yourself on the market and seek the advice of a professional if necessary. With a well-diversified portfolio and a comprehensive understanding of the different investment types available, you can take control of your financial future and achieve your economic development goals.

INVESTING IN CRYPTOCURRENCY

The rise of digital assets has made investing in cryptocurrencies like Bitcoin, Ethereum, and others increasingly popular, thanks to their significant growth in value in recent years. These digital currencies leverage blockchain technology to establish a decentralized, secure, and transparent ledger for recording transactions.

Cryptocurrency investment offers the possibility of high returns, but it is accompanied by a high level of volatility and risk. Prospective investors should conduct extensive research and acquire a deep understanding of both the technology behind cryptocurrencies and the current market dynamics before committing funds.

A notable advantage of investing in cryptocurrencies is the bypassing of traditional government regulations and financial institutions, facilitating direct transactions between individuals. This aspect makes cryptocurrencies particularly appealing in regions with unstable national currencies or limited access to conventional banking systems, offering a more accessible and inclusive financial option.

The cryptocurrency market, being in its early stages and undergoing swift evolution, presents unique challenges. Its emerging nature, coupled with a lack of solidified regulations and inherent volatility, often leads to significant price swings, and exposes it to risks like hacking and digital asset theft. Prospective investors should be aware of these risks and carefully assess their financial situation and risk tolerance before venturing into cryptocurrency investments.

It is advisable to consult a financial advisor and extensively educate oneself about the possible risks and benefits associated with cryptocurrency investment before making any financial decisions in this area.

BITCOIN, IS IT A GOOD INVESTMENT?

Bitcoin is a decentralized digital currency created in 2009 that operates on a peer-to-peer network without a central authority. It allows for secure, fast, and inexpensive transactions without the need for intermediaries. Transactions are verified through a public ledger known as the blockchain.

Whether Bitcoin is a good investment or not is a highly debated topic. On the one hand, it has seen significant price appreciation over the years, with some investors becoming overnight millionaires. On the other hand, Bitcoin is a highly speculative and volatile asset that can be subject to significant price swings.

Investing in Bitcoin should be approached with caution and a thorough understanding of the risks involved. It is important to consider your investment goals, risk tolerance, and overall financial situation before investing in Bitcoin.

Additionally, it is important to research and understands the technology behind Bitcoin, as well as any potential regulatory changes or security risks that may impact its value. It is also recommended to diversify your investment portfolio rather than putting all your eggs in one basket.

In conclusion, investing in Bitcoin can be a high-risk, high-reward opportunity, and it is important to approach it with caution and a solid understanding of the underlying technology and risks involved.

ETHEREUM, IS IT A GOOD INVESTMENT?

Ethereum is a decentralized, open-source blockchain platform that enables the creation of smart contracts and decentralized applications (dApps). Unlike Bitcoin, which was primarily created as a digital currency, Ethereum was designed to be a platform for developers to build decentralized applications on top of its blockchain.

As for whether Ethereum is a good investment, the answer is not simple. On the one hand, Ethereum has seen tremendous growth since its creation in 2015 and has become the second-largest cryptocurrency by market capitalization. This growth has been driven in part by the increasing popularity of decentralized finance (DeFi) and non-fungible tokens (NFTs), both of which have been built on the Ethereum blockchain.

On the other hand, investing in cryptocurrency is inherently risky, and Ethereum is no exception. The value of Ethereum is highly volatile, and its price can change rapidly in response to news events and market sentiment. Additionally, the cryptocurrency market is still relatively unregulated, which means that investors face a higher risk of fraud and other types of financial crime.

While Ethereum has tremendous potential as a platform for decentralized applications, investing in it carries a significant amount of risk. Before investing in Ethereum, it is important to carefully consider your investment goals, risk tolerance, and overall financial situation. As with any investment, it is always a good idea to do your research, consult with a financial professional, and diversify your portfolio to reduce risk.

WHAT IS BLOCKCHAIN?

Blockchain is a distributed digital ledger that is used to record transactions securely and transparently. It was originally designed for the digital currency Bitcoin but has since been adapted for many other uses.

A blockchain is comprised of a series of blocks, each of which contains several transactions. Each block is linked to the previous block in the chain, creating a secure and unalterable history of all transactions. (Nakamoto, 2008)

One of the key benefits of blockchain technology is that it eliminates the need for intermediaries, such as banks, to validate transactions. Instead, transactions are validated by a decentralized network of computers, making the system much more secure and resistant to fraud.

Another benefit of blockchain is that it allows for greater transparency in transactions. All participants in the network can view and verify all transactions, creating a more trust-based system.

There are many potential applications for blockchain beyond just cryptocurrency. For example, it can be used in supply chain management, voting systems, and even in the creation of new financial instruments.

As blockchain continues to evolve and mature, it is likely that we will see an increasing number of new and innovative uses for this technology. Whether it is a good investment or not will depend on a few factors, including market trends and adoption rates, as well as regulatory and technological developments.

I will seek to break it down for better understanding. Think of it as a public ledger that is shared between many computers, making it almost impossible to change the information recorded in the blocks. Once a block is added to the blockchain, it cannot be deleted or altered, which makes it a secure way to store important information.

Imagine you have a big notebook that is used by everyone in your class to keep track of their allowance money. Each time you receive money or spend money, you write it down in the notebook, and everyone in the class can see what you have recorded. The notebook is like the blockchain, and the transactions are like the blocks.

The information in the blocks is secured by complex mathematical algorithms, making it very difficult for anyone to alter the information in the blockchain. This is why it is considered a secure and trustworthy way to store important information.

DIFFERENT TYPES OF INVESTMENTS

Investing is a crucial aspect of financial planning, and there are many types of investment options available to individuals. Here are some of the most common types of investments:

Stocks - These are ownership shares in a company and can be bought and sold on stock exchanges. Stocks are a form of equity investment and can provide both short and long-term growth.

Bonds - Bonds are debt instruments in which an investor loans money to an entity (such as a corporation or government) and receives interest payments in return. Bonds are less risky than stocks but typically provide lower returns.

Real Estate - Real estate investments can include purchasing property for rental income, investing in real estate investment trusts (REITs), or buying into a real estate investment group. Real estate can provide a stable income stream and long-term appreciation.

Real estate investment involves buying, managing, renting, or selling properties for the purpose of making a profit. This can include residential, commercial, or industrial properties. It can be a good investment option for those looking for a long-term investment with the potential for appreciation over time.

One of the advantages of real estate investment is the potential for stable income through rental earnings. Additionally, property values may increase over time, leading to a potential increase in the asset's value. Real estate also has tax benefits, as expenses such as mortgage interest, insurance, and property taxes can be deductible.

However, real estate investment also comes with risks. The real estate market can be volatile and subject to economic changes, and properties may take longer to sell in a declining market. Property management can also be time-consuming and expensive, particularly if the property is not generating positive cash flow.

Ultimately, the suitability of real estate investment depends on an individual's financial situation, investment goals, and risk tolerance. It is important to conduct thorough research and analyze the market and property before making any investment decisions and to consult with a financial advisor to determine the best options for you.

Real estate investment can come in many forms, including residential and commercial properties, land, and real estate investment trusts (REITs).

Investing in real estate can provide diversification to your portfolio, generate passive income, and offer the potential for long-term capital appreciation.

Although investing in real estate requires a large amount of capital, the rewards can be substantial. Rental properties can provide a stable source of passive income, while commercial properties can offer high returns if leased to a successful business. Furthermore, owning physical property can provide a sense of security, as it is a tangible asset.

However, real estate investment is not without its challenges. The real estate market can be unpredictable and subject to fluctuations, and owning and managing property can be time-consuming and require a lot of effort. It is crucial to thoroughly research and understand the local real estate market and the specific property you are considering before making any investment decisions. It is also advisable to seek the advice of a financial advisor or real estate professional before making a significant real estate investment.

REAL ESTATE & AIRBNB

Investing in real estate for the Airbnb market refers to purchasing a property specifically for the purpose of renting it out on the short-term rental platform Airbnb. This type of investment aims to generate income through the rental of the property to travelers rather than traditional long-term tenants.

One of the key benefits of investing in real estate for the Airbnb market is the potential for high rental income. Airbnb properties are often in high demand, especially in popular tourist destinations or urban areas, and can command higher nightly rates than traditional long-term rentals. Additionally, the flexible rental periods offered by Airbnb can lead to a higher occupancy rate and more rental income compared to long-term rentals.

Another benefit of investing in real estate for the Airbnb market is the ability to tap into the growing trend of short-term rentals. The popularity of Airbnb and other short-term rental platforms continues to grow, driven by the increased demand for alternative and more affordable accommodation options for travelers.

However, investing in real estate for the Airbnb market is not without its risks. The short-term rental market is subject to fluctuations, and demand for Airbnb properties can vary depending on the time of year and local events. Additionally, local regulations and zoning laws can impact the ability to rent a property on Airbnb, and property management can be more complex and time-consuming compared to traditional long-term rentals.

It is important to carefully research and understand the local market, demand for Airbnb properties, and any regulations and laws before deciding to invest in real estate for the Airbnb market. This can include consulting with a real estate professional or financial advisor, as well as analyzing comparable rental properties and Airbnb occupancy rates.

In brief, investing in real estate for the Airbnb market can be a good option for those looking to generate high rental income and tap into the growing trend of short-term rentals. However, it is important to understand the market, demand, and regulations before making any investment decisions and to seek the guidance of a professional if needed.

Mutual Funds - Mutual funds are professionally managed portfolios that pool together money from many investors. They allow individuals to invest in a diversified portfolio of stocks, bonds, and other securities.

Exchange-Traded Funds (ETFs) - Like mutual funds, ETFs are professionally managed portfolios that can be bought and sold like individual stocks. They offer the diversification benefits of mutual funds with the ability to trade like individual securities.

Commodities - Commodities refer to raw materials such as precious metals, energy, or agricultural products that are traded on commodity exchanges. Commodities can provide an opportunity for diversification and can act as a hedge against inflation.

Cryptocurrencies - Cryptocurrencies are digital or virtual currencies that use cryptography to secure transactions. The most well-known cryptocurrency is Bitcoin, but there are many others, such as Ethereum, Ripple, and Litecoin. Cryptocurrency investments are considered high-risk due to their volatility.

In conclusion, when deciding on an investment strategy, it is important to consider one's risk tolerance, investment goals, and overall financial situation. It may also be helpful to consult a financial advisor for guidance.

DIVERSIFYING YOUR INVESTMENT PORTFOLIO

Diversification is a key component of a well-rounded investment portfolio. It involves spreading out investments across different asset classes, such as stocks, bonds, real estate, and commodities, to minimize risk and maximize returns. A diversified portfolio is less vulnerable to market fluctuations and can help you reach your investment goals with more stability.

There are several ways to diversify your investment portfolio:

Asset Class Diversification: This involves investing in a mix of different types of assets, such as stocks, bonds, real estate, and commodities. Each asset class has its own unique risk-return characteristics, and by investing in a mix of assets, you can reduce the overall risk of your portfolio.

Sector Diversification: This involves investing in a mix of industries or sectors within a particular asset class. For example, you can invest in a mix of technology, healthcare, and financial stocks to reduce the risk of investing in a single sector.

Geographical Diversification: This involves investing in a mix of companies or real estate properties located in different regions or countries. This helps to reduce the risk of investing in a single economy or market.

Investment Style Diversification: This involves investing in a mix of growth and value stocks or actively managed and passively managed funds. Growth stocks are focused on future growth potential, while value stocks are focused on undervalued companies. Actively managed funds are managed by a fund manager, while passively managed funds follow a specific index.

Remember, diversification does not assure profits or guard against losses, but it can help diminish the overall risk in your investment portfolio and boost the chances of meeting your long-term investment objectives.

Diversification is a critical component of a well-rounded investment portfolio. It involves spreading out investments across different asset classes, sectors, regions, and investment styles to reduce risk and maximize returns. To ensure effective diversification, it is recommended to consult with a financial advisor to understand the best options for your unique investment goals and risk tolerance.

BUILDING WEALTH

Building wealth is a long-term financial goal that involves creating a strong financial foundation and growing assets over time. Wealth-building strategies are focused on creating income streams, reducing debt, and making wise investment decisions.

A farmer that does not sow seed will never reap another harvest.

One of the key steps in building wealth is creating a budget and following it closely. This will help to ensure that expenses are under control and that there is a surplus of income that can be saved or invested. The next step is to pay off high-interest debt, such as credit card balances, personal loans, and car loans, as this will help to reduce the amount of money spent on interest and increase the amount available for investment.

Building wealth also requires a focus on saving and investing. This can be achieved by contributing to a 401(k) or individual retirement account (IRA), setting up automatic savings plans, and investing in a diverse range of assets, such as stocks, bonds, and real estate. Diversification helps to spread risk and reduce the impact of market fluctuations on an investment portfolio.

In addition to traditional investment options, it is important to consider alternative investment strategies, such as starting a business, buying rental properties, or investing in peer-to-peer lending platforms. These strategies can provide additional income streams and help to build wealth over time.

Another important aspect of building wealth is education. Taking the time to learn about financial literacy, investment strategies, and the principles of wealth creation can greatly enhance an individual's ability to make informed financial decisions and achieve their long-term wealth-building goals.

Ultimately, building wealth takes time, discipline, and patience. It is important to have a clear financial plan in place and stick to it, even during periods of market volatility or financial uncertainty. With a focus on saving, investing, and diversifying, it is possible to build a strong financial foundation and achieve long-term wealth.

ENTREPRENEURSHIP AND SMALL BUSINESS OWNERSHIP

Entrepreneurship and small business ownership refer to the process of starting, managing, and growing a new business. Entrepreneurs and small business owners are individuals who identify an opportunity, start a business from scratch, and work to make it successful. They are the drivers of economic growth and job creation, and they play a crucial role in shaping the future of the global economy. Entrepreneurship is a challenging and rewarding path that requires a combination of vision, creativity, hard work, and risk-taking. Starting a business from scratch is not easy, but it can provide a sense of accomplishment and financial freedom. The process of entrepreneurship involves identifying a market opportunity, developing a business plan, securing financing, building a team, and executing the business strategy. It also requires a high degree of resilience, as many businesses fail in the early stages.

Small business ownership offers many benefits, including the opportunity to be your own boss, the ability to create and control your financial future, and the satisfaction of building something from scratch. Owning a small business can also provide a sense of purpose and fulfillment, as you are able to make a positive impact on your community.

However, small business ownership also comes with its own set of challenges. Running a successful business requires a lot of hard work, dedication, and perseverance. It also requires the ability to adapt to change and make quick decisions, as well as the willingness to take calculated risks. There are also financial risks involved, as small business owners are personally responsible for the success or failure of the business.

Despite the challenges, entrepreneurship and small business ownership remain popular career paths for individuals who are seeking financial independence and a sense of purpose. For those who are willing to put in the time, effort, and dedication required, the rewards can be substantial. Building a successful small business can provide financial stability, personal fulfillment, and the satisfaction of creating something of lasting value.

Embarking on entrepreneurship and small business ownership is a demanding yet fulfilling journey, necessitating relentless effort, commitment, and resilience. If you are driven by problem-solving, ready to embrace risks, and eager to create something from the ground up, then becoming a small business owner could be your calling. Conduct thorough research, craft a robust business plan, and consult with seasoned professionals before you start this venture.

Starting a business can be an exciting and rewarding experience, but it also requires careful planning and preparation. Here are five steps to help you get started:

- **Identify your business idea:** The first step in starting a business is to determine what you want to do. Consider your skills, interests, and the needs of the market to come up with an idea for your business.
- **Conduct market research:** Once you have a business idea, research the market to determine the viability of your idea. Analyze your competition, identify your target market, and gather data on the industry and market trends.
- **Create a business plan:** A business plan is a comprehensive document that outlines your business objectives, strategies, and financial projections. It is a critical tool for securing funding and tracking your progress.
- **Secure funding:** Starting a business often requires a significant investment of capital. Determine how much funding you need and explore your financing options, such as loans, grants, or investments from friends and family.
- **Launch and grow your business:** Once you have secured funding, it is time to launch your business. This will involve establishing your legal and financial structure, building your team, and developing a marketing and sales strategy. Over time, you will need to continually evaluate and adjust your business strategies to stay competitive and achieve your goals.

Starting a business can be difficult, but with proper planning and effort, it can also be a fulfilling and rewarding experience. Therefore, Get a copy of my book other book "A New Start in Business" from Amazon.com for a comprehensive and in-depth understanding of entrepreneurship, including how to write a business plan and launch a business.

BUILDING PASSIVE INCOME STREAMS

Building passive income streams is a strategy for generating income without the need for active involvement on a day-to-day basis. This type of income can provide a steady source of funds, even when you are not actively working and can help you to reach your financial goals faster. Here are five ways to build passive income streams:

Investing in stocks, bonds, or mutual funds: Investing in stocks, bonds, or mutual funds can provide a steady stream of passive income in the form of dividends or interest. This type of investment requires initial capital, and it is important to understand the risks involved.

Rental properties: Owning rental properties can provide a steady stream of passive income from rent payments. This type of investment requires significant capital and ongoing management but can provide a significant return over time.

Online businesses: Building an online business, such as an e-commerce store or a blog, can provide a steady stream of passive income. Once established, these businesses can generate income with little ongoing effort, although they may require an initial investment in time and resources.

Royalties from creative work: If you have a creative talent, such as writing, photography, or music, you can earn passive income by licensing your work for use by others. This type of passive income requires an initial investment of time and effort but can provide a steady stream of income over time.

Investing in peer-to-peer (P2P) lending platforms: P2P lending platforms allow you to lend money to individuals or small businesses and earn interest on your investment. This type of investment requires initial capital and carries some level of risk but can provide a steady stream of passive income.

In conclusion, building passive income streams is a smart financial strategy that can help you to reach your financial goals and provide a steady source of funds without active involvement. By diversifying your income streams, you can reduce risk and ensure a steady stream of income, even during difficult economic times.

MANAGING DEBT

Managing debt is a critical aspect of personal finance, as it can have a significant impact on your financial stability and future wealth. Here are some steps for managing debt effectively:

Know your debt: The first step in managing debt is to understand exactly what you owe and to whom. Make a list of all your debts, including the creditor, interest rate, minimum payment, and due date.

Create a budget: Once you have a clear picture of your debt, create a budget to help you manage your expenses and allocate funds to debt repayment. A budget can help you to prioritize debt repayment and avoid taking on additional debt.

Prioritize debt repayment: Consider paying off high-interest debt first, as this will save you money in the long run. You can also consider consolidating your debt with a personal loan or balance transfer credit card, which may offer a lower interest rate and simplify the repayment process.

Make more than the minimum payment: Making only the minimum payment on your debt can result in paying more in interest over time. Consider making extra payments to pay off your debt faster and save money in the long run.

Avoid taking on additional debt: Avoid taking on new debt, especially high-interest debt, while you are working to pay off your existing debt. Instead, focus on paying down your existing debt and building an emergency fund to protect against future financial emergencies.

Seek professional help if needed: If you are having difficulty managing your debt, consider seeking the help of a financial advisor or credit counselor. They can help you create a debt repayment plan and negotiate with creditors to lower interest rates or monthly payments.

Managing debt requires discipline, commitment, and a clear understanding of your financial situation. By prioritizing debt repayment, avoiding new debt, and seeking professional help if needed, you can take control of your debt and achieve financial stability.

Managing debt is a crucial aspect of personal finance, and it is important to develop a plan to repay your debt as quickly and efficiently as possible. Here are some additional tips for effectively managing debt:

- **Automate payments:** Automating your debt payments can help ensure that you never miss a payment, which can help you avoid late fees and damage to your credit score.

- **Consider a debt repayment strategy:** There are several debt repayments strategies, such as the Snowball Method and the Avalanche Method, which prioritize paying off debts based on either their balance or interest rate. Consider using one of these methods to help you prioritize your debt repayment.
- **Make extra payments:** Making extra payments, even if they are small, can help you pay off your debt faster and save money in interest charges.
- **Increase your income:** Consider increasing your income by working overtime, taking on a side job, or freelancing to help you pay off your debt more quickly.
- Reduce expenses: Reducing your expenses can free up money to put towards paying off your debt. Consider cutting back on unnecessary expenses, such as entertainment, dining out, and subscriptions, and use the extra funds to pay off debt.
- Avoid using credit cards: Using credit cards can increase your debt, especially if you are not paying off your balance in full each month. Consider using cash or a debit card instead to avoid accruing additional debt.

In addition to these tips, it is also important to monitor your debt regularly and adjust your repayment plan as needed. With discipline, commitment, and a clear plan, you can effectively manage your debt and achieve financial stability.

UNDERSTANDING DIFFERENT TYPES OF DEBT

Debt is an important aspect of personal finance, and it is important to understand the different types of debt in order to make informed financial decisions. Here are some common types of debt:

Mortgages: A mortgage is a loan used to purchase a home. It is typically the largest debt that an individual will have in their lifetime. Mortgages have long repayment terms, typically ranging from 15 to 30 years, and have lower interest rates compared to other types of debt.

Auto Loans: An auto loan is a loan used to purchase a vehicle. Auto loans typically have a repayment term of 3 to 7 years and a higher interest rate compared to a mortgage.

Student Loans: Student loans are loans used to pay for college tuition and related expenses. Student loans can have a repayment term of up to 20 years, and the interest rate can vary depending on the type of loan.

Credit Card Debt: Credit card debt is debt that is incurred by using a credit card. Credit card debt has a high-interest rate and is considered unsecured debt, which means that there is no collateral securing the loan.

Personal Loans: Personal loans are unsecured loans that can be used for a variety of purposes, including debt consolidation, home improvements, or large purchases. Personal loans have a repayment term of 2 to 7 years and an interest rate that varies based on the lender and the borrower's credit score.

Secured Loans: Secured loans are loans that are secured by collateral, such as a vehicle or savings account. Secured loans typically have lower interest rates compared to unsecured loans, but if the borrower defaults on the loan, the lender can seize the collateral.

It is important to understand the different types of debt, their interest rates, and repayment terms to make informed financial decisions and avoid taking on too much debt. Consider seeking the help of a financial advisor if you have questions about managing your debt.

PAYING OFF DEBT EFFICIENTLY

Paying off debt efficiently requires a combination of discipline, a clear plan, and a commitment to reducing your debt. Here are some tips for paying off debt efficiently:

- **Create a budget:** Creating a budget is the first step in paying off debt efficiently. Your budget should include all your income and expenses, including your debt payments. This will help you see where your money is going and identify areas where you can reduce expenses and free up money to put towards debt repayment.

- **Prioritize high-interest debt:** High-interest debt, such as credit card debt, should be a priority because it is the most expensive debt to carry. Consider using a debt repayments strategy, such as the Snowball Method or the Avalanche Method, to prioritize paying off high-interest debt first.

- **Make extra payments:** Making extra payments, even if they are small, can help you pay off your debt faster and save money in interest charges. Consider rounding up your payments or making bi-weekly payments instead of monthly payments.

- **Increase your income:** Consider increasing your income by working overtime, taking on a side job, or freelancing to help you pay off your debt more quickly.

- **Reduce expenses:** Reducing your expenses can free up money to put towards paying off debt. Consider cutting back on unnecessary expenses, such as entertainment, dining out, and subscriptions, and use the extra funds to pay off debt.

- **Avoid taking on additional debt:** Avoid taking on additional debt while you are paying off debt. This will help you focus your resources on reducing your debt instead of accruing additional debt.

- **Monitor your progress:** Monitoring your progress is important to stay motivated and on track. Consider setting up a debt repayment tracker to see how much you have paid off and how much you have left to pay.

With discipline, a clear plan, and a commitment to reducing your debt, you can pay off your debt efficiently and achieve financial stability. Consider seeking the help of a financial advisor if you have questions about paying off debt efficiently.

To elaborate further, it is important to understand that paying off debt efficiently is not just about making minimum payments but rather taking a proactive approach to reducing debt as quickly and effectively as possible. Here are some additional tips for paying off debt efficiently:

- **Consolidate debt:** Consolidating debt can simplify the debt repayment process and potentially lower your interest rate. Consider using a balance transfer credit card or a personal loan to consolidate high-interest debt into one manageable payment.

- **Negotiate with lenders:** If you are struggling to make your debt payments, consider negotiating with your lenders. You may be able to negotiate a lower interest rate, extended repayment terms, or a temporary suspension of payments.

- **Use windfalls wisely:** If you receive a windfall, such as a bonus, inheritance, or tax refund, consider using it to pay off debt. This will help you reduce your debt faster and save money on interest charges.

- **Practice good credit habits:** Building and maintaining good credit habits is important to reduce the cost of debt and improve your chances of being approved for credit in the future. Consider paying your bills on time, keeping your credit card balances low, and monitoring your credit report regularly.

- **Stay motivated:** Paying off debt can be a long and difficult process, but it is important to stay motivated and focused on your goal. Consider setting achievable debt repayment goals and celebrating small victories along the way.

By following these tips and incorporating them into your debt repayment strategy, you can make progress in reducing your debt and achieving financial stability. Remember to be patient and persistent and to seek help if you need it. A financial advisor can help you create a personalized debt repayment plan that is tailored to your individual needs and circumstances.

AVOIDING DEBT TRAPS

Avoiding debt traps is a crucial aspect of managing debt and achieving financial stability. A debt trap refers to a situation where a person takes on debt that they are unable to repay, resulting in high-interest charges, penalties, and additional debt. Here are some tips for avoiding debt traps:

- **Know the terms of your debt:** Before you take on any debt, make sure you understand the terms of the debt, including the interest rate, repayment terms, and any fees or penalties associated with the debt.

- **Avoid high-interest debt:** High-interest debt, such as payday loans, title loans, and credit card cash advances, can quickly lead to a debt trap. Consider avoiding high-interest debt whenever possible and opt for low-interest alternatives, such as personal loans or balance transfer credit cards.

- **Be cautious of debt consolidation offers:** Debt consolidation offers can be tempting, but it is important to be cautious and do your research before committing. Some debt consolidation companies charge high fees, and the terms of the debt may not be any better than the terms of the original debt.

- **Don't overuse credit:** Overusing credit can lead to a debt trap, as it can quickly become difficult to keep up with the payments. Consider limiting your use of credit to emergency situations and using cash or debit instead of credit whenever possible.

- **Seek help if you need it:** If you are struggling with debt, do not hesitate to seek help. Consider talking to a financial advisor or credit counselor to help you create a debt repayment plan and avoid debt traps.

By following these tips and avoiding debt traps, you can reduce the cost of debt and achieve financial stability. Remember to be disciplined, proactive, and informed in your approach to debt and to seek help if you need it. A financial advisor can help you create a personalized debt management plan that is tailored to your individual needs and circumstances.

CONCLUSION

In concluding this chapter, developing yourself economically is a crucial aspect of achieving financial stability and security. By building an emergency fund, understanding different types of debt, paying off debt efficiently, avoiding debt traps, and building passive income streams, you can reduce the cost of debt, improve your credit score, and achieve financial security. Moreover, adopting a long-term outlook and being informed, proactive, and disciplined in financial management is essential. Consulting a financial advisor can prove immensely beneficial, as they can assist in devising a personalized financial strategy that aligns with your unique needs and situation.

Remember, developing yourself economically takes time and effort, but with the right strategies and support, you can achieve financial stability and peace of mind.

Developing oneself economically involves several different strategies and approaches, all aimed at achieving financial stability and security. A key aspect of this process is building an emergency fund, which provides a financial cushion that can be used in times of unexpected expenses or emergencies. This helps to reduce the need for high-interest debt and improves financial stability.

Another important aspect of developing oneself economically is understanding different types of debt and paying off debt efficiently. By paying off debt, you can reduce the cost of debt, improve your credit score, and achieve financial security. Additionally, avoiding debt traps, such as high-interest debt or debt consolidation offers, can help you reduce the cost of debt and avoid financial hardship.

Building passive income streams is also a key aspect of developing oneself economically. By building multiple streams of passive income, you can reduce your reliance on active income and improve your financial stability. This can include strategies such as investing in stocks or real estate, starting a side hustle, or participating in affiliate marketing.

It is important to have a long-term perspective when developing oneself economically and to be informed, proactive, and disciplined in your approach to finances. Seeking help from a financial advisor can also be extremely valuable, as they can help you create a personalized financial plan that is tailored to your individual needs and circumstances. Remember, developing oneself economically takes time and effort, but with the right strategies and support, you can achieve financial stability and peace of mind.

"Wealth consists not in having great possessions but in having few wants" - Epictetus.

This quote by Epictetus highlights the importance of contentment and simplicity in achieving financial stability and wealth. Rather than focusing on acquiring more possessions and material goods, this quote suggests that having few wants and a simple lifestyle can lead to a sense of wealth and financial stability. By reducing the number of wants and desires, individuals can reduce their expenses and increase their financial stability, allowing them to focus on what truly matters. This perspective on wealth emphasizes the importance of contentment, mindfulness, and simplicity in achieving financial stability and happiness.

Chapter Seven
DEVELOPING YOURSELF SPIRITUALLY

What does it profit a man to gain the whole world, yet loses his soul for what can a man give in exchange for his soul?

INTRODUCTION

Man Shall not live by bread alone...

"Man shall not live by bread alone..." This profound statement sets the tone for our final chapter "Developing Yourself Spiritually." It is a reminder that life is more than just material possessions or physical abundance. This statement poses a significant question: what is it other than bread that man is in need off? In this chapter, we delve into this concept, focusing on the true essence of life and the true bread that man needs.

Our discourse in this chapter, centers on the idea that life's most valuable aspects are not our belongings or our physical condition, but rather our ongoing search for deeper truths and spiritual bread. This quest for truth is found through spiritual growth. Spiritual development is about gaining a better understanding of ourselves and building a closer relationship with the God. It is a path available to everyone, regardless of wealth, status, or size. Each of us has an inherent desire to connect with a higher power.

In this journey of spiritual growth, we embark on a personal exploration. It involves introspecting on our beliefs, values, and the purpose of our existence. This path is not just about finding peace and contentment within; it also enhances our mental and emotional health. It deepens our connections with others and brings a greater sense of purpose and fulfillment to our lives.

Throughout this chapter, we will explore various aspects of spiritual growth. We will discuss self-awareness, the importance of values and beliefs, and how to cultivate a deeper sense of connection with the God. Spiritual growth is not a mere aspect of life; it is a transformative journey that shapes our understanding of the world and ourselves.

DEFINITION OF SPIRITUAL DEVELOPMENT

The concept of spiritual development is central to this chapter's exploration of personal spiritual growth. By defining this term, we lay the groundwork for everything that follows, offering clarity on what spiritual development truly means and involves.

At its core, spiritual development entails strengthening our connection to a higher power or the divine, fostering inner peace, contentment, and a sense of purpose. This profound journey of self-discovery and growth is deeply personal, involving the exploration and deepening of our understanding of our spirituality. It also calls for aligning our beliefs and values with those of the Creator. Through this journey, we not only seek a better understanding of ourselves but also aim to harmonize our lives with the spiritual principles that guide us.

Throughout this chapter, I will adopt the Judeo-Christian value perspective to delve into spirituality. While recognizing that people may hold diverse views on spirituality, I personally embrace the path of the kingdom of God.

A prevalent misconception surrounding spiritual development is the belief that it can be advanced independently of a relationship with and belief in God. This misperception frequently emerges in modern dialogues about spirituality, reflecting a growing inclination to disassociate spiritual growth from conventional religious convictions, especially those centered on a higher power. This notion often stems from individuals who yearn for spiritual growth but wish to sidestep the concept of God.

In contemporary discussions about spirituality, there is an increasing emphasis on self-discovery, mindfulness, and personal transformation. Numerous people endeavor to delve into their inner selves and develop a sense of purpose and fulfilment, often without adhering to conventional religious doctrines or recognizing the existence of a supreme divine entity.

This shift reflects a broader societal trend toward secularism and the desire for more personalized, inclusive approaches to spiritual development.

However, it is essential to recognize that spirituality and belief in a higher power are not inherently incompatible. While some may choose a more secular path, others find spiritual nourishment and growth through their relationship with God. The diversity of perspectives on spirituality highlights the complexity and richness of this deeply personal and subjective journey.

In this chapter, we challenge and explore this notion by emphasizing the integral role that a belief in God can play in true spiritual development. The journey towards spiritual enlightenment, in many traditions, is deeply intertwined with the recognition and understanding of a divine presence. This connection is not just about religious rituals or practices; it is about cultivating a relationship with God that permeates every aspect of one's life.

Belief in God, in this context, serves as a guiding force that shapes one's values, actions, and understanding of the world. It is a source of strength, comfort, and moral grounding. When individuals embark on spiritual development with this belief, they often find a more profound sense of purpose and direction in their lives. This spiritual path is about aligning one's personal values, goals, and actions with the will of God, leading to a more harmonious and fulfilling life.

Moreover, this belief in God often brings a sense of community and belonging, as it connects individuals with others who share similar spiritual values and practices. This communal aspect of spirituality can be a powerful force for personal growth and support, further enriching the spiritual journey.

Expanding on this, the Book of Psalms in the Bible is a treasure trove of poetic expressions that deeply explores the theme of reliance on God. It portrays Him as the quintessential source of guidance, strength, and spiritual fulfillment.

In **Psalm 16:8,** David wrote, **"I have set the LORD always before me; because he is at my right hand, I shall not be shaken,"** there is a powerful declaration of unwavering trust in God. This verse reflects a deep-seated belief in the constant presence and support of the Divine. It teaches us about placing God at the center of our lives, suggesting that such a focus brings stability and resilience. In the context of spiritual development, this verse emphasizes the importance of continually acknowledging God's presence, relying on Him not just in times of need, but as a constant companion and protector.

Psalm 119:105, "Your word is a lamp for my feet, a light on my path," highlights another crucial aspect: God as the guiding force in life. This metaphor of light guiding the way in darkness speaks to the role of God's teachings and wisdom in providing direction and clarity in our lives. It suggests that the principles and values derived from a spiritual understanding of God's word can illuminate our decisions and the paths we choose, leading us towards righteousness and spiritual growth.

Finally, **Psalm 42:1-2, "As the deer pants for streams of water, so my soul pants for you, my God. My soul thirsts for God, for the living God. When can I go and meet with God?"** vividly expresses the soul's deep longing for a connection with God. This imagery of a deer thirsting for water powerfully conveys the natural, intrinsic desire of the human soul for spiritual nourishment and communion with the Divine. It reflects a profound yearning not just for knowledge about God, but for a personal, experiential relationship with Him. This longing is at the heart of spiritual development – it is about seeking to experience God's presence, love, and wisdom in a deeply personal and transformative way.

Together, these Psalms offer a holistic view of spiritual development: it is about steadfast reliance on God, guidance through His teachings, and a heartfelt longing for a direct, personal relationship with the Divine. This journey of spiritual growth is rooted in a deep commitment to and desire for a life lived in close communion with God.

IMPORTANCE OF SPIRITUAL DEVELOPMENT

The importance of spiritual development in one's personal growth is profoundly captured in Jude 1:20, **"But you, beloved, building yourselves up in your most holy faith and praying in the Holy Spirit."** This scripture not only underscores the significance of active engagement in nurturing one's faith but also highlights how this process enriches every aspect of life.

This scripture highlights two key aspects:

Self-Edification in Faith: The phrase **"building yourselves up in your most holy faith"** suggests that faith is not static but dynamic. It can and should be developed and strengthened. This building up is akin to a spiritual exercise, where believers are encouraged to deepen their understanding, conviction, and practice of their faith.

Prayer as a Tool for Growth: The importance of **"praying in the Holy Spirit"** indicates that prayer is a vital mechanism for spiritual growth. It is not just a ritual or a request but a means of deeper communion with the divine. Praying in the Holy Spirit can be understood as praying with sincerity, guidance, and inspiration from the Holy Spirit, fostering a deeper spiritual connection and understanding.

In the broader context of spiritual development, these elements play a crucial role. Spiritual growth involves more than self-improvement; it is about cultivating a connection with the creator of the universe who greater than oneself, which in turn enriches life. This process involves expanding consciousness, aligning values and actions with deeper truths, and developing qualities like compassion, patience, and understanding.

Moreover, the journey of spiritual growth is intrinsically linked to enhancing one's overall well-being. This journey leads to an increased sense of self-awareness, which is fundamental in understanding one's unique purpose and place in the world. As this awareness deepens, it cultivates emotional resilience, equipping individuals with the strength to face life's myriad challenges with greater composure and peace of mind.

Just as a tree is identified by its fruits, the spirit within an individual also yields distinct fruits as they grow spiritually. This idea is beautifully encapsulated in Galatians 5:22-23, where it is expressed:

"But the fruit of the Spirit is love, joy, peace, patience, kindness, goodness, faithfulness, gentleness, and self-control. Against such things there is no law."

These fruits—love, joy, peace, patience, kindness, goodness, faithfulness, gentleness, and self-control—are not just virtues to be admired but are tangible indicators of a life transformed by spiritual growth. Each of these qualities reflects a different facet of spiritual maturity and character development, shaping an individual's interactions with themselves, others, and the larger world. They serve as a compass guiding one towards a more fulfilling, purpose-driven existence.

Additionally, spiritual development deeply enriches one's relationships. As individuals progress in their spiritual journey, they often embody the fruits of the Spirit—love, joy, peace, patience, kindness, goodness, faithfulness, gentleness, and self-control. These qualities, as outlined in Galatians 5:22-23, foster enhanced empathy, compassion, and presence in interactions with others. This transformation not only strengthens personal relationships but also cultivates a profound sense of connectedness with the broader human community.

The Importance of Spiritual Development is indeed a crucial aspect of personal growth and understanding one's purpose. It is a multifaceted journey that involves exploring and deepening one's inner life and connection to a higher power or set of values. This exploration is not only about seeking answers to life's big questions but also about finding a sense of peace, direction, and fulfillment that transcends everyday experiences.

Dr. Myles Monroe, my teacher and pastor of more than 30 years, has made significant contributions to this field. Dr. Monroe's work often centers around the concept of purpose, particularly how individuals can discover and fulfill their unique purposes in life. His approach to spiritual development is deeply intertwined with understanding one's innate potential and the divine plan for everyone.

Dr. Monroe emphasizes that spiritual development is not a passive process but an active pursuit. It involves introspection, the cultivation of a personal relationship with God, and the application of spiritual principles in daily life. He often discusses how a deepened spiritual understanding can lead to a life that is not only more fulfilling but also more aligned with a greater, divinely orchestrated purpose.

Furthermore, Monroe's teachings frequently highlight the idea that every person is created with a specific purpose in mind, and that part of spiritual development involves discovering and living out this purpose. This perspective offers a powerful framework for personal growth, as it encourages individuals to look beyond superficial goals and achievements and to connect with a deeper sense of meaning in their lives.

UNDERSTANDING YOUR SPIRITUALITY

The Book of 3 John 1:2, reads: **"Beloved, I pray that you may prosper in all things and be in health, just as your soul prospers."** This verse beautifully ties together the concepts of spiritual well-being, physical health, and overall prosperity, offering a holistic view of what a fulfilled life can look like.

Relation to the Scripture

Prosperity in All Things: The phrase **"that you may prosper in all things"** suggests a desire for holistic success. This is not limited to material wealth or achievements but includes emotional, intellectual, and spiritual richness. In the context of spirituality, this prosperity means living a life aligned with one's values and beliefs, fulfilling one's potential, and contributing meaningfully to the world.

Health: The mention of being "in health" implies a state of well-being that is more than just the absence of illness. It encompasses mental, emotional, and physical health. Spirituality often plays a vital role in maintaining health, as it can provide coping mechanisms, a sense of peace, and a positive outlook, all of which contribute to overall well-being.

Soul's Prosperity: The condition **"just as your soul prospers"** is particularly significant. It implies that the foundation of all prosperity and health is the state of one's soul or inner self. This points to the idea that spiritual health is the cornerstone of all other forms of health and prosperity. A flourishing soul, one that is connected, content, and at peace, paves the way for a flourishing life in other areas.

Expanding on the concept that a soul can prosper and, conversely, that it can also experience poverty, it is essential to explore what constitutes the wealth and poverty of a soul, and how one can take steps to strengthen and enrich their soul or spirit.

The Prosperity and Poverty of the Soul

Prosperity of the Soul: A prosperous soul is often characterized by a deep sense of peace, contentment, and fulfillment. It is not merely about religious observance but encompasses a sense of connection and harmony with God, others. Attributes of a prosperous soul include empathy, love, inner peace, a sense of purpose, and the ability to find joy and gratitude in life's experiences.

Poverty of the Soul: In contrast, a soul experiences poverty when it lacks these qualities. This can manifest as a feeling of emptiness, disconnection, chronic dissatisfaction, or a lack of purpose and direction. Such a state can lead to negative emotions like bitterness, envy, and despair, indicating a need for spiritual nourishment and growth.

Steps to Strengthen the Soul/Spirit

Pray, Fasting and Meditation: Regular Pray, fasting and meditation can help in understanding the inner self, identifying areas of spiritual neglect, and fostering a sense of peace and connection.

Cultivating Relationships: The development and preservation of deep, meaningful relationships play a vital role in enriching the soul. This involves creating a sense of community and belonging, along with the practice of empathy and compassion in our dealings with others. As the principle **"Love your neighbor as you love yourself"** suggests, treating others with the same care and consideration we reserve for ourselves is essential for a fulfilled and spiritually healthy life.

Engaging in Purposeful Activities: Engaging in activities that align with one's values and contribute to a greater good can provide a sense of purpose and fulfillment.

Learning and Growth: Actively seeking and absorbing knowledge, whether it pertains to spirituality, emotional understanding, or intellectual subjects, is essential for the enrichment of the soul. This process of learning is beautifully encapsulated in the scripture **"Thy word have I hid in mine heart, that I might not sin against thee"** (Psalm 119:11). This verse highlights the importance of studying, internalizing, and meditating on spiritual teachings. By delving into religious texts, philosophical works, and engaging in reflective conversations, we not only expand our worldview but also embed these insights deeply within ourselves. This internalization is akin to meditating on the teachings, allowing them to shape our thoughts, actions, and spiritual understanding, leading to a more grounded and enlightened existence.

Gratitude and Positivity: Cultivating an attitude of gratitude and focusing on positive aspects of life can significantly impact the state of the soul, leading to greater contentment and joy.

Just as the body and mind can experience health or illness, so too can the soul prosper or suffer. By taking intentional steps to nurture and strengthen the soul, individuals can cultivate a richer, more fulfilling spiritual life, enhancing their overall well-being and sense of purpose.

Norman Vincent Peale, on the other hand, was an American minister and author known for his teachings on positive thinking and the power of prayer. In his most famous book, **"The Power of Positive Thinking,"** Peale lays out a philosophy of positive thinking that has helped millions of people around the world overcome challenges and improve their lives.

Peale believed that positive thoughts and affirmations have the power to shape a person's experiences and circumstances. He argued that by focusing on positive thoughts and replacing negative ones with positive ones, individuals can develop a more hopeful outlook on life and improve their mental, emotional, and physical well-being. (Peale, 1952.)

Understanding Spirituality

Spirituality, in its deepest essence, encompasses much more than routine practices or superficial expressions. It represents the dimension of human experience that is intimately involved in the search for a profound sense of meaning, purpose, and connection with the Almighty. This quest is not merely about adhering to religious rituals or doctrines; it is a journey that delves into the core of one's being, seeking to understand the larger questions of existence and one's place within the universe.

True spirituality involves an inner transformation, where individuals explore their deepest values, beliefs, and aspirations. It is about developing a personal relationship with the Father, however one chooses to define or understand that concept. This relationship often brings a sense of peace, guidance, and resilience in the face of life's challenges.

Moreover, this pursuit transcends mere intellectual understanding; it involves the heart and soul, leading to experiences and realizations that are deeply personal and transformative. In this light, anything that does not contribute to this profound exploration of meaning, purpose, and divine connection can be seen as superficial, lacking the depth and authenticity that true spirituality seeks to offer. This perspective elevates spirituality from mere tradition or habit to a vital, enriching part of the human experience, central to personal growth and understanding.

WHAT IS SPIRITUALITY?

In relating Saint Paul's interaction with the Athenians to the question of "What is spirituality?", we find a profound illustration of the exploration and expression of spiritual understanding in diverse cultural contexts. Paul's encounter with the Athenians, particularly his discussion about the 'Unknown God', sheds light on the universality and varied dimensions of spirituality.

Spirituality, at its core, is about seeking and connecting with the divine, or a higher truth, which is precisely what Paul encountered in Athens. The Athenians, with their altar to an **'Unknown God',** were expressing a spiritual longing and recognition that there was something greater beyond their current understanding. This reflects a key aspect of spirituality: the quest for a deeper understanding of the unknown or the divine.

Further, The Apostle Paul's perspective on spirituality is rooted in the belief that salvation comes through faith in Jesus Christ. According to Paul, spirituality is not just a matter of following certain rituals or rules, but it involves a personal, transformative relationship with God. This relationship is made possible by the indwelling of the Holy Spirit, who gives believers the power to live a holy and righteous life.

One key passage that reflects Paul's perspective on spirituality is Romans 8:1-4, where he writes, **"There is, therefore, no condemnation for those who are in Christ Jesus. For the law of the Spirit of life has set you free in Christ Jesus from the law of sin and death. For God has done what the law, weakened by the flesh, could not do. By sending His own Son in the likeness of sinful flesh and for sin, He condemned sin in the flesh in order that the righteous requirement of the law might be fulfilled in us, who walk not according to the flesh but according to the Spirit."**

Here, Paul makes it clear that the only way to live a spiritual life is through the power of the Holy Spirit, who sets believers free from the power of sin and death. He also emphasizes that living a spiritual life is not about following the law but about being transformed by the Spirit and walking in obedience to God.

Another important passage that reflects Paul's perspective on spirituality is found in Colossians 3:1-3, where he writes, **"If then you have been raised with Christ, seek the things that are above, where Christ is, seated at the right hand of God. Set your mind on things that are above, not on things that are on earth. For you have died, and your life is hidden with Christ in God."**

In this passage, Paul encourages believers to set their minds on things above, where

Christ is seated, and to live their lives in a way that reflects their relationship with God. He emphasizes that through their faith in Jesus Christ, believers have died to their old way of life and have been raised to a new life in the Spirit.

The Apostle Paul's perspective on spirituality emphasizes the importance of a personal, transformative relationship with God through faith in Jesus Christ and the power of the Holy Spirit. He encourages believers to live their lives in a way that reflects this relationship by setting their minds on things above and living in obedience to God.

In Romans 8:6, Apostle Paul writes, **"For to be carnally minded is death, but to be spiritually minded is life and peace."** This passage reflects Paul's perspective on the importance of living a spiritual life rather than a life focused on worldly desires and pursuits.

For Paul, being **"carnally minded"** refers to living according to the flesh or the desires of the physical body rather than the desires of the Spirit. This way of living is characterized by a focus on worldly desires, such as pleasure, power, and wealth, rather than on the things of God.

Paul contrasts this with being **"spiritually minded,"** which refers to living according to the guidance and power of the Holy Spirit. This way of living is characterized by a focus on the things of God, such as love, joy, peace, and righteousness. In this passage, Paul makes it clear that living a carnal life leads to death, both physical and spiritual, while living a spiritual life leads to life and peace. He emphasizes that living according to the desires of the flesh is a path that ultimately leads to destruction, while living according to the desires of the Spirit is a path that leads to life and peace in this world and in the world to come.

The Apostle Paul's phrase **"to be carnally minded is death"** reflects his belief that living a spiritual life, focused on the things of God and guided by the Holy Spirit, is essential for both physical and spiritual well-being. By contrast, living a carnal life, focused on worldly desires, ultimately leads to death and destruction.

The pursuit of vanity, money, and worldly glory as the sole focus in life often leads to a destination of death and emptiness. This is evident in the high rates of suicide, drug overdoses, and self-hatred that we see in society today. The temporary happiness that these worldly pursuits bring is often short-lived and is often accompanied by feelings of loneliness and emptiness.

On the other hand, true inner peace and fulfillment can only be found through a spiritual connection. When an individual is connected to their spirituality, they experience a deep sense of peace and joy that transcends their temporary worldly pursuits. This inner peace leads to a life that is abundant and fulfilling, one that is filled with joy and contentment.

Paul, in his writings, further emphasizes the importance of living a life guided by spiritual principles and a relationship with God. He encourages individuals to focus their minds on things above rather than on the temporary and fleeting pleasures of this world.

By doing so, they can experience a life that is abundant and filled with true inner peace and joy.

Living a life solely focused on vanity, money, and worldly glory leads to death and emptiness while living a life guided by spirituality and a relationship with God leads to inner peace and a fulfilling life. Paul encourages individuals to set their minds on things above and to live a life that is guided by spiritual principles to experience true inner peace and fulfillment.

The Way

Numerous religions across the world, including Islam, Hinduism, and Confucianism, propose various paths to connect with a divine entity or a supreme being, often referred to as God or the Father. These faiths generally embrace the idea that there are multiple routes to achieving this divine connection, reflecting the diverse tapestry of spiritual beliefs and practices.

In contrast, within Christianity, there is a unique claim made by Jesus Christ, setting it apart from other religions. Jesus asserted a singular path to God the Father, famously stating, **"I am the way, the truth, and the life. No one comes to the Father except through me."** This statement, found in the Christian scriptures, underscores a fundamental tenet of Christianity: the belief that the only way to reach God the Father is through Jesus Christ himself.

This claim highlights a pivotal aspect of the Christian faith, focusing on the uniqueness of Jesus as not just a spiritual leader, but as the sole mediator between humanity and God. It suggests that while the pursuit of spirituality and truth is common across various religions, Christianity offers a distinct perspective on this quest. According to this view, true spiritual fulfillment and the ultimate understanding of truth are found uniquely through Jesus Christ, defining him as the central figure in the Christian pathway to God.

To reinforce his claim as the singular way to God the Father, Jesus employs vivid metaphors that highlight his exclusive role in spiritual salvation. He describes himself as both the door and the gate for the sheep, as captured in his teachings. This imagery, rich in pastoral symbolism, is used to underscore his unique position as the gateway to spiritual safety and fulfillment.

In the Gospel of John, specifically John 10:7-10, Jesus articulates this concept clearly. He states, **"I am the gate for the sheep. All who have come before me** are thieves and robbers, but the sheep have not listened to them. I am the gate; whoever enters through me will be saved. They will come in and go out, and find pasture."

Here, the image of Jesus as the gate reflects his role as the protector and provider, much like a shepherd who guards the entrance to a sheepfold. This sheepfold symbolizes a place of security, belonging, and nurturing – akin to the spiritual haven offered by God. By declaring himself the gate, Jesus is asserting that it is through him alone that one gains access to God the Father and his divine blessings.

Moreover, his warning about those who attempt to enter 'by another way' being thieves and robbers serves as a caution against false teachings or misleading paths claiming to offer spiritual enlightenment or a route to God. This analogy is a critical element in Christian theology, emphasizing the legitimacy and integrity of the path Jesus offers compared to others that may seem appealing but are ultimately deceptive and lead away from true spiritual safety.

Thus, in John 10:7-10, Jesus reinforces the central Christian belief in his indispensable role in bridging humanity with God, asserting that genuine spiritual fulfillment and access to God are achievable solely through faith in him.

Who was Jesus Before coming to earth?

Why is Jesus Considered 'The Way'?

Throughout history, few figures have ignited as much debate and fascination as Jesus Christ. His uniqueness stems not just from his teachings or miracles, but from his extraordinary claims - claims unparalleled in human history. Jesus asserted himself to be both the Son of Man and the Son of God, intertwining human and divine natures in a singular identity. This claim alone distinguishes him from all leaders, prophets, or spiritual guides who either preceded or followed him.

To truly grasp the essence of Jesus' identity, one must explore his existence before his earthly incarnation. Christian doctrine posits that Jesus existed prior to his birth in Bethlehem, a belief grounded in scriptural references such as John 1:1-14. Here, Jesus is described as the Word (Logos), existing with God from the beginning and participating in the creation of the universe. This pre-existence underscores his divine nature, as espoused in the Nicene Creed, which describes him as begotten, not made, and being of one substance with the Father. In this theological framework, Jesus is not just a historical figure but a pre-existent divine entity, integral to the understanding of God's plan and purpose.

Furthermore, Jesus' claim to be 'the way' to the Father is a cornerstone of Christian theology. This assertion, found in John 14:6, underlines his unique role as the mediator between God and humanity. In Christian belief, Jesus' life, death, and resurrection are not mere historical events but pivotal moments in the divine narrative of salvation. His sacrificial death is seen as the atonement for human sins, offering a path to redemption and reconciliation with God. This salvific role, exclusive to Jesus, sets him apart from other religious leaders and prophets.

His connection to Old Testament prophecies further cements his position within the Christian faith. Jesus is often seen as the fulfillment of these ancient predictions, linking his life and mission to a longstanding divine plan. This fulfillment not only validates his messianic role but also connects the Christian narrative to its Judaic roots.

In understanding who Jesus is and why he is considered 'the way' to the Father, one must delve into these theological and historical dimensions. His identity, as portrayed in Christian doctrine, transcends mere mortal understanding, embodying a complex interplay of divine and human, historical and eternal, fulfilling a role unparalleled in any other spiritual or historical narrative.

Jesus Before the Coming to Earth

Let us delve into ancient texts beyond the traditional biblical canon, which provide a compelling depiction of who Jesus was before his earthly incarnation. The text in focus, revered as one of the most ancient writings, is the Book of Enoch. Authored by the patriarch Enoch, who stood merely seven generations from Adam, this book occupies a unique place in religious history. While it is not a part of the canonical Bible used by most Christian denominations, it holds a significant position in the Ethiopian Orthodox Bible. Furthermore, its authenticity is bolstered by the discovery of numerous copies among the Dead Sea Scrolls, lending credence to its historical and religious value.

Chapter 46 Vs 1-8 of the Book of Enoch presents a fascinating and mystical portrayal of a figure believed by many to prefigure Jesus. Enoch describes a vision of one he calls **"the Ancient of days,"** whose head was **"white like wool,"** symbolizing wisdom and agelessness. Accompanying this figure was another being, whose countenance bore the appearance of a man, radiating graciousness akin to that of the holy angels. This depiction aligns with traditional representations of divine wisdom and purity.

In this enigmatic chapter, Enoch, guided by an angel, inquires about the identity of this **man-like being.** The response he receives is profound: this being is identified as **"the son of man,"** distinguished by his righteousness and intimate association with all that is good and just. He is depicted as the one in whom righteousness dwells and as the revealer of hidden treasures, a figure chosen by the Lord of Spirits.

This portrayal in the Book of Enoch not only provides insight into ancient text and apocalyptic literature but also offers a glimpse into how early interpretations of Jesus' pre-earthly existence might have been shaped. The description of the **"son of man"** in the Book of Enoch echoes the later Christian understandings of Jesus as a pre-existent divine figure, associated with wisdom, righteousness, and the revelation of God's will.

The Book of Enoch, thus, stands as a fascinating and significant ancient text. It bridges the worlds of Jewish mysticism and early Christian thought, offering a unique perspective on the figure of Jesus Christ long before his birth in Bethlehem. This exploration into such extra-biblical texts enriches our understanding of the complex stories of religious and historical narratives that surround one of history's most profound and enigmatic figures.

Fast-forwarding to the Book of Matthew, we observe that Jesus refers to Himself as the **"Son of Man"** on eleven distinct occasions. To a modern Westerner, familiar with Christianity, this title might not seem particularly striking or significant. However, in the context of Jesus' time and within the Jewish cultural and religious setting, this term carried profound implications.

In first-century Judaism, the populace was well-versed in their religious texts, including works like the Book of Enoch, which was influential in shaping their understanding of certain messianic terms. The Book of Enoch, though not part of the Hebrew Bible, was known and respected in various Jewish sects. It contained references to the **"Son of Man,"** as a celestial figure, associated with righteousness and divine judgment. This background is crucial for understanding the impact of Jesus' use of the term.

When Jesus called Himself the **"Son of Man,"** it was not just a reference to His human nature. Instead, He was invoking a title steeped in rich theological and apocalyptic connotations. To His Jewish audience, this was a direct connection to the "Son of Man," depicted in Jewish apocalyptic literature — a figure who was expected to play a pivotal role in God's divine plan, often associated with the coming of the kingdom of God and the final judgment.

Therefore, Jesus' use of this title was far from being a mere self-reference; it was a powerful claim about His identity and role. By adopting this title, Jesus was positioning Himself within the prophetic traditions of Judaism, identifying Himself with a figure who had deep roots in their religious understanding.

This claim did not sit well with the Jewish leaders of the time. To them, Jesus, a Galilean carpenter, claiming such a lofty title was not only audacious but potentially blasphemous. It challenged their established religious authority and interpretations of the Messiah. This tension between Jesus' claims and the Jewish leaders' expectations is a recurring theme in the Gospels, culminating in the events of Jesus' trial and crucifixion.

The term **"Son of Man,"** as used by Jesus in the Gospel of Matthew, was a deliberate and profound declaration of His divine position and mission. It connected Him to a deep-seated Jewish expectation of a divine-messianic figure, a connection that was both revolutionary and controversial in His time. Understanding this context allows us to grasp the full weight and significance of Jesus' self-identification as the "Son of Man" in the Jewish setting of the first century.

From The Prophet Daniel View

The prophetic visions of Daniel in the Hebrew Bible offer remarkable parallels to the earlier visions described in the Book of Enoch. Particularly, in Daniel 7:13, the prophet recounts a vision strikingly similar to what Enoch witnessed: **"I saw in the night visions, and behold, with the clouds of heaven there came one like a son of man, and he came to the Ancient of Days and was presented before Him."** This imagery of 'one like a son of man' approaching the 'Ancient of Days,' who is traditionally interpreted as God the Father, echoes the description found in Enoch's writings.

The significance of this parallel extends beyond the mere similarity of the visions. Firstly, it illustrates a continuity and consistency in Jewish apocalyptic literature. The figure of the 'son of man' in both Enoch and Daniel is depicted not just as a human being but as a celestial or divine figure, endowed with authority and destined to play a crucial role in God's plan. This common imagery across different texts and time periods indicates a deep-rooted theological concept within Jewish tradition.

Secondly, the consistency between these visions is noteworthy given the historical gap between the two texts. The Book of Enoch is believed to predate the Book of Daniel by over a millennium and a half. This substantial time difference yet striking similarity in visions lends weight to the authenticity and importance of the 'son of man' motif in Jewish eschatological thought.

Furthermore, the appearance of this motif in Daniel, a canonical book of the Hebrew Bible, also validates and reinforces the themes found in the more esoteric and less widely recognized Book of Enoch. Daniel's vision of the 'son of man' is particularly influential, as it was written during a time of significant upheaval and persecution for the Jewish people. This context might have shaped the imagery of a divine figure who intervenes in human history, providing hope and assurance of God's sovereignty and ultimate justice.

In Christian theology, these visions from both Enoch and Daniel take on additional significance. Christians interpret the 'son of man' as a reference to Jesus Christ, seeing these ancient visions as prophetic anticipations of His coming and role. The image of the **'son of man'** coming on the clouds and being presented before the Ancient of Days is often associated with the ascension of Christ and his enthronement in heaven, as well as his future return in glory. This interpretation is rooted in the way Jesus Himself used the title "Son of Man" in the Gospels, particularly in contexts speaking of His coming in glory and His role in judgment and redemption.

The alignment of these prophetic visions across different eras and texts – from Enoch to Daniel – highlights a thematic thread in Jewish and Christian eschatology. It underscores a shared anticipation of a divinely appointed figure who transcends time, playing a central role in the cosmic narrative of creation, judgment, and redemption. This thread weaves through the fabric of biblical prophecy, contributing to a deeper understanding of the figure of the Messiah in both Jewish and Christian traditions.

Jude the Brother of Jesus

To further bolster our discussion regarding the Book of Enoch and its profound revelations, we can draw upon a direct reference to it in the New Testament. This reference significantly strengthens the argument for the relevance and influence of the Book of Enoch within early Christian thought. In the New Testament, specifically in the Epistle of Jude, there is a notable instance where Jude, identified as the brother of Jesus Christ, explicitly quotes from the Book of Enoch.

Jude's citation of Enoch is particularly compelling because it illustrates the early Christian recognition of the Book of Enoch's theological significance. This is not a casual reference; rather, it is an acknowledgment of the Book of Enoch as a source of religious and prophetic insight. Jude 1:14-15 states, **"Enoch, the seventh from Adam, prophesied about these men also, saying, 'Behold, the Lord comes with ten thousands of His saints, to execute judgment on all, to convict all who are ungodly among them of all their ungodly deeds which they have committed in an ungodly way, and of all the harsh things which ungodly sinners have spoken against Him.'"**

This quotation is significant for several reasons. **First,** it confirms the existence and recognition of the Book of Enoch during the time of the New Testament authors. **Second,** it shows that Jude, a figure closely connected to the early Christian community, considered the teachings of Enoch authoritative enough to use in his admonitions against ungodliness and to support his teachings about divine judgment. The inclusion of Enoch's prophecy in Jude's epistle suggests that the early Christian community have been very familiar with Enoch's writings and held them in high regard.

The reference in Jude's epistle serves as a bridge linking the Jewish apocalyptic literature, represented by the Book of Enoch, with early Christian teachings. It demonstrates the continuity of religious thought and the enduring impact of Enoch's visions on the Judeo-Christian tradition. This connection enriches our understanding of the development of early Christian theology and its roots in Jewish apocalyptic thought.

God's Messiah

Drawing from the intriguing references in the Book of Enoch and connecting them with the narrative of Jesus in the New Testament, we arrive at a profound conclusion: Jesus is God's Messiah. The term **"Messiah"** is derived from the Hebrew word **"Mashiach,"** meaning **"anointed one."** This concept of anointing, prevalent in Jewish tradition, symbolizes being chosen and empowered by God for a specific, divine purpose.

In the Book of Enoch, particularly Chapter 46, Verse 3, there is a notable passage that says, **"because the Lord of spirits has chosen him,"** which can be interpreted as a reference to the anointing of a chosen one. This idea aligns with the portrayal of Jesus in the New Testament. The anointing of Jesus is vividly illustrated at His baptism by John the Baptist. The Gospels describe a moment of divine affirmation where the Spirit descends upon Jesus in the form of a dove, and a voice from heaven proclaims, **"This is my beloved Son, in whom I am well pleased."** This event is a critical juncture in the New Testament, signifying Jesus' public anointing and divine endorsement as the Messiah.

Moreover, the New Testament further reinforces this understanding of Jesus as the anointed one. John the Baptist, a pivotal figure in the Gospels, explicitly recognizes Jesus as **"the Lamb of God."** This title is rich in symbolism, drawing from Jewish sacrificial traditions and pointing to Jesus' role as the ultimate sacrifice for the sins of humanity. This imagery aligns with the Messianic expectation of a savior and redeemer, as foretold in the Hebrew scriptures.

The synthesis of these scriptural elements – from the mystical texts of the Book of Enoch to the historical narratives of the New Testament – paints a comprehensive picture of Jesus as the Messiah. The term **"Messiah"** in this context embodies more than the notion of an anointed leader; it encapsulates a deeply spiritual and redemptive role. In Christian theology, Jesus as the Messiah is not merely a political savior or a restorer of earthly kingdoms, but a divine figure who brings spiritual salvation and reconciliation between God and humanity as sated in the book of Ephesians 2:14 **"For He Himself is our peace, who has made both one, and has broken down the middle wall of separation."**

The concept of the Messiah in the Hebrew Bible is illuminated through various prophecies and expectations. Prophets such as Isaiah and Daniel spoke of a future figure characterized by peace, justice, and righteousness. Christians have traditionally interpreted these prophecies as prefiguring the life and mission of Jesus.

Isaiah, for instance, provides a prophecy that is often associated with the birth of

Jesus. In Isaiah 9:6, it is stated: **"For unto us a child is born, unto us a son is given: and the government shall be upon his shoulder: and his name shall be called Wonderful, Counsellor, The mighty God, The everlasting Father, The Prince of Peace."** This passage is seen as significant in Christian theology, hinting at the divine nature and messianic role of Jesus.

Furthermore, Isaiah offers another prophecy in Chapter 53, which is interpreted as a depiction of the suffering servant. This text is often seen as a foreshadowing of Jesus' sacrificial death. Isaiah 53 describes a figure who suffers and bears the sins of many, a passage that Christians see as directly correlating with Jesus' life, his suffering, and his role in atonement.

These prophecies from Isaiah, along with others from the Hebrew Bible, form a foundational element in the Christian understanding of Jesus as the Messiah. They are seen as not only predictive but also as integral in shaping the narrative of Jesus' life and his redemptive mission as understood in Christian theology. The New Testament's depiction of Jesus aligns with these Messianic prophecies, presenting Him as fulfilling these ancient expectations. His teachings, miracles, death, and resurrection are portrayed as the culmination of God's plan for human redemption. The title **"Messiah"** in relation to Jesus thus transcends a mere label; it signifies the fulfillment of a long-awaited hope and the embodiment of God's promise to redeem the world.

Is Jesus God?

The question of whether Jesus Christ is God stands as one of the most profound and debated inquiries in religious scholarship. This perplexity stems from the challenge of reconciling the notion of a divine being existing within a human form. Christianity, distinctively, upholds the belief that Jesus Christ was God incarnate - God in human flesh. This belief is not just a matter of faith but is also supported by historical and scriptural evidence.

Drawing from earlier discussions, the Book of Enoch describes a figure known as the **"son of man,"** seen by some as a prefiguration of Jesus. Furthermore, the writings of New Testament authors like Paul and Peter contribute to this understanding. They often speak of Jesus in terms that elevate Him beyond a mere mortal or prophet, suggesting a divine nature.

One of the key scriptural references that support this view comes from the prophecy of Isaiah, specifically Isaiah 9:6, which states: **"For unto us a child is born, unto us a son is given: and the government shall be upon his shoulder: and his name shall be called Wonderful, Counsellor, The mighty God, The everlasting Father, The Prince of Peace."** This verse presents a child, understood by Christians to be Jesus, with titles that attribute divinity, such as **"Mighty God"** and **"Everlasting Father,"** which significantly support the concept of Jesus' divine nature.

In the rich words of Isaiah's prophecies, a profound declaration is made in Isaiah 7:14: Therefore the Lord himself will give you a sign: The virgin will conceive and give birth to a son, and will call him **Immanuel.'** The name Immanuel, translating to **'God with us,'** encapsulates a deeply significant theological concept. This prophecy is embraced by Christians as a definitive prediction of Jesus' birth, symbolizing not merely a remote divine influence, but God's direct presence in human form.

This prophecy holds a critical place in Christian theology, embodying the concept of the incarnation — the melding of the divine with the human. It presents the revolutionary notion that God would not just interact with humanity from afar but would enter into human existence as a tangible, living entity. This vision, as set forth by Isaiah, establishes a key tenet of Christian belief, affirming Jesus as God made flesh.

The name Immanuel powerfully communicates the dual nature of Jesus: simultaneously fully divine and fully human. It highlights the essence of Jesus' mission on Earth — to act as a conduit between the divine and the mortal, integrating God's presence into the fabric of human life and its challenges. The realization of this prophecy through Jesus' birth provides believers with a concrete assurance of God's active participation in the world, forging a tangible connection with the divine.

Etymologically, 'Immanuel' is a blend of Hebrew words **'Immanu' (with us) and 'El' (God),** creating a profound statement about God's presence within humanity. This element of the prophecy not only sheds light on the intimate nature of God's relationship with humanity but also highlights the transformative aspect of this divine-human interaction as depicted in Christian theology. This understanding further reinforces the argument that Jesus was, indeed, God in the flesh, providing a compelling foundation for faith and reflection in your narrative.

However, beyond what others have said about Him, it is crucial to consider Jesus' own declarations about His identity. In the New Testament, Jesus makes several statements that have been interpreted as claims to divinity. For example, in the Gospel of John 10:30, Jesus states, **"I and the Father are one."** This statement has been seen by many as a direct claim of unity with God. Additionally, in John 8:58, Jesus says, **"Before Abraham was, I am," using the phrase "I am,"** which echoes the name of God revealed to Moses in Exodus 3:14, **"I AM WHO I AM."**

In the Book of Revelation, where the Apostle John recounts his visionary experiences, there is a profound declaration by Jesus that reinforces the idea of His divinity. In Revelation 1:8, Jesus proclaims, **"I am the Alpha and the Omega, says the Lord God, who is and who was and who is to come, the Almighty."** This statement, identifying Himself as the **"Alpha and Omega"** and **"the Almighty,"** is a powerful assertion of divinity, equating Jesus with the eternal and omnipotent nature of God.

This declaration in Revelation is further supported by the Gospel of John, particularly in its opening verses. John 1:1-3 states: **"In the beginning was the Word, and the Word was with God, and the Word was God. He was in the beginning with God. All things were made through Him, and without Him, nothing was made that was made."** Here, John refers to Jesus as the "Word" (Logos in Greek), asserting His preexistence and participation in creation. This passage not only identifies the Word as God but also emphasizes that the Word was with God, indicating a distinct personhood within the Godhead.

The Gospel of John continues this theme by stating in John 1:14, **"And the Word became flesh and dwelt among us."** This verse encapsulates the Christian doctrine of the Incarnation – the belief that Jesus, the Word, became human while still retaining His divine nature.

These scriptural references – from the Book of Revelation and the Gospel of John – are central to the Christian understanding of Jesus as both God and man. Revelation 1:8 highlights His eternal and all-encompassing nature, while John 1:1-3 and 1:14 affirm His role in creation and His incarnation. Together, they provide a scriptural foundation for the belief in Jesus Christ as a divine being, integral to Christian theology.

These references, from both the Old and New Testaments, form a tapestry of evidence that many Christian theologians and believers cite to affirm Jesus' identity as both the Son of God and God Himself. This belief, while appearing paradoxical, is central to the Christian understanding of the nature of Jesus Christ.

To deepen the exploration of the concept that Jesus was at God's side during the creation of the universe, it is beneficial to examine a passage from the Hebrew Bible. While this passage is not explicitly about Jesus, it is frequently interpreted within Christian theology as symbolically prefiguring or representing His role. The reference comes from the Book of Proverbs, often attributed to King Solomon, a key figure in Jewish wisdom literature.

The specific verse is Proverbs 8:30, in which wisdom is personified, taking on the role of a collaborator in the act of creation. The verse reads: **"Then I was beside Him, as a master workman; and I was daily His delight, rejoicing always before Him."** In this imagery, wisdom is depicted not just as a characteristic of God but as an active, personified presence alongside God.

Christian theologians have often seen this personification of wisdom as a metaphorical representation of Jesus Christ. This perspective is influenced by and harmonized with the New Testament, particularly the Gospel of John. In John 1:1-

3, Jesus is described as the **"Word"** (Logos), through whom all things were made, a concept that parallels the idea of wisdom being beside God in Proverbs.

This connection between the Old Testament wisdom literature and the New Testament depiction of Jesus emphasizes the belief in Jesus' preexistence and active participation in creation alongside God. It illustrates how Christian theology often interprets Hebrew Bible texts in light of the New Testament, seeing in them foreshadowing's or symbolic representations of Jesus' divine nature and role.

This linkage between the Old Testament and the New Testament writings reflects the Christian theological perspective that sees Jesus as preexistent and participating in the creation of the universe alongside God the Father. It underscores the belief in the divine nature of Jesus, harmonizing the Old Testament wisdom literature with the teachings of the New Testament.

Numerous scriptural references enhance the study of Jesus Christ's divinity, presenting a topic ripe for individual exploration. As a reader, you are invited to independently navigate these texts, scrutinize the evidence and interpretations offered, and draw your personal conclusions regarding this deep theological matter.

To conclude this discussion on the divinity of Jesus, it is fitting to reflect on a pivotal moment recorded in the New Testament. This moment involves Thomas, one of Jesus' disciples, in the aftermath of Jesus' resurrection. The account, found in the Gospel of John, vividly captures Thomas' transformation from doubt to belief.

After Jesus' crucifixion and reported resurrection, Thomas expressed skepticism about the resurrection, famously declaring that he would not believe until he saw and touched the wounds of Jesus himself. This moment of skepticism is resolved in John 20:27-28, where Jesus appears to Thomas and invites him to put his hand into the wounds. Thomas' response upon seeing and touching Jesus is a profound declaration of faith and recognition of Jesus' identity: **"My Lord and my God."**

Thomas' exclamation, **"My Lord and my God,"** is more than just an expression of astonishment; it is a declaration of Jesus' divine nature. In this moment, Thomas recognizes and affirms the full identity of Jesus – not only as his teacher and Lord but also as God. This acknowledgment from a disciple, especially one initially doubtful, is seen as a powerful testament to Jesus' divinity.

The journey to understanding Jesus' nature is a deeply personal one, enriched by scriptural study and reflection. The example of Thomas, moving from doubt to a profound declaration of Jesus' divinity, serves as a compelling conclusion to the exploration of whether Jesus is God, encapsulating the journey from skepticism to faith.

Flavius Josephus, Account of Jesus

In our in-depth exploration of Jesus as the Messiah from a biblical viewpoint, the insights of Josephus Flavius, an esteemed Jewish historian from antiquity, offer an invaluable third-party perspective. His distinguished work, **"Antiquities of the Jews,"** meticulously documents the history, victories, and struggles of the Jewish people and includes a significant account of Jesus' life. Josephus's description of Jesus as "a wise man" enriches our understanding of Jesus' historical significance.

Here is the pertinent excerpt from Josephus: "At this time, there was a wise man named Jesus. If it is appropriate to call him a man, for he performed remarkable deeds and was a teacher of those who gladly embrace truth. He attracted many followers, both from among the Jews and the Gentiles. **He was the Christ.** When Pilate, upon the accusation of our leading men, had condemned him to the cross, his original followers did not abandon him. He appeared to them alive again on the third day, as the divine prophets had foretold these and countless other marvelous things about him. The sect of Christians, named after him, persists to this day." **(Whiston)**

This passage, found in Book 18, Chapter 3, Part 3 of "Antiquities of the Jews," is one of the earliest non-Christian references to Jesus. Not only does it acknowledge Jesus' profound impact but also the formation of Christianity. Remarkably, Josephus refers to Jesus as the Messiah or Christ. He also notes the belief that Jesus' disciples witnessed him alive three days post-crucifixion, a prophecy foretold by prophets. This third-party corroboration not only bolsters the Gospel narratives but also lends a broader perspective to the recognition of Jesus as the Messiah and the anointed one of God.

SPIRITUALITY WITH A PURPOSE

In the preceding sections, we embarked on a journey through history and scripture, exploring three pivotal questions: 1) Who was Jesus Christ before His earthly incarnation? 2) What does it mean to be God's Messiah? 3) Is Jesus truly God? This exploration is crucial because genuine spirituality is anchored in a divine purpose. Without this specific purpose, spiritual practices risk becoming mere meditation without deeper significance.

As outlined in Chapter One, human beings are comprised of three elements: body, soul, and spirit. For authentic spiritual growth, it is essential to recognize that true spiritual development is attainable only through a connection with God, as facilitated by Jesus Christ. Contemporary thought often suggests that there are multiple paths to God. However, this idea diverges from the central Christian teaching that the sole route to God the Father is through Jesus Christ. Therefore, the first step in spiritual development is establishing a relationship with Jesus Christ. He Himself stated, **"I am the way, the truth, and the life: no man cometh unto the Father, but by me"** (John 14:6). This declaration underscores the importance of first forming a bond with Jesus to truly connect with God.

There is a common misconception that practices like yoga or deep meditation alone constitute spiritual development. While these can be beneficial practices, in the Christian context, true spiritual growth involves communion with God through Jesus Christ. This communion is primarily achieved through prayer and fasting. These practices are not just ritualistic exercises; they are means of deepening one's relationship with God, facilitated by Jesus.

Later in this chapter, we delve deeper into the significance and relevance of prayer and fasting. We will explore how these practices are not merely religious obligations, but are vital tools for spiritual growth, providing a pathway to a more profound understanding and connection with the divine. The importance of these practices lies in their ability to draw us closer to God, fostering a deeper spiritual maturity that aligns with the Christian faith's core teachings.

ENHANCING YOUR SPIRITUAL AWARENESS

Enhancing your spiritual awareness involves developing a deeper understanding of your own spirituality and connecting with a higher power, the universe, or your own inner consciousness. It is a personal journey that requires dedication, reflection, and growth. Here are some ways to enhance your spiritual awareness:

Meditation: Meditation is a powerful tool for enhancing spiritual awareness. It involves quieting the mind and focusing on the present moment. It can be as simple as sitting quietly and breathing, or you can use guided meditations to help you focus.

Gratitude: Cultivating an attitude of gratitude can help you feel more connected to the world around you.

Practice taking time each day to reflect on what you are grateful for.

Nature: Spending time in nature can help you feel more connected to the world and the larger universe. Go for walks, sit in the park, or simply observe the beauty of nature.

Service to others: Helping others can bring a sense of purpose and fulfillment to your life. Find ways to serve your community, whether through volunteering, donating to charity, or simply being there for a friend in need.

Self-reflection: Take time each day to reflect on your thoughts, feelings, and behaviors. Consider what you can do to become a better person, both for yourself and for others.

Spirituality practices: Explore different spiritual practices, such as yoga, tai chi, or journaling, to find what resonates with you.

Remember, enhancing your spiritual awareness is a lifelong journey, and there's no right or wrong way to do it. The key is to be open, curious, and dedicated to your own growth.

PRAYER AND FASTING

How To Pray?

"Teach us how to pray" is a fundamental request, one that every person, as they transition from childhood to adulthood, might benefit from asking. This pivotal question was posed by the disciples of Jesus Christ, recognizing the vital role of prayer in their spiritual journey. Jesus, understanding the importance of prayer and being a practitioner of it Himself, provided His disciples with a structured guide for prayer. This guide is what we now know as the **"Our Father"** prayer, or the Lord's Prayer.

The Lord's Prayer begins by establishing a connection with God: **"Our Father, who art in heaven."** This opening line not only identifies to whom the prayer is addressed but also acknowledges the transcendent nature of God. The next line, **"Hallowed be Thy name,"** further emphasizes God's holiness, instilling a sense of reverence at the outset of the prayer.

As the prayer progresses, it speaks to the coming of God's kingdom: **"Thy kingdom come, Thy will be done, on earth as it is in heaven."** This is a significant aspect of the prayer, as it reflects a desire for God's sovereign will to manifest on earth, aligning human intentions with divine purposes.

The prayer then shifts to more personal requests, starting with **"Give us this day our daily bread."** This line symbolizes the need for sustenance, both physical and spiritual, acknowledging our dependence on God for all provisions. Following this, the prayer addresses the need for forgiveness: **"And forgive us our trespasses, as we forgive those who trespass against us."** This part emphasizes the importance of confession and the practice of forgiveness, essential aspects of Christian living.

Finally, the prayer seeks divine guidance and protection: **"And lead us not into temptation but deliver us from evil."** Here, there is a recognition of the challenges and dangers in life, alongside a request for God's protection and guidance to navigate these challenges.

While the Lord's Prayer is often recited verbatim, its true essence lies in its function as a template for daily prayer. It encompasses key elements of worship, petition, confession, and reliance on God's guidance. This prayer serves as a comprehensive framework, guiding believers in their personal communication with the divine. It is not just a ritualistic recitation but a profound guide to developing a deeper, more meaningful prayer life.

Why Should we Pray?

The act of prayer holds a significant place in various religious practices, serving as a profound connection between the devotee and the divine. In Islam, for instance, adherents engage in prayer five times a day, a practice known as Salah, reflecting their devotion and submission to Allah. Similarly, in Hinduism, offerings and prayers are made, often at home shrines, as a way of honoring and seeking blessings from their deities.

The fundamental question, however, revolves around the purpose and impact of prayer. Does prayer primarily benefit the individual, or is it an offering to the divine? The Apostle Paul, in his teachings, urges believers to **"pray without ceasing"** (1 Thessalonians 5:17), highlighting the continuous nature of this spiritual practice. This suggests that prayer is not just a ritualistic act, but a persistent state of communion with God.

Dr. Myles Munroe, in his insightful book on prayer, emphasizes that prayer is a key that unlocks divine action on Earth. He posits that, according to Christian belief, God granted humanity authority and dominion over the Earth (Genesis 1:28). Consequently, God respects this autonomy and requires human invitation or permission to intervene in earthly matters. Thus, prayer becomes a medium through which believers invite or authorize God's involvement in their lives and the world.

This concept aligns with the teachings of Jesus, who said, **"Whatever you bind on earth will be bound in heaven, and whatever you loose on earth will be loosed in heaven"** (Matthew 18:18). This implies that human actions and decisions, especially in the realm of prayer, have spiritual significance and consequences.

Furthermore, the Apostle Paul speaks of engaging in various forms of prayer, including psalms and spiritual songs (Ephesians 5:19), suggesting a diverse and expressive approach to this spiritual discipline. This variety in prayer practices highlights its multifaceted nature, serving not only as a request or intercession but also as an expression of gratitude, worship, and spiritual reflection.

The act of prayer in religious traditions is multifunctional. It serves as a channel for spiritual communication, a means of inviting divine intervention, and a practice that fosters a deeper, continuous relationship with the divine. As we delve deeper into this topic in this chapter, we will explore the transformative power of prayer in personal and communal spiritual development.

My objective in this discussion is not to delve exhaustively into the subject, but rather to point you towards a valuable resource. I strongly recommend acquiring Dr. Myles Munroe's book, **"The Power of Prayer,"** which offers profound insights into the role of prayer in spiritual growth. True spiritual development, as Dr. Munroe illustrates, is closely intertwined with both the understanding and practice of prayer.

Prayer, in its essence, should be strategic and intentional, rather than random or haphazard. This concept is echoed in the teachings of Jesus Christ, who emphasized the importance of how we pray. In John 14:13-14, Jesus states, **"Whatever you ask in my name, this I will do, that the Father may be glorified in the Son. If you ask me anything in my name, I will do it."** This instructs believers to pray to God the Father, yet to do so invoking Jesus' name. This invocation is not merely a formula; it signifies recognition of Jesus' role as a mediator and his authority granted by God.

By praying in Jesus' name, believers align their requests with the character and will of Jesus, ensuring that their prayers are not just self-centered petitions but are in harmony with the greater divine plan. Dr. Munroe's book delves deeper into these concepts, illustrating how strategic prayer shapes our spiritual journey and connects us more deeply with the divine purpose.

In summary, the practice of prayer is a fundamental aspect of spiritual life, requiring both understanding and intentionality. Dr. Myles Munroe's **"The Power of Prayer"** is an invaluable guide in exploring these dimensions of prayer, helping believers to realize a richer, more meaningful spiritual experience.

Fasting

Fasting, often perceived as a challenging discipline for many Christians, holds a significant place in spiritual practice. The saying, **"He who controls his belly controls the world,"** aptly encapsulates the essence of fasting: it is a practice of self-discipline and spiritual mastery over physical desires.

In exploring the biblical perspective on fasting, it is enlightening to consider Jesus Christ's teachings on the subject. When questioned by His disciples about fasting, Jesus provided a profound insight. He explained that there would be an appropriate time for fasting, as mentioned in the Gospel of Matthew (9:15): **"The time will come when the bridegroom will be taken from them; then they will fast."** This indicates that fasting is not merely a ritualistic act but a deeply personal and situational practice, especially significant in times of spiritual seeking or mourning.

Additionally, the New Testament recounts an incident where a disciple struggled to cast out a demon and sought Jesus' guidance. Jesus' response, as recorded in Mark 9:29, was, **"This kind can come out by nothing but prayer and fasting."** This statement underscores the power of fasting combined with prayer, suggesting that some spiritual battles require a greater depth of spiritual discipline and commitment.

Fasting, therefore, is not just a physical abstention but a spiritual exercise that enhances one's prayer life and spiritual fortitude. It is a voluntary act of surrender and humility before God, seeking deeper communion and greater spiritual authority. This practice, when undertaken in the right spirit and for the right reasons, can lead to profound personal transformation and spiritual breakthroughs.

To emerge victorious in spiritual battles, it is essential to cultivate a robust prayer life and a disciplined approach to fasting. As the Apostle Paul advises in Ephesians 6:10, **"Finally, my brethren, be strong in the Lord and in the power of His might."** This strength in the Lord is not just a matter of physical or intellectual capability; it encompasses spiritual fortitude, which is nurtured through consistent and dedicated practices of prayer and fasting.

Prayer serves as a direct line of communication with God, a way to seek guidance, strength, and wisdom from a higher power. It is through prayer that one can find the courage and insight to face spiritual challenges. Fasting, on the other hand, is a practice of self-denial, a deliberate abstinence that sharpens spiritual focus and demonstrates a commitment to seeking God's will above earthly desires.

The combination of prayer and fasting is a powerful tool in spiritual development. It is not merely about abstaining from food or uttering words of prayer; it is about aligning one's spirit with the will of God, surrendering personal desires to embrace God's plan. This alignment empowers believers to stand firm against spiritual adversities, fortified by the strength that comes from a deep and intimate relationship with God.

Spiritual strength and victory in battles are closely tied to the depth of one's spiritual disciplines. A committed practice of prayer and fasting is crucial in developing this spiritual strength, enabling believers to stand steadfast in the Lord and in the power of His might, as exhorted by Apostle Paul.

NATURE AND SPIRITUAL DEVELOPMENT

Connecting with nature is indeed a profound way to achieve spiritual harmony and deepen one's connection with the divine. Many spiritual traditions view nature as a manifestation of God's presence, a living tapestry reflecting the beauty and intricacy of divine creation. This natural world, with its seamless interplay of elements, serves as a vivid reminder of the interconnectedness of all life.

The act of immersing oneself in nature can be a deeply spiritual experience, offering a sense of peace, rejuvenation, and a unique space for reflection and prayer. The natural world, in its tranquility and simplicity, provides a stark contrast to the often chaotic and noisy human-made environments, enabling individuals to connect more easily with the divine.

The life of Jesus Christ offers profound examples of this connection with nature in spiritual practice. The Gospel of Matthew (26:36-46) recounts how Jesus prayed in the Garden of Gethsemane, a moment of deep spiritual anguish and communion with God before his crucifixion. In these quiet, natural settings, away from the distractions of daily life, Jesus found strength and clarity.

Moreover, following his baptism, as described in the Gospel of Mark (1:12-13), Jesus was led into the wilderness. This time in the wilderness was not just a period of temptation but also an opportunity for spiritual fortification and oneness with nature. Away from the bustle of society, Jesus could engage in deep reflection and connection with God.

These biblical accounts underscore the importance of nature as a setting for prayer and spiritual growth. The solitude and beauty of natural environments provide a unique backdrop for introspection and communion with the divine, fostering a sense of inner peace and spiritual renewal. In a world where distractions are abundant, turning to nature can be a powerful way to reconnect with oneself and the divine presence that permeates all creation.

The Garden of Eden, as depicted in the Bible, indeed stands as a profound symbol of the idyllic harmony between humanity, nature, and the divine. This biblical garden represents not only the physical beauty and abundance of the natural world but also embodies the spiritual connection humans once enjoyed with God in a state of pristine communion.

In the narrative of Genesis, the Garden of Eden is portrayed as a place where God and humans interacted intimately. Genesis 3:8 poignantly describes how God walked in the garden in the cool of the day, a powerful image of divine closeness and accessibility. This scenario paints a vivid picture of a time when the boundary between the human and the divine was permeable, with nature serving as the sacred space for this profound interaction.

The Garden of Eden thus serves as more than a historical or mythological setting; it is a metaphor for the potential of living in spiritual harmony with nature and experiencing a close, unmediated relationship with the divine. It suggests a world where the spiritual and the natural are intertwined, where the presence of the God is palpable in the living elements of nature.

This narrative underscores the importance of nature as a conduit for spiritual growth and connection. Just as the Garden of Eden was a place of communion between God and humans, spending time in nature in the present day can facilitate a deeper spiritual relationship with the divine. Nature, in its inherent beauty and tranquility, offers a unique environment for reflection, prayer, and connection with God.

Reflecting on the Garden of Eden inspires a longing for a return to that original state of harmony and serves as a reminder of the profound spiritual benefits of connecting with the natural world. It encourages us to seek moments of tranquility and closeness with the God amidst the beauty of the natural world, thereby deepening our spiritual lives and our understanding of the sacred interconnectedness of all creation.

A God Walk

In contemporary times, the concept of a **"God walk"** or a walk in nature has become a meaningful spiritual practice for many individuals seeking to deepen their connection with the God. This practice involves intentionally spending time in natural surroundings to foster a sense of spiritual harmony and closeness to God.

The act of taking a walk in nature offers a respite from the fast-paced and often overwhelming rhythms of modern life. It allows individuals to slow down, immerse themselves in the beauty and serenity of the natural world, and reflect on the presence of the God in their lives. This slowing down is not just physical but also mental and spiritual, creating space for introspection, prayer, and mindfulness.

Nature, in its vast and varied forms, reflects the complexity and wonder of creation. Being amidst nature can heighten one's awareness of the presence of God that permeates all things. The tranquility of natural settings – the rustling of leaves, the gentle flow of a stream, the vast expanse of the sky – can facilitate a profound sense of peace and spiritual rejuvenation. This peaceful environment makes it easier for individuals to listen for God's voice, perceive His handiwork, and engage in meaningful spiritual reflection.

Moreover, the practice of a **"God walk"** aligns well with the biblical tradition of seeking solitude in nature for spiritual connection, as exemplified by Jesus Christ. It reinforces the idea that the natural world is not just a backdrop for human activity but a living, sacred space where one can encounter the divine.

In essence, engaging in a **"God walk"** is a powerful way to nurture one's spiritual life. It offers a simple yet profound means to reconnect with God, deepen spiritual awareness, and experience the restorative power of nature. This practice reminds us of the enduring relevance of nature as a source of spiritual inspiration and a place of communion with the divine in our modern world.

My Secret Place

My garden holds a special place in my heart; it is where I find a deep connection with God. Whenever I am seeking guidance, comfort, or simply a word to lift my spirits, I retreat to this little haven of mine. Surrounded by the vibrant colors of hibiscus, the cascading beauty of bougainvillea, and the delicate fragrance of roses, I feel a profound sense of peace and spiritual connection.

This place is not just about the flowers or the greenery; it is where I feel most in tune with nature, and in turn, feel my spiritual bond with God strengthen. I recall a conversation with my wife where I shared an enlightening moment: an answer to a troubling question had come to me while I was in the garden. In response, she expressed her curiosity, wondering why she had not experienced such moments of clarity in the same way. With a smile, I suggested, **"Maybe you should try spending some time in the garden."**

For me, this garden is more than a place; it is my personal sanctuary, a sacred space where I feel God's presence most acutely. It is not a church building or a traditional place of worship, but it is where I find my most honest and profound moments of prayer and reflection. This garden is my secret place, a testament to the unique ways we each can find and nurture our connection with the divine.

Experiencing nature offers a profound path to spiritual harmony and a deeper connection with the divine. Engaging in simple activities like walking in a park or pausing to appreciate the natural world's beauty can significantly enhance one's spiritual well-being. These moments spent in nature not only foster a connection with the divine but also imbue a sense of peace and rejuvenation, enriching the soul and mind.

Practicing Spiritually

Now that we have embraced fasting and prayer, it is essential to delve into the true essence of practicing spirituality. Common misconceptions suggest that spirituality is about outward piety, appearing holy, or adopting a certain style of dress. However, the practice of spirituality is much simpler and more profound than these external expressions.

Jesus Christ taught the essence of spirituality through his words and actions. He emphasized that serving others, especially those in need, is at the heart of true spirituality. In the Gospel of Matthew (25:40), Jesus says, **"Truly I tell you, whatever you did for one of the least of these brothers and sisters of mine, you did for me."** This statement highlights that acts of kindness and compassion towards the less fortunate are acts of service to God Himself.

Furthermore, Jesus illustrates this principle in another passage (Matthew 25:31-46), where He describes the final judgment. He speaks of people who did great things in His name but neglected the fundamental acts of caring for those in need, like feeding the hungry or clothing the naked. To these people, He says, **"Depart from me, you who are cursed, into the eternal fire prepared for the devil and his angels."** This stark warning underscores that true spirituality is not about grandiose religious acts but about compassionate actions towards others.

Practicing spirituality, therefore, is fundamentally about being a keeper of our brothers and sisters. It involves feeding the poor, clothing the naked, and extending a helping hand to those in need. These acts of love and compassion are the true measures of one's spiritual life, reflecting the heart of Jesus' teachings. In essence, to walk in spirituality is to walk in love, empathy, and service to others, embodying the love of Christ in our daily lives.

It may seem paradoxical to assert that the practice of something as intangible as spirituality is rooted in physical acts, yet this is precisely the case. These physical acts, embodied in the form of love, sharing, and caring, are deeply spiritual in nature. They represent the tangible expression of an inner spiritual reality.

This concept is grounded in the understanding that love, though a spiritual emotion, manifests most authentically through physical actions. When we help, share with, and care for others, we are enacting spiritual principles in a concrete way. As the biblical teaching goes, it is incongruent to claim love for God while harboring hatred or indifference towards one's neighbor (1 John 4:20). True spirituality, therefore, is not confined to inner feelings or beliefs but is demonstrated through our interactions and generosity towards those around us.

Continuing to grow spiritually, then, involves a consistent practice of this art of love. This means actively giving to those who are less fortunate - the poor, the sick, the needy. Such acts of giving are not merely charitable deeds; they are profound expressions of spiritual growth and maturity. Each act of kindness and generosity is a step towards embodying the love and compassion that lie at the heart of spiritual practice.

In essence, the journey of spiritual growth is intrinsically linked to how we treat and support others. It is through these acts of love and service that our spiritual lives gain depth and meaning, reflecting the core teachings of many spiritual traditions.

Indeed, according to the teachings of Jesus, the true measure of one's spirituality is not found in the number of miraculous deeds performed, such as speaking in tongues, performing miracles, or even raising the dead. Rather, it is deeply rooted in the compassion and care shown towards the less fortunate - the poor, the sick, and the needy.

Jesus emphasized this principle in his teachings, particularly in the parable of the Sheep and the Goats (Matthew 25:31-46). In this parable, he starkly contrasts the eternal destinies of those who have shown compassion to those in need with those who have not. The key message is that acts of kindness to the least fortunate are viewed as acts done unto Jesus himself. Conversely, neglecting to show compassion to those in need is akin to neglecting Jesus.

This teaching is a profound reminder that spiritual life is not just about personal piety or supernatural manifestations. Rather, it is fundamentally about how we treat and care for others, especially those who are vulnerable or marginalized. The failure to live out this compassionate aspect of faith, regardless of other religious achievements, is seen as a serious spiritual shortfall. Jesus' words that he "never knew" such individuals highlight the importance of aligning one's actions with the core values of compassion and empathy that he taught and exemplified.

In summary, the teachings of Jesus place a significant emphasis on compassion and service to others as the true indicators of a person's relationship with God. This perspective challenges and broadens our understanding of what it means to live a spiritually fulfilling life.

The Value of the Soul

In conclusion, the essence of all that has been discussed in this book can be encapsulated in one profound question posed by Jesus: **"What does it profit a man to gain the whole world, yet forfeit his soul? Or what can a man give in exchange for his soul?"** This question is the cornerstone of my entire book, encapsulating its central message.

You might pursue material wealth, seek extensive knowledge, or strive for physical health, but the ultimate question remains: what value do these achievements hold if, in the process, you lose your soul? In the journey of spiritual development, the primary goal is the salvation of your soul, which is found in believing in Jesus Christ. He said, **"I have come that they may have life, and have it to the full"** (John 10:10). This promise suggests that true life, both in this world and beyond, is found in Him.

Jesus' statement, **"The Son has life in himself"** (John 5:26), signifies that eternal life, the ultimate aspiration of all mankind, is a gift that only He can bestow. Therefore, developing oneself spiritually is not merely about self-improvement or religious rituals; it is fundamentally about cultivating a personal relationship with Jesus Christ. This relationship is the capstone of spiritual growth, the crucial element that brings coherence and completeness to all that has been discussed in this book.

In the end, if a person loses their soul, then all other achievements are rendered meaningless. The pursuit of spiritual growth, therefore, should be centered on securing one's soul through a relationship with Christ, which not only promises eternal life but also brings meaning and purpose to our existence in this life.

King Solomon, renowned for his wisdom and wealth as the king of Israel, engaged in deep reflection towards the end of his life. His insights, particularly about the significance of revering God and adhering to His commandments, are profoundly captured in the book of Ecclesiastes. Through this introspective journey, Solomon, who experienced unparalleled riches and wisdom, came to understand a fundamental truth.

In Ecclesiastes, Solomon explores various facets of life, from the pursuit of pleasure and knowledge to the accumulation of wealth and power. Despite having access to all the worldly things, one could desire, he ultimately discerns that these pursuits are fleeting, likening them to 'chasing after the wind'. This realization leads him to a powerful conclusion: the greatest wisdom and purpose of life lie in fearing God and keeping His commandments.

This conclusion represents a significant shift from the temporal to the eternal, highlighting a recognition that true fulfillment and meaning are found not in earthly achievements or pleasures, but in a life lived in reverence and obedience to God. Solomon's reflection thus serves as a timeless reminder of the importance of prioritizing spiritual values and living in alignment with divine principles.

"Fear God and keep His commandments, this is the whole and only duty of man,"

BIBLIOGRAPHY

Bible. (n.d.).

The Buddha's Teachings on Greed and Possession.Buddhism.org, T. B. (n.d.). www.buddhanet.net/e-learning/history/buddha_teachings.htm.

Chopra, D. (1994). The Seven Spiritual Laws of Success. . Amber-Allen Publishing,

Gandhi, M. K. (1994). Life is an Indivisible Whole.The Gandhi Reader: A Sourcebook of His Life and Writings. edited by Homer A. Jack, Grove Press,p. 312.

Gandhi, M. K. (1994). Life is an Indivisible Whole." The Gandhi Reader: A Sourcebook of His Life and Writings. Homer A. Jack, Grove Press,p. 312.

2:7., B. K. (n.d.).

Descartes, R. (1641.). "Meditations on First Philosophy." .

Augustine, S. B. (397-400.). "The Confessions." .

Aquinas, T. S. (1265-1274.). "Summa Theologiae." .

Bible. (n.d.). King James Version. Genesis 4:7.

"Emotional Processing in the Brain." Brain Facts and Figures, S. f. (n.d.). www.brainfacts.org/thinking-sensing-and-behaving/emotions/articles/2012/emotional-processing-in-the-brain.

Brain., ". P. (2014.). Current Opinion in Neurobiology, vol. 26. pp. 36-41.

Smith, J. T. (2015.). The Cingulate Gyrus, Frontiers in Human Neuroscience. A Key Player in Brain Function and Disorder, vol. 9, no. 194, .

James, W. (vol. 1, 1890,). "The Emotions aren't always immediately subject to reason, but they are always immediately subject to action.". pp. 442-443.

Buddha. (1993). "The mind is everything; what you think, you become." Sayings of the Buddha, ed. John Ross Carter and Mahinda Palihawadana.

Lovelace, R. (n.d.). Stone walls do not a prison make. In To Althea from Prison, (p. 1642.).

Plato. (n.d.). The Republic. In The Republic (p. Book VI).

Churchill, W. (Speech, Unknown.). "The empires of the future are the empires of the mind.".

Aurelius., M. (19XX.). "The soul becomes dyed with the color of its thoughts.". In Meditations, (pp. Book X, section Y,).

Carson, B. (1992). In Think Big. HarperCollins Publishers.

King Jr., M. L. (n.d.). "Education is that particular something that will lift men from the dark depths of ignorance to the majestic heights of knowledge and prosperity.".

X., M. (1965). The Autobiography of Malcolm X. Grove Press.

A., A. ((2001)). Journal of Child Language. https://doi.org/10.1017/S0305000901003077, 28(3), 567-576.

A., A. (2010). Title of the study. Journal of Experimental Psychology,, https://doi.org/10.1037/a0020157. 45(5), 123-456.

Paul. (n.d.). "Faith comes by hearing, and hearing by the word of God." Romans 10:17. New Living Translation.

Hill, N. (2010). Think and Grow Rich. Wilder Publications,.

Bible, P. 4. (n.d.). "Above all else, guard your heart, for everything you do flows from it." . . New International Version.

Jul, H. C. (2018 Mar 30). https://www.ncbi.nlm.nih.gov/pmc/articles/PMC6037301/.

Murphy, J. (. (1963). The Power of Your Subconscious Mind. Simon & Schuster.

Lomas, S. H. (2012). individuals who possess a balance of cognitive and emotional intelligence have better mental health outcomes and more successful personal relationships. The journal Personality and Social Psychology Review.

colleagues, L. a. (2018). Individuals who can balance their emotions and cognitive thinking tend to make more rational and effective decisions. The journal Emotion.

Darwin, C. (1859). On the Origin of Species. Means of Natural Selection,.

Spinoza. (n.d.). The Ethics of Spinoza.

Joseph LeDoux. (n.d.). Emotions are a subjective experience, a powerful intrusion into our consciousness, and a feeling.

Paul, A. (n.d.). 1 Corinthians 13:2. New International Version.

Goleman, D. (1995.). Emotional Intelligence. Bantam Books.

Fables, A. (2008,). The Goose That Laid the Golden Eggs. Translated by George Fyler Townsend, Project Gutenberg, www.gutenberg.org/files/21/21-h/21-h.

htm#link2H_4_0005.

Gandhi, M. K. (1948). Key to Health. Ahmedabad, . Navajivan Publishing House.

Mindell, E. a. (2011). The Vitamin Bible. Grand Central Publishing.

Quigley, D. T. (January 1, 1943). The national malnutrition. Lee Foundation for nutritional Research; 2nd edition .

Capiello, P. (2012). Prostate Cancer: Prevention and Cure.

Society, A. C. (2022). Cancer Facts & Figures 2022. American Cancer Society.

Foundation, P. C. (2016). State of the Prostate Cancer Patient 2016. Prostate Cancer Foundation.

Society, A. C. (2019). Cancer Facts & Figures for African Americans 2019-2021. 21.

Perron, N. J. (2016). Social Determinants of Health Among African-American Men. Journal of Men's Health, 69-87.

Rebbeck, T. R. (2017). Prostate cancer disparities by race and ethnicity: From nucleotide to neighborhood. American Journal of Preventive Medicine Vol 52, S34-S42.

Denmeade, S. R. (2000). The Cancer Complexity: Exploring Advanced Prostate Cancer. Springer Science & Business Media.

Etzioni, R. P. (2008). Overdiagnosis due to prostate-specific antigen screening: lessons from US prostate cancer incidence trends. The American Journal of Medicine, Volume: 121 Issue: 5, 419-426.

Society, A. C. (2022). https://www.cancer.org/cancer/prostate-cancer/about/key-statistics.html.

Rebbeck TR, D. S. (207). Prostate Cancer in Other Populations: An Overview. Prostate Cancer, Biology, Genetics, and the New Therapeutics. 3rd edition, 491-502.

Walsh, P. C. (2012). Dr. Patrick Walsh's guide to surviving prostate cancer. Grand Central Life & Style.

Shimizu, H. R. (n.d.). Cancers of the prostate and breast among Japanese and white immigrants in Los Angeles County. British Journal of Cancer, 63(6), 963-966. doi: 10.1038/bjc.1991.215.

Sakamoto H, T. H. (2008). Prostate cancer incidence in Japan. Journal of the National Cancer Institute., 949-950. doi:10.1093/jnci/djn202.

Walsh, P. C. (2007). Dr. Patrick Walsh's Guide to Surviving Prostate Cancer. Hachette Books.

Gomez, S. C. (2008, doi: 10.1016/j.annepidem.2008.06.003.). Incidence of prostate cancer in Latino men: A population-based study in California. Annals of Epidemiology, 18(10), . pp. 771-776.

Medicine, A. J. (2015 Aug). Breast cancer: an overview of risk factors, diagnosis, treatment, and survivorship. American Journal of Medicine, 128(8):733-41.

Society., A. C. (2020-2021). Breast Cancer Facts & Figures.

figures, B. c. (2021-2022). https://www.cancer.org/content/dam/cancer-org/research/cancer-facts-and-statistics/breast-cancer-facts-and-figures/breast-cancer-facts-and-figures. American Cancer Society.

Oncology, J. o. (n.d.). Black women had a 2.2 times higher risk of being diagnosed with triple-negative breast cancer than white women. In https://ascopubs.org/doi/abs/10.1200/JCO.2009.23.2100).

DeSantis, C. E. (2020). Breast cancer statistics, 2019. CA: a cancer journal for clinicians .

Chen, X. L. (2015). Breast cancer molecular subtypes and survival in a hospital-based sample in China. In Cancer Epidemiology, Biomarkers & Prevention, 24(12),https://doi.org/10.1158/1055-9965.EPI-15-0453 (pp. 1791-1797.).

Society., A. C. ((2020)). Breast cancer facts & figures 2019-2020. Atlanta:. In I. American Cancer Society.

John, E. M. (2017). Genetic ancestry and risk of breast cancer among US Latinas. Cancer Epidemiology, Biomarkers & Prevention, 26(8).

Prevention, C. f. ((2021)). https://www.cdc.gov/stroke/facts.htm.

Prevention, C. f. ((2017)). Sleep and Chronic Disease. https://www.cdc.gov/sleep/about_sleep/chronic_disease.html. St-Onge, M. P., & McReynolds, A. . Metabolic Consequences of Sleep and.

Whitbourne, S. K. ((2019)). Social psychology. New York: Routledge.

Cacioppo, J. T. ((2009)). Perceived social isolation and cognition. Trends in Cognitive Sciences, 13(10).

Hawkley, L. C. (2010). . Loneliness matters: A theoretical and empirical review of consequences and mechanisms. Annals of Behavioral Medicine, 40(2).

House, J. S. (1988). Social relationships and health. Science, 241(4865).

Parke, R. D. (2010). Social Development. In Handbook of Child Psychology and Developmental Science: Socioemotional Processes (Vol. 3, . John Wiley & Sons.

Komives, S. R. (2018). Leadership for a Better World: Understanding the Social Change Model of Leadership Development (3rd ed.). . Jossey-Bass.

Tzu., L. (n.d.). The Philosophy of History. In T. M. (n.d.). Tao Te Ching. In G. W. F. Hegel. Dover Publications.

Confucius. (2003). The Analects. Penguin Classics.

Barlow, D. H.-Z.-R. (2017). Unified Protocol for Transdiagnostic Treatment of Emotional Disorders: Workbook. Oxford University Press.

Health, N. I. ((2021)). Social anxiety disorder: More than just shyness. . In https://www.nimh.nih.gov/health/publications/social-anxiety-disorder-more-than-just-shyness/index.shtml.

Furmark, T. (2002). Social phobia: overview of community surveys. Acta Psychiatrica Scandinavica, 105(2).

Carnegie, D. (1936). How to Win Friends and Influence People . New York: Simon & Schuster.

Tolle, E. (1997). The Power of Now: A Guide to Spiritual Enlightenment . Novato, CA: New World Library, .

Lee, K. Y. (2000). From Third World to First: The Singapore Story 1965-2000. Singapore. Times Editions.

Ripley, A. (2021). High Conflict: Why We Get Trapped and How We Get Out. In A. Ripley. Simon & Schuster.

Folger, J. P. (2014). The Handbook of Conflict Resolution: Theory and Practice. . John Wiley & Sons.

Doran, G. T. (1981). The paper, titled "There's a S.M.A.R.T. way to write management's goals and objectives,".

Warren, E. a. (2006). All Your Worth: The Ultimate Lifetime Money Plan. . Free Press.

Nakamoto, S. (2008). "Bitcoin: A Peer-to-Peer Electronic Cash System." Bitcoin. org, , https://bitcoin.org/bitcoin.pdf.

Hagee, J. (2013). Four Blood Moons: Something is About to Change . Worthy Publishing.

Peale, N. V. (1952.). The Power of Positive Thinking. Prentice-Hall.

Covey, S. R. (1989). The 7 Habits of Highly Effective People. Free Press, .

Huxley, A. (1932). Brave New World. Chatto & Windus.

Munroe, M. (1998). Understanding the purpose and power of prayer. . Whitaker House.

Munroe, M. (2007). The Principles and Power of Fasting . Whitaker House.

Bible. (1993). New Revised Standard Version. Luke 12:15.

Society, A. C. (2021). Breast Cancer in Men: https://www.cancer.org/cancer/breast-cancer-in-men/about/key-statistics.html.